THE POLITICS OF NATIONHOOD

The Politics of Nationhood

Sovereignty, Britishness and Conservative Politics

Philip Lynch
Department of Politics
University of Leicester

First published in Great Britain 1999 by
MACMILLAN PRESS LTD
Houndmills, Basingstoke, Hampshire RG21 6XS and London
Companies and representatives throughout the world

A catalogue record for this book is available from the British Library.

ISBN 0–333–65612–1

First published in the United States of America 1999 by
ST. MARTIN'S PRESS, INC.,
Scholarly and Reference Division,
175 Fifth Avenue, New York, N.Y. 10010

ISBN 0–312–21835–4

Library of Congress Cataloging-in-Publication Data
Lynch, Philip, 1967–
The politics of nationhood : sovereignty, Britishness and
conservative politics / Philip Lynch.
 p. cm.
Includes bibliographical references and index.
ISBN 0–312–21835–4 (cloth)
1. Conservative Party (Great Britain) 2. Conservatism—Great
Britain. 3. Nationalism—Great Britain. 4. Great Britain—Politics
and government—1979–1997. I. Title.
JN1129.C69L96   1998
324.24104—dc21
                                                                98–28308
                                                                   CIP

© Philip Lynch 1999

All rights reserved. No reproduction, copy or transmission of this publication may be made without written permission.

No paragraph of this publication may be reproduced, copied or transmitted save with written permission or in accordance with the provisions of the Copyright, Designs and Patents Act 1988, or under the terms of any licence permitting limited copying issued by the Copyright Licensing Agency, 90 Tottenham Court Road, London W1P 9HE.

Any person who does any unauthorised act in relation to this publication may be liable to criminal prosecution and civil claims for damages.

The author has asserted his right to be identified as the author of this work in accordance with the Copyright, Designs and Patents Act 1988.

This book is printed on paper suitable for recycling and made from fully managed and sustained forest sources.

10 9 8 7 6 5 4 3 2 1
08 07 06 05 04 03 02 01 00 99

Printed and bound in Great Britain by
Antony Rowe Ltd, Chippenham, Wiltshire

For my parents

Contents

Preface	ix
List of Abbreviations	x
Introduction	xi

1 Conservatism and the Politics of Nationhood — 1
  Historical Perspectives — 1
  The Conservative Nation — 4
  The Conservative Party and the Politics of Nationhood — 9
  Conclusions — 20

2 Heath and Powell – Two National Strategies — 22
  The Changing Politics of Nationhood — 23
  Heath's National Strategy — 28
  Powell's Nationalist Strategy — 38
  Conclusions — 45

3 Thatcherism and the Politics of Nationhood — 48
  Thatcherism and Thatcher — 50
  Ideology, Ideas and Thatcherite Discourse — 51
  Thatcherism – a Political Project — 59
  A Coherent Project? Sceptical Views — 61
  Conclusions — 63

4 European Integration — 66
  Conservative Policy and European Integration, 1979–97 — 67
  Nationhood and Europe — 77
  Sovereignty and Autonomy — 80
  European Integration and Conservative Politics — 89
  Conclusions — 101

5 Territorial Politics — 103
  Scotland — 105
  Wales — 115
  Northern Ireland — 116
  The European Dimension — 127
  Conclusions — 128

Contents

6	**'Race' and Immigration**	131
	Conservatism, 'Race' and Nationhood	132
	Citizenship, Immigration and Asylum	135
	Race Relations and Public Policy	144
	The Politics of 'Race' and the Conservative Party	149
	Conclusions	152
7	**Conclusions**	154
	The Conservative Politics of Nationhood after 1997	157
	Rethinking the Conservative Nation	162
Notes and References		168
Select Bibliography		195
Index		197

Preface

This book is the result of a number of years of research on British Conservative politics, the nation and the nation-state during which time I have incurred many debts. Some of the themes examined here were first explored in a PhD at the University of Warwick, where my supervisors Lincoln Allison and Zig Layton-Henry, and examiners Jim Bulpitt and Andrew Gamble, provided much valuable guidance. Significant developments in the Conservative politics of nationhood under the Major Governments, plus an extension and refocusing of the project, mean that large parts of the book draw upon research conducted at the University of Leicester. The Department of Politics and Centre for European Politics and Institutions have provided a stimulating and friendly environment for academic study. In particular, I have benefited from the advice and expertise of a number of colleagues working on areas relevant to my own research, particularly Alasdair Blair, John Hoffman, Stephen Hopkins, Jörg Monar and John Young. Responsibility for any errors is of course mine alone. The Economic and Social Research Council provided funding for the original doctoral research and I received a small research grant from the Social Sciences Faculty Research Board at the University of Leicester. My thanks also to Tim Farmiloe at Macmillan for granting extensions to the original deadline, allowing me to assess the whole of the Major Governments' period in office.

Personal thanks are owed to my brother Martin for not letting distance prevent us growing closer; to friends who provided (too) welcome distractions from writing; to a girl from the north country; and to Alex and Eric for the glory and their genius. My greatest debt is to my parents, whose support has been invaluable and whose kindness is greatly appreciated. It is to them that this book is dedicated with love and respect.

PHILIP LYNCH Leicester, 1998

List of Abbreviations

AIA	Anglo-Irish Agreement
BDTC	British Dependent Territories Citizen
BNA	British Nationality Act 1981
CAP	Common Agricultural Policy
CBI	Confederation of British Industry
CFSP	Common Foreign and Security Policy
CRE	Commission for Racial Equality
CUKC	Citizenship of the United Kingdom and Colonies
DSD	Downing Street Declaration
EC	European Community
ECB	European Central Bank
ECJ	European Court of Justice
Ecu	European Currency Unit
EFTA	European Free Trade Association
EMU	Economic and Monetary Union
EPC	European Political Cooperation
ERM	Exchange Rate Mechanism
EU	European Union
GATT	General Agreement on Tariffs and Trade
IGC	Intergovernmental Conference
IRA	Irish Republican Army
JHA	Justice and Home Affairs
MP	Member of Parliament
NAFTA	North American Free Trade Agreement
NATO	North Atlantic Treaty Organization
QMV	Qualified Majority Voting
SDLP	Social Democratic and Labour Party
SEA	Single European Act
SEM	Single European Market
SNP	Scottish National Party
TEU	Treaty on European Union
UK	United Kingdom
UKREP	United Kingdom Personal Representation to the European Communities
VAT	Value Added Tax
WEU	Western European Union

Introduction

> I am not sure what is meant by those who say that the Party should return to One Nation Conservatism. As far as I can tell by their views on European federalism, such people's creed would be better described as 'No Nation Conservatism'.
>
> Margaret Thatcher
>
> To argue against the European Union is to argue against Britain's profoundest self-interest, against her place in the world, and flies in the face of the patriotic instinct that is one of the defining elements of Conservatism.
>
> Tristan Garel-Jones
>
> The Conservative Party is the nationalist party *par excellence*.
>
> A Conservative Party which cannot present itself to the country as a national party suffers under a severe handicap.
>
> Enoch Powell
>
> I will negotiate in the interests of the United Kingdom as a whole, not in the convenient party political interests of the Conservative Party. If that is unhappy politically for some then I regret that. I have to answer to my conscience and my nation and history for what I actually decide to do.
>
> John Major.[1]

The nation and nation-state have had a central place in British Conservative politics for more than a century, the Conservative Party's status as the patriotic party defending the constitution, Union and Empire being at the heart of party statecraft and a key factor in its political success. Since the 1960s, however, the Conservatives have been forced to re-examine their statecraft and values in respect of the politics of nationhood in the light of decolonization, membership of the European Community (EC), difficulties in territorial management and the development of a multicultural society. By the 1980s, relations with the EC, tougher immigration policies, the Falklands conflict and Margaret Thatcher's instinctive Englishness were being cited as evidence of a new patriotic orientation in Conservative politics. But given the intensified factionalism on European issues and territorial management problems under John Major's leadership, the politics of nationhood appears problematic territory for Conservatives.

This book aims to provide an integrated study of the Conservative politics of nationhood. It examines the visions of national identity and the nation-state which inform Conservative politics, plus Conservative policy in areas which have a decisive impact on national identity and the nation-state, notably European integration, territorial politics and the politics of immigration and 'race'. The importance of the politics of nationhood to Conservative statecraft and the extent to which the Conservatives have developed a successful national strategy are guiding themes. A coherent and successful national strategy would have a number of elements, namely (1) a clear vision of the nation and nation-state which informs Conservative politics; (2) a political strategy in which the defence of national identity, the territorial integrity of the nation-state and national sovereignty have a leading place, and (3) Conservative predominance in the politics of nationhood, including an appropriation of patriotic discourse and identification as the patriotic or national party. Though often offering tangible political benefits for the Conservative Party, the politics of nationhood is not necessarily easily manageable territory for Conservatives: tariff reform, the Irish Question and European integration illustrating the intense ideological divisions and statecraft problems it can provoke.

The first chapter provides an overview of Conservatism and the politics of nationhood, tracing the development first of a distinctive conservative concept of the nation, then the rise to predominance of the Conservative Party in the politics of nationhood under Disraeli and Salisbury. Chapter 2 explores the alternative strategies developed by Heath and Powell in the 1960s and 1970s as means of adapting Conservative statecraft and the politics of nationhood to a post-imperial environment.

The Thatcher period marked a critical stage in the development of a revised Conservative politics of nationhood, Thatcherism seeking to defend the nation-state and revitalize national identity. Chapter 3 notes that despite commitments to defend national sovereignty, curb immigration and protect the Union, plus its populist patriotic discourse, Thatcherism did not produce a coherent national strategy or achieve hegemony in the politics of nationhood. Instead European integration, the management of the Union and of a multicultural society posed significant problems for the Conservatives, ultimately contributing to their 1997 election defeat.

Introduction

European integration, territorial politics and the politics of 'race' and immigration are then explored in more detail. Chapter 4 focuses on Britain and the European Union (EU), examining government policy, the significance of European integration for Conservative views of nationhood and national sovereignty. The statecraft problems raised by further European integration, including an erosion of executive autonomy, problems of party management and dilemmas over electoral strategy, are also assessed. Chapter 5 then examines Conservative statecraft and the management of the Union, noting developments in, and differences between, policy towards Scotland, Wales and Northern Ireland under the Thatcher and Major Governments. Conservative policy and attitudes on immigration and the management of a multicultural society are then explored in Chapter 6. In each chapter, particular attention is paid to the relative importance of ideology and statecraft considerations, and the successes and failings of Conservative policy. The book concludes by assessing the opportunities and problems which the politics of nationhood raises for the Conservative Party at the end of the twentieth century. It argues that a reassessment of party policy on European integration and devolution, plus a rethinking of the conservative idea of the nation, is required if the Conservatives are to maintain their predominance in this area.

1 Conservatism and the Politics of Nationhood

To understand the contemporary significance of the politics of nationhood in British Conservative politics, it is important to briefly trace its historical and ideological roots, noting the opportunities and constraints the politics of nationhood has provided for the Conservative Party. The Conservative Party is often depicted as having enjoyed a predominance over the politics of nationhood during the last hundred years. The party's status and self-image as a national party became a central element of Conservative statecraft, while Conservatives also developed a coherent account of the nation and state patriotism, and made effective use of patriotic discourse. This appropriation of the politics of nationhood occurred under Disraeli's leadership, when the Conservatives became identified as the patriotic party supporting national institutions, the Union and Empire. Disraeli's legacy was a One Nation strategy which ensured the political success of the Conservative Party in a new era of democratic politics. Recent historical research has, however, noted that conservative state patriotism was not the only significant political expression of patriotism. Disputes within Conservative politics about the appropriate national strategy – for example, over tariff reform, Ireland or withdrawal from Empire – meant that the politics of nationhood often proved problematic territory for Conservatives.[1]

HISTORICAL PERSPECTIVES

National identities are dynamic rather than static, developing gradually over time in response to external and internal developments. Conservative accounts of British national history may include both a Tory focus on authority and organic development and a Whig emphasis on individual liberty and the balanced constitution, often fusing elements of the two and building myths into their account. National identity is contested: there is no necessary or inevitable relationship between Britishness (or Englishness) and conservative politics, although a number of factors in the development of British national consciousness can be viewed as favourable to a conservative account of nationhood. Thus the emergence of the English then British nation-state and national identities prior to the era of ideological nationalism and democratic politics limited the scope for the emergence of ethnic or oppositional patriotisms. However, neither the limited state-based nature of British identity nor the populist character of conservative patriotic discourse negated the potential for disputes about national identity, either between radical and conservative patriotisms or within conservative politics.

In the United Kingdom's (UK) multinational state, the balance between a state-based British identity and older ethnic or national identities has been a complex one. The nations of the UK maintained important aspects of their ethnic, political and cultural identities, with a British state patriotism added to these to provide a sense of shared identity and interests, thereby limiting the scope for separatist sub-state nationalisms. This state-based or civic sense of Britishness drew heavily upon English traditions, notably the principle of parliamentary sovereignty and a Whig history of progress and exceptionalism, plus the values and interests of an Anglicized elite, but the UK did not become a truly homogeneous state in either its social make-up or its institutional arrangements.[2]

In the case of England, the relatively early development of the nation-state (including an emerging bureaucratic system of taxation and law, a developing national economy, a standing army and a territorial state which was for the most part linguistically homogenous) helped the emergence of an English national identity among a ruling elite.[3] Tracing the origins of English national consciousness is problematic, especially given the presentation of 'invented traditions' as long-lived phenomena.[4] Although local identities were predominant in the late-Tudor period, among the Elizabethan gentry a cult of monarchy and a Protestant foreign policy fostered English consciousness.[5] The language of patriotism became more politically significant during the English Civil War when it was linked to ideas of liberty, Puritan destiny and national honour in radical thought, but to hierarchy and the divine right of kings in Tory language.[6] Whigs presented the Glorious Revolution as a key moment in national history, stressing progress and constitutional balance; Tories accepted the mixed constitution but focused on state authority, social hierarchy and private property. Gerald Newman's study of English nationalism in the late eighteenth century notes how writers, artists and intellectuals popularized an English consciousness through literary quests for 'national sincerity', the propagation of national symbols, such as John Bull and Britannia, and anti-French sentiment. Individual liberty, tolerance, sincerity and the idea of the gentleman, property rights, parliamentary sovereignty and parochialism have variously been cited as key attributes of Englishness.[7] Studies of radical patriotism have focused on opposition to despotic rule and support for the liberties of the 'freeborn Englishmen' against monarchical rule, while New Right historians have depicted enterprise, free trade, private property and the rule of law as key elements of English history and identity.[8]

Linda Colley's work on the formation of British identity traces how in the eighteenth century the identification of an external enemy (Catholic France) which threatened the distinctive life of the British state and society (essentially its Protestantism) was a critical factor in the forging of a British consciousness superimposed on older identities and allegiances.[9] Scottish identity survived the 1707 Act of Union: its distinctive civic identity drew the separate legal and educational systems, while the legacy of statehood and popular sovereignty ensured a continuing political dimension. But the Anglicization of Scottish elites – their incorporation into the state structure, the economic opportunities offered by Union and Empire – helped the spread of Britishness.

Despite the largely successful creation of a British identity which linked the nations of Great Britain without submerging their distinctive identities and a system of administrative devolution which allowed local elites some autonomy in 'low politics', the UK multinational state required careful management. The centre had to ensure balance within the Union, for the enduring ethnic, cultural and political facets of old allegiances were never far below the surface of British identity. English elites resisted an English nationalist outlook, instead developing in the nineteenth century a 'Whig imperialist' statecraft concerned with the successful management of the multinational UK.[10] But this strategy and the spread of Britishness as an integrative identity was least successful in Ireland, this having heightened political repercussions for the centre, a factor following the Act of Union in 1800 when Ireland was brought into Westminster.

By the end of the eighteenth century, British national identity was strengthening, propagated by the state but also emerging at lower levels, while patriotic rhetoric was used by both radical and loyalist patriots. During the French Revolutionary wars, state elites further developed British identity and sought to benefit from the appeal of patriotism. The gradual conservative appropriation of the politics of nationhood which followed took a number of forms, from the deliberate identification of the monarchy with the British nation to the rise of loyalist patriotic groups and the intellectual development of a conservative concept of the nation.[11] Patriotic discourse was not, though, consistently or actively taken up by the state during this period; that would not reach its peak for another century, by which time mass participation, education and communications provided the necessary conditions for an effective state-sponsored patriotism. Pitt the Younger's Government viewed appeals to national unity and loyalty as useful in mobilizing the war effort and countering domestic radicalism. But it also feared that an active campaign of popular patriotism might have the unwelcome effect of increasing demands for political reform as radical patriotisms remained potent.[12]

THE CONSERVATIVE NATION

Although David Hume and Henry Bolingbroke had written on 'national character' in the eighteenth century, neither provided a recognizably modern conservative doctrine or a coherent account of the nation.[13] Instead, Edmund Burke provided the English ruling elite with its first coherent conservative statements and one which developed a conservative view of nationhood (the 'conservative nation').[14] Burke's account of the nation was an important counterpart to radical patriotism, evident in the work of Richard Price and then Thomas Paine, and furthered the appropriation of patriotic discourse by conservative forces. The key elements of the Burkean nation are found in his writings on the constitution and history of the English nation-state plus the national character of its people. It was built around and reflected the core conservative themes of community, organic development, tradition, authority, hierarchy and anti-rationalism.[15]

The National Community

For Burke, the nation is a key form of human community, providing common allegiance, shared values and a 'moral essence'. Through the nation, society becomes 'a partnership ... between those who are living and those who are dead and those who are yet to be born'.[16] Human beings are social animals who belong in a number of associations or 'little platoons' ranging from the family, through local community to nation and ultimately to humanity as a whole. The conservative view of human nature stresses individual identification with the particular but, unlike the deterministic nationalisms of the continental Right, defends individual liberty against an overpowerful state and activist politics. An individual's character is in part framed by his or her socialization in the national community, but he or she is not exclusively dependent on the nation for their moral values. The individual has multiple and diverse allegiances, though patriotism and duty are essential attributes of human nature which need to be fostered. Cultural differences between nations are the result of differing habits and prejudices, not human nature. These form man's 'second nature': people from different societies have different traditions and 'prejudices'.[17] The customs and values of a society are the basis of its national character, yet these are not static or racially determined.

A nation is not an idea only of local extent and individual momentary aggregation, but it is an idea of continuity which extends in time as well as in numbers and in space. And this is the choice not of one day or one set of people, not a tumultuary and giddy choice, it is a deliberate election of ages and generations. It is a constitution made by what is ten thousand times better than choice; it is made by the peculiar circumstances, occasions, tempers, dispositions and moral, civil and social habitudes of the people, which disclose themselves only in a long space of time. It is a vestment which accommodates itself to the body.[18]

The nation provides a sense of solidarity and belonging: it is an integrative community binding together those who share the same 'second nature', traditions and values. Instead of being defined in ethnic or racial terms, conservative accounts of the nation focus on allegiance to common institutions, a shared history and a political culture which fosters common values. Patriotism is a natural and moral disposition, providing a sense of unity, solidarity and identity.

Tradition and Organic Evolution

The strength of the English nation-state lies in its longevity and gradual organic development. Institutions and traditions are socially and historically shaped. The constitution has evolved over the course of centuries, reflecting the wisdom of past generations: it is not an artificial creation based on abstract principle, but one built on tradition, shaped by the national past and reflecting the national character. Burke's account of English history mixes a Whig emphasis on progress towards a balanced constitution with Tory themes of hierarchy, order and a defence of existing institutions against the dictates of reason. It employs myths of historical continuity and national prestige to bolster the conservative nation, disputing the radical patriotic reading of the Glorious Revolution, instead depicting it as running with the grain of tradition and as the final act of the constitutional settlement.[19]

Conservatism rejects activist or ideological politics based on abstract principle or end-state goals, being instead a form of limited politics shaped by philosophical scepticism and a concern with specific circumstance.[20] The nation is defined in terms of its constitutional order and shared traditions: 'our country is not a thing of mere physical locality ... the place that determines our duty to our country is a social, civil relation'.[21] The English constitution is depicted as reflecting the accumulated wisdom of the past and the essential character of the English people, Burke suggesting that in a stable polity institutions accord with the values and habits of the nation. National character and the constitution are intrinsically linked: English values such as the rule of law, individual liberty and allegiance to authority are reflected in its constitutional settlement. As the constitution reflects morality, natural law and national habits, the English have adopted a deferential attitude.[22]

In his writings on America, India and his native Ireland, Burke continued his focus on English constitutionalism.[23] He was critical of Warren Hastings' rule in India and also policy towards the American colonies, arguing that the government was wrong not to apply the English tradition of individual liberty there. Colonial policy should be formulated according to circumstance not abstract rights: Americans should have the chance of self-government and political liberty because they share the values and habits of the English. Burke also criticized the Protestant Ascendancy in Ireland and supported Irish Catholic Emancipation, but believed that responsible British rule would best suit its people. The French Revolution, meanwhile, is presented not just as a threat to English traditions, but also to European civilization and the common fund of traditions, laws and morals – based on Christianity, Roman Law and feudalism – which European nation-states share.[24]

Prescriptive Authority and Hierarchy

The Burkean nation is an ordered, hierarchical community. Whereas the Jacobin concept of the nation looks to popular sovereignty and equal citizenship, Burke's is based on prescriptive authority and rule by a natural aristocracy. The nation is neither democratic nor identified with 'the people': in terms of political participation and resource distribution, the nation only consisted of those with landed or financial interests. But Burke's is a paternalistic conservatism in which the governing class has duties towards the rest of society and represents the interests of the nation as a whole. Legitimate claims to property and authority rest on prescriptive authority, that is on longevity and tradition rather than abstract principle. Individual freedom and rights exist within a framework of ordered liberty, reciprocal obligations and a hierarchical social order. Prescription or long-lived usage of property or office brings stability and order as the natural aristocracy accumulates experience of governing and the national character.

Political and Cultural Accounts

Burke laid the foundations of the conservative concept of the nation, providing a significant conservative counterpart to radical patriotism. The Burkean nation is a hierarchical community deriving its strength from the weight of tradition and the proximity of its ruling institutions to the national character. It is an integrative community, but not an oppressive one: the individual flourishes within the nation as he is a social animal, naturally patriotic with his character shaped in part by the national community into which he is born. The nation is not the single overriding focus of loyalty, but one link in a chain of membership extending from the family unit to humanity. Human beings are not racially divided, but differ because of their environmentally shaped 'second nature'. Burke's is not an ethnically defined concept of the nation, but one based around the values and traditions of the ruling elite of the dominant English ethnic group.

The conservative nation is a mix of the often-counterpoised political (or civic) and cultural (or ethnic) accounts of national identity. Ethnic accounts define the nation in terms of common descent from a distinct ethnic group, focusing on objective factors such as language and history.[25] It is an exclusivist, pre-political community determining the identity of its individual members. The civic model stresses political features within a territorially bound political community, either equal citizenship rights (for civic humanist accounts) or constitutional stability and limited politics (conservative state patriotism). Nationhood is a state-based rather than ethnically defined identity, one of a number of diverse allegiances. The division between the two accounts is not, though, clear cut: the national community is the location of ethnic memories which link man to the past, to the national territory, and provides shared expectations of a national future. But equally it is the primary location of political and social relations, of citizenship and civil society.

The conservative nation, especially in its Burkean mode, is a hybrid of the moderate elements of the civic and cultural accounts, recognizing both the political and pre-political elements of identity and community. National identity is shaped by both cultural factors (whether ethnic memories, shared values) and political factors (state patriotism, 'invented traditions'). Given the multinational nature of the UK and the translation of the conservative concept of the nation into a fully-fledged conservative state patriotism, British national identity is a political one based on state patriotism rather than ethnic identity, although one which coexists with the cultural identities of its component nations.

The conservative nation is a limited one, shunning ideological nationalism and universalist end-state prescriptions in favour of empiricism, parochialism (including nostalgia and myths) and philosophical scepticism. It is shaped by core conservative values, by historical circumstance and by opposition to the politics of its rivals. Rather than a static account, the conservative idea of the nation has developed over time, adapting or reacting to change, but gradually absorbing some of the themes espoused by its rivals. The Burkean nation is one of the clearest expositions of conservative thought, but a number of different strands of thought have existed within British Conservatism emphasizing various elements of the political or cultural accounts of the nation.[26] The Right has often embraced activist politics, espousing an ideological nationalism or racial account of politics. More recently, as will be covered in Chapter 3, the neo-liberal and cultural conservative branches of New Right have fractured the Burkean account of the nation.

THE CONSERVATIVE PARTY AND THE POLITICS OF NATIONHOOD

Burke's account of the nation was a significant early stage in the gradual appropriation of patriotic discourse. But his was not a state-sponsored official nationalism, the Tory Party, split by the repeal of the Corn Laws, not achieving predominance in the politics of nationhood until the late nineteenth century. Political ideas are important to Conservative politics, but are not its defining feature. British Conservatism is essentially a tradition of political practice, a concern with statecraft or government rather than ideological principle. Conservative ideas form an important backcloth, a support mechanism for Conservative Party statecraft, rather than the guiding principles of a purposive ideology.[27] Thus, in an examination of conservatism and the politics of nationhood, the prime focus should be on Conservative Party statecraft, assessing the means and ends of Conservative politics plus the relationship between populist patriotism and political strategy. The identification of the Conservative Party with the nation and nation-state was not one born solely (or even primarily) from an ideological attachment to the national community, but from considerations of party statecraft.

Disraeli's leadership was the pivotal moment in the development of a conservative state patriotism which formed a central plank of Conservative statecraft and self-image. For Lord Blake, 'that then is Disraeli's most lasting contribution to the success of this party. He made it the "national party"'.[28] The Conservative national strategy which developed in the late nineteenth century, whereby the politics of nationhood became a central feature of party statecraft, had a number of core elements. (1) A concerted use of patriotic discourse in which the Conservative Party was portrayed as the 'national party' and contrasted with an 'anti-patriotic' opposition. This was coupled with the popularization of conservative state patriotism through the myths and symbols of monarchy, Empire and national history. (2) A One Nation political strategy looking to national unity rather than sectional politics, rejecting alternative strategies such as a reactionary defence of landed interests staunchly opposing social and economic change. An integrative politics of nationhood would broaden Conservative support and counter democracy's radical impetus, while allowing the party in office to defend the existing social structure and balance of power. (3) The identification of Conservative strategy and populist patriotism with imperialism, offering the prospect of UK-wide domestic benefits and potent myths of imperial mission. (4) Support for the territorial integrity of the Union and opposition to Home Rule. Though the Conservative's support and ethos were largely English, party statecraft looked to the successful management of the multinational UK state rather than to the Conservatives as an English national party.

One Nation Politics and Conservative State Patriotism

Disraeli utilized and developed the Burkean account of the nation in his early work, portraying the Tory Party as the national party and criticizing the development of 'two nations' in British society.[29] In his 1872 speeches at Manchester and Crystal Palace, Disraeli identified the upholding of national institutions, the 'elevation of the condition of the people' and imperialism as the party's 'three great objects'.[30] The politics of nationhood had a leading place within this One Nation political strategy. One Nation politics aimed to locate the Conservative defence of the constitution and existing distribution of power and property within the new political, economic and social circumstances of Britain's emerging democracy. Industrialization and urbanization threatened the interests of key Tory supporters, but to defend them effectively the party would have to adapt.

Disraeli is often credited with modernizing the Conservative Party, mapping out progressive policies and fashioning its appeal as a national party, but the legend is an exaggerated one. Despite the rhetoric of national unity and social progress, the defence of traditional Conservative causes remained paramount, though support for existing institutions was framed so as to appeal to latent patriotism. The British people were depicted as patriotic and deferential. The 'elevation of the condition of the people' would ensure social stability, while its patriotic appeal would secure popular loyalty to continued rule by a hierarchical, but paternalist, elite. One Nation Conservatism envisaged a national community in which people were bound together by reciprocal obligations plus patriotic respect for the Constitution, Church and social hierarchy.

Behind the One Nation rhetoric of a party with cross-class appeal and a clear social programme, the reality was one of limited social legislation, though educational reforms helped the dissemination of British national identity. The governments of Disraeli and Salisbury generally followed pragmatic free market policies, with little state intervention in social or economic affairs, and sought low taxation and the protection of property rights.[31] Careful management and the defence of existing interests were the watchwords of Salisbury's statecraft, appealing to natural conservatives, opposing Home Rule and forming an alliance with the Liberal Unionists.[32] Adapting the party to meet the demands of a new democratic era while defending the interests of its traditional supporters was the central challenge to Conservative statecraft, and one which provoked differing strategies. Neither Disraeli nor Salisbury thus accepted the range of reforms envizaged by Randolph Churchill's 'Tory Democracy' programme or Joseph Chamberlain's social imperialism.[33]

The Conservatives' image as the patriotic party was electorally significant, helping it win votes from disillusioned Liberals and newly enfranchised groups. The Disraelian party concentrated on cementing its support among a middle class fearful of Gladstonian radicalism.[34] But the lower middle and working classes in urban constituencies also became important sources of Conservative support, the party seeking their support through patriotic, imperialist and Orange rhetoric rather than specific social reform programmes.[35] To this extent, the Conservatives remained predominantly the party of the Establishment. The party also became more professional during this period, though the most important role in organizing grassroots popular conservatism was played by the Primrose League, a voluntary organization which mobilized patriotic and imperialist sentiment.[36] The leadership depicted the Liberals as an anti-patriotic party, criticizing Gladstone's reluctance towards imperial expansion, his support for Irish Home Rule and reliance on the parliamentary support of the Irish Nationalists. As Robert McKenzie and Allan Silver note,

> The central argument which appears in the popular party literature is that the Conservatives are uniquely qualified to govern Britain and that the institutions of the country are safe in their hands alone ... Because of their understanding of the nation and its history, their devotion to the interests of the whole community, and their inherently superior governmental skills, they alone are qualified to rule.[37]

In the late-Victorian era conservative state patriotism was popularized and mobilized through a concerted use of myths and symbols, one of the most significant being the monarchy. Though the monarchy had previously been promoted as a symbol of tradition and unity, it was most explicitly presented in these terms in the 1880s and 1890s. The ritualization and commercialization of the monarchy reached new levels in the popular ceremonials marking Victoria's Jubilees.[38] Eric Hobsbawm notes how the state dramatized the national community by reviving civic rituals as expressions of official state nationalism. These 'invented traditions' symbolized social cohesion and nationhood, legitimized the state and harnessed support for the conservative nation.

The monarchy became an important element in conservative state patriotism, enhancing themes of tradition, a continuous national history and British identity. The popularization of the monarchy promoted deferential acceptance of the conservative political settlement, its hierarchical social order and pre-democratic institutional framework, and was closely associated with imperialism. Tom Nairn depicts the monarchy as the central element in a pre-modern surrogate British identity which emerged without the ethnic, modernizing or participatory elements associated with nationalist politics.[39] It was important in shaping a limited rather than participatory state patriotism which fostered support for the existing distribution of power. But Nairn over-states his case as the monarchy was not politicized in the sense of being explicitly identified with the Conservative Party, for, as Hugh Cunningham notes, 'the most potent symbol of the nation, one capable of harmonizing the divergent patriotisms of church, chapel, locality, nation, kingdom and Empire, was monarchy; and monarchy was above party'.[40]

Imperialism

Imperialism also emerged as a central component of Conservative statecraft, the politics of nationhood and British identity in this period. The expansion, then defence, of the British Empire became guiding themes of economic and foreign policy, while its populist promotion by the Conservatives heightened Empire's place in the national consciousness. Imperial extension seemed to policy-makers to protect British economic, commercial and military interests; it provided the necessary finance and raw materials for the domestic social reforms some Conservatives felt were necessary in Britain's emerging democracy; it could be linked to a newly activist conservative state patriotism as the overseas counterpart to the Whig formula of national progress, as a patriotic foreign policy, and as the 'civilizing mission' of an elect nation; and it was a key weapon in the patriotic armoury ranged against Gladstone's Liberals. However, in the longer term, imperialism's centrality to conservative state patriotism and British identity became problematic as the political costs of defending the Empire rose and public support for it waned.

The association of the Conservative Party with imperialism was shaped by the consolidation of British colonies under Disraeli, his portrayal of foreign policy in terms of national interest (following Palmerston) and his critique of Liberal foreign policy. An active policy of imperial expansion was taken up by Salisbury and Chamberlain, the latter becoming one of its foremost exponents, depicting imperialism as the extension of British governing skills, constitutional practices and capitalism.[41]

The jingoism and propaganda surrounding imperial expansion furthered the portrayal of the Conservatives as the patriotic party and helped popularize conservative state patriotism. New modes of communication such as the popular press, the music halls and later the cinemas acted as agents for the spread of imperialism into the popular psyche.[42] Populist imperialism was also linked with the spread of racial accounts of politics, Conservative discourse making frequent appeals to racial mission and the supposed superiority of the British 'race'. Racial theories and discourse of the coloured 'other' were commonplace in the late-Victorian period, often expressed in the crude pseudo-scientific language of Social Darwinism, with myths of Anglo-Saxon superiority accompanied by xenophobia aimed at the urban Irish population and the indigenous populations of the colonies.[43] The 1905 Aliens Act reflected this general air of prejudice and intolerance.

Though a key element in the Conservative national strategy, the organization of Empire also posed problems for the politics of nationhood, tensions existing between the goal of upholding the integrity and character of the British nation-state and those of imperial or racial unity. Dilkes and Seeley depicted the self-governing colonies as part of a 'Greater Britain' united by 'race', language and law. The Empire was perceived as an expansion of the British nation and nation-state, and a range of political opinion supported stronger bonds between Anglo-Saxon settlers and the UK.[44] Imperialism also helped cement the Union between England and Scotland: Glasgow's economic strength increased with its role as the second city of the Empire, while a disproportionately high number of Scots played key administrative and economic roles in the colonies. But tensions in Conservative statecraft intensified when the government of Empire became bound up with the Irish Question.

Empire and myths of the Anglo-Saxon race shaped British state patriotism and national identity, being actively fostered by the state and the Conservative Party. Given the economic opportunities it offered, the populist patriotism it engendered and the concept of imperial kinship it produced, imperialism legitimated and gave substance to a multinational British identity, but in doing so made for a vacuum at the heart of Britishness.[45] Although Empire was bound up with conservative state patriotism and Whig imperialism, expansionist imperialism and universalizing themes of racial mission sat uneasily with the particularism and limited politics of the conservative nation, moving conservative state patriotism closer to the activist politics associated with ideological nationalism and racism.

Chamberlain's tariff reform campaign, launched in 1903, presented the Conservative Party with a different political strategy. At its heart was an alternative mode of political economy, a system of imperial protection which would involve tariffs on manufactured goods and duties on foodstuffs imported from outside the Empire, securing colonial markets for British producers through preferential tariff agreements. E. H. H. Green traces the progression of the tariff reform campaign, developing from a piecemeal response to Liberal free trade and reluctant imperialism, into a fully-fledged policy structure.[46] By the 1908 Unauthorized Programme it embraced 'social imperialism', tying protectionism with domestic social reforms, the economic benefits accruing from tariffs being used to finance pensions and national insurance. Tariff reform was also presented as a means of revitalizing Conservative identity and addressing the dilemmas the party faced in protecting its traditional interests and supporters while attempting to expand its electoral base.

According to its supporters, tariff reform would boost the party's cross-class appeal, protecting British industry and regenerating the agricultural sector, while financing social reform and mobilizing populist patriotism. It would also bring imperial unity, economically significant in a world where British hegemony was fading, aiding British defence and restoring Empire to centre stage following the Boer War. But within the strategy lay a series of problems: the self-governing colonies were not convinced of the merits of the scheme as they built their own markets; tariff reform meant higher food prices which were electorally damaging; and, finally, the ideological basis of the campaign split the Conservative Party, its nationalistic rhetoric undermining the non-doctrinaire, limited politics of the conservative nation.[47]

Tariff reform was the clearest indication that the politics of nationhood could prove difficult territory for the Conservative Party. One Nation statecraft was faced by an alternative political and economic strategy in the shape of tariff reform: both emphasized the centrality of the politics of nationhood to Conservatism, but differed fundamentally on the means and ends of Conservative governance. A doctrinaire nationalist Right had emerged in Edwardian Britain and, on the Irish question, the constitution and imperial protection, its supporters were prepared to put principle before party.

The Union

Defence of the territorial integrity of the Union had been a cornerstone of Conservative statecraft for much of the period since 1886, when Gladstone's first Home Rule Bill pushed the territorial management of the United Kingdom into the realm of 'high politics'. The UK had become an increasingly integrated state during the nineteenth century: industrialization brought greater internal migration, economic integration and urbanization, while the dissemination of a state-based British identity, populist imperialism and the acquiescence of local elites laid the foundations for a relatively stable territorial settlement in Great Britain. But the development of the UK multinational state was not a uniform process. British society, culture and identity developed unevenly and regional differences persisted.

The period from 1880 to 1922 was one of upheaval as the Irish Question in particular moved issues of territorial management to political centre stage. Ethnic consciousness and class politics were forcefully combined in demands for Home Rule and land reform. The Conservative Party developed a Unionist strategy, the territorial side of a statecraft in which the politics of nationhood played a leading role and which was a clear alternative to the Liberal vision of British identity and territorial politics. Central to Conservative unionism were the defence of Union and Empire, the protection of the constitution and parliamentary sovereignty plus the existing distribution of power and resources, including the defence of property rights and the two-party system in which the Conservatives competed as a national party.

Jim Bulpitt's influential study of Conservative territorial management views the desire of the party leaders to protect the relative autonomy of the centre from peripheral demands as the cornerstone of the Unionist territorial code.[48] In order to maintain their predominance in 'high politics', win the acquiescence of local elites and prevent themselves from becoming enmeshed in local politics, Tory leaders granted peripheral elites a significant amount of administrative and cultural autonomy. Conservative leaders did not seek greater centralization or a uniform state, but fostered a complex pattern of indirect rule and administrative devolution, while defending the sovereignty of parliament and executive autonomy, and promoting British identity.

This pattern of territorial management was evident in Scotland, where administrative and cultural distinctiveness, the economic benefits of Empire and Union and tactical concessions such as the creation of the Scottish Office in 1885 defused Scottish nationalism. Cross-party support existed for the creation of the Scottish Office under Salisbury's new administration in 1885, the Secretary of State for Scotland gaining Cabinet status in 1892. The creation of the Scottish Office confirmed the pattern of limited administrative devolution on Scottish issues, but its main purpose was 'to redress the wounded dignities of the Scottish people' and stifle demands for Home Rule.[49] Irish issues had particular resonance in Scotland, fuelling demands for Home Rule in the 1880s and again after the First World War. The Conservatives were electorally weaker in Scotland than in their southern English heartlands, but Home Rule brought periodic upturns in party fortunes, winning the Orange vote in Protestant areas and bringing an alliance with the Liberal Unionists. Unionism was the major element of Scottish Conservatism (the party being named the Scottish Unionist Party from 1912 to 1965), though the party clearly had a Scottish national as well as unionist identity.[50] Wales was still less favourable electoral ground for the Conservatives, where the Liberal Party tapped into a tradition of dissent.

Territorial upheaval revolts in Scotland and Wales were limited, and management by the centre relatively effective, but this did not apply to Ireland which was governed in quasi-colonial style. Local administration here was not aided by significant cooperation from Anglicized local elites. Neither was Britishness as a form of plural identity accepted by Ireland's Catholic middle class who turned in increasing numbers to Irish nationalism, while the Ulster version of Britishness differed significantly from conservative state patriotism.[51] Gladstone's land and Church reforms signalled a move towards 'the government of Ireland by Irish principles', before Ireland became the central issue in British party politics with his 1886 Home Rule Bill.[52] Here the complexities of territorial politics were condensed into a struggle between, on the one hand, a Liberal Party identified with a policy of Irish self-government (Home Rule) and in parliamentary alliance with the Irish Nationalists and, on the other, a Conservative Party (renamed the Unionist Party) committed to the defence of the constitution, property, Empire and Union.

Differing conceptions of the British state and identity were employed within these formulas for management of the Union. D. G. Boyce claims that Gladstone's version of Britishness acknowledged that the state was multinational and should be governed according to the identities and traditions of its historic nations. The Liberals became identified with dissent, Irish Home Rule and Welsh Nonconformism, enjoying strong electoral support in Scotland and Wales.[53] For the Conservatives, the British state represented a constitutional high-point, the key to its world power; Home Rule would mean a weakening, or even the break-up, of the United Kingdom and the Empire. Albert Dicey offered the clearest defence of the Union, depicting federalism as a concept alien to the British constitution and dismissing Irish claims to nationhood. Only the Union could maintain justice, freedom and state authority.[54] Defence of the Union was a core component of Salisbury's statecraft, using the Irish Question 'to consolidate his primacy over the party, to stiffen its reflexes, to forge an alliance with the Unionist defectors from the Liberal Party, to get rid of Churchill, and hence to establish himself in office for almost fourteen years'.[55]

Conservative unionism was expressed in more emotive terms by Randolph Churchill whose support for Ulster was encapsulated by the phrase 'Ulster will fight and Ulster will be right'. The Orange card and anti-Irish rhetoric brought electoral success for the Conservatives in Protestant Glasgow and Lancashire, unfavourable territory on purely class grounds. Considerations of party statecraft were as significant as those of Conservative principle. Home Rule broke the Liberal's spell of dominance. Following the defeat of the first Home Rule Bill, Salisbury came to power with a majority resting on support from the Liberal Unionists, newly formed following Chamberlain's and Hartington's break from the Liberals.[56] The Liberal Unionist MPs became firmly allied with the Conservative

Party after the 1893 Home Rule Bill, though remained a separate entity until the merger of the party organizations in 1912. Analysis of the voting behaviour of Liberal Unionist and Conservative MPs has shown that support for the Union was the main area of agreement, policy differences existing on other issues.[57]

The Edwardian era was one of crisis in Conservative politics as Salisbury's statecraft unravelled and the politics of nationhood provoked serious internal divisions. Tariff reform was the main catalyst of these, but a hardening of attitudes towards Irish Home Rule on the Tory Right also contributed to intra-party tensions. Arthur Balfour's 'constructive Unionism' mixed coercion and conciliation, hoping that a series of reforms would stifle Home Rule demands ('killing Home Rule with kindness').[58] But a range of popular leagues – mobilizing support for issues such as conscription, 'national efficiency', tariff reform and the defence of Ulster – emerged as the 'radical Right' constructed a nationalist strategy on the fringes of Conservative politics.[59] The determination of this 'diehard' Right to defend the constitution and Union, by unconstitutional needs if necessary, was hardened by the disputes over the Lloyd George budget in 1909–10, fusing questions of class, property and territory. Meanwhile federalism or 'Home Rule all Round' was attracting intellectual support, though Austen Chamberlain was one of only a handful of leading Conservatives to flirt with it.[60]

By the third Home Rule Bill of 1912, much Conservative energy was directed towards safeguarding Unionist Ulster. The significance of Ulster to Conservative unionism owed much to pressure from Ulster Unionists and to the backing of Andrew Bonar Law, for whom 'the insurmountable objection to Home Rule is the injustice of attempting to impose it against their will upon the Unionists of Ulster'.[61] But the defence of Ulster threatened further factional strife and saw considerable energy expended on an area which would bring the party few electoral rewards and tarnish it with the brush of doctrinaire nationalism.[62] Ulster's Unionists articulated a British identity, but one stressing Ulster's Protestant heritage, loyalty to the Crown rather than to a Westminster parliament which was threatening to 'transfer a people's allegiance without their consent', plus Anglo-Saxon links with Britain and Empire.[63] Compromise over Ulster appeared unlikely given the Right's threats of violent resistance, until European war, coalition government and uprising in Ireland dictated change in Conservative strategy. Party leaders accepted that Irish nationalism in the south could not be contained within the United Kingdom, but insisted that Protestant Ulster should be excluded from the Irish Free State. Following the 1922 Anglo-Irish Treaty, six Ulster counties duly remained in the Union as Northern Ireland and British territorial politics entered a more stable period.[64]

A relationship built on non-interference emerged between centre and locality, a territorial code characterized by Bulpitt as a 'dual polity' in which local and sub-national politics existed in separate arenas. The centre, lacking the resources or inclination to become embroiled in local matters, granted limited administrative autonomy in Scotland and significant executive autonomy to the new Stormont regime in Northern Ireland, concentrating itself on economic and foreign affairs. The decline of the Liberals and emergence of a Labour Party concentrating on winning power at the centre helped ensure that party competition would be played out over national issues in Great Britain.

Baldwin's State Patriotism

The Conservative Party under Baldwin's leadership reverted to a moderate state or constitutional patriotism, acting as a national rather than nationalist party, though one which continued to have an English hue. As leader, Baldwin re-established the Conservative's credentials as the party of national unity rather than sectional interests, praising the settled constitution and national character, and attacking class-based socialist politics. His speeches set out a depoliticized conservative patriotism, but one essentially English and rural in its imagery, evoking nostalgic and parochial images of a 'golden age' of rural life and the English country gentleman, and idealizing the English character.[65] In Scotland, the Unionist Party maintained its Scottish identity, linking a defence of Scottish identity and interests with conservative state patriotism.

Baldwin's rhetoric was designed to soothe Conservative nerves as the country entered a period of economic and social dislocation, including a brief readoption of tariff reform in 1923. A depoliticized politics of nationhood emphasizing social cohesion and the nation's ability to integrate and tolerate diverse groups within its ranks would ease the absorption of the working class into the political nation: 'in Baldwin's hands, "democracy" was tamed by identification with constitutionalism and patriotism'.[66] Imperialism still figured in conservative state patriotism, but was cleansed of some of its messianic and aggressively nationalist elements as a retreat from Empire began, marking a clearer distinction between moderate conservatism and the nationalist Right. Appeasement tarnished Conservative patriotism, while Labour politicians and intellectuals also began to prove adept at using the language of state patriotism and Whig imperialism.[67]

CONCLUSIONS

Conservative predominance in the politics of nationhood is neither permanent nor inevitable, but a product of historical conditions and political strategy. A coherent conservative concept of the nation was first systematically developed by Burke, fusing Whig and Tory themes in its account of British history, identity and political structure. Conservatives gradually appropriated the language of nationhood, constructing a non-ethnic, non-democratic account which emphasized tradition, continuous progress towards the balanced constitution, limited politics and a deferential national character, and a rejection of ideological politics in favour of particularism and practical statecraft. Added to this were myths and symbols of conservative state patriotism, which in the late nineteenth century became a key pillar of Conservative politics. Patriotic rhetoric, national cohesion, imperialism and the defence of the Union and constitutional settlement were central to Conservative statecraft in a period of challenges to the party's role.

However, as well as bringing political advantage, the politics of nationhood also produced fundamental disputes about the means and ends of Conservative politics. Tariff reform and the Irish Question provoked fundamental disputes about party strategy and British identity in which the limited politics of conservative state patriotism was challenged by a Right-wing nationalism whose adherents put principle before concerns of party. At a doctrinal level, the Burkean blend of Whig and Tory themes also proved a difficult balancing act. For much of the period studied in this chapter, conservative state patriotism drew upon a Whig reading of British nationhood which emphasized national progress and a balanced constitution. But this was periodically challenged by Tory or 'radical Right' accounts of nationhood and Conservative politics. The centrality of imperialism (and associated racial myths) to conservative state patriotism also hindered the development of a coherent sense of British identity, a problem which became particularly apparent in the post-war era.

The relationship between the Conservative Party and the politics of nationhood ran into difficulties by the late 1950s. The foundations of conservative state patriotism were undermined by a number of factors: British political and economic decline, the retreat from Empire and reluctant turn to Europe, a renewal of substate nationalism, immigration from the New Commonwealth and a Keynesian welfare state political settlement in which the Conservatives had lost their distinctive patriotic voice and had not developed a coherent post-imperial idea of Britishness. From the late 1960s leading Conservatives thus began to seek a renewed politics of nationhood, a quest which produced fundamentally different views of the nation-state, national identity and Conservative statecraft.

2 Heath and Powell – Two National Strategies

The politics of nationhood, central to Conservative political strategy since the 1880s, offered the party fewer political advantages in the post-war period. By 1945, the Conservative claim to be the patriotic party had lost resonance given their association with the pre-war depression, the emergence of a popular patriotic discourse on the Left and a new period of consensus politics.[1] Within the parameters of this bipartisan consensus, Conservative predominance in the politics of nationhood receded – the party could no longer credibly resort to patriotic rhetoric which challenged Labour's legitimacy and depicted the Conservatives as the only party understanding the interests and values of the British people. The foundations of the Conservative politics of nationhood also crumbled as Britain's world-power status waned, economic decline became more apparent, the retreat from Empire gathered pace and immigration from the New Commonwealth changed British society.

Internal and external challenges to the Conservative politics of nationhood provoked intra-party disputes, notably in the rearguard action fought by Tory imperialists, although they were isolated following Suez, accelerated decolonization and the 1961 application for membership of the European Community. The 1950s and 1960s were a confused period for the Conservative politics of nationhood: imperialist voices were heard over Suez and Rhodesia, while immigration became a key concern of the Right, but one which the leadership approached with obvious unease. Although aware that promoting the Conservatives as the 'party of Europe' was a significant departure, Macmillan presented EC membership as neither an abandonment of Britain's global pretensions, nor a serious challenge to British sovereignty or the Conservative's status as the patriotic party.

Heath's leadership (1965–75) was a critical period in the Conservative politics of nationhood as questions about the modernization of Conservative politics came to the fore. Heath's programme was built on EC membership and a relative modernization of the state which, together with a concern to avoid an overt politicization of 'race' issues, support in Opposition for Scottish devolution and his Government's imposition of direct rule for Northern Ireland, contributed to intra-party disputes about Conservative statecraft and the politics of nationhood. Enoch Powell provided a New Right authoritarian individualist critique of Heath's programme, offering in its place a vision of the Conservatives as the party of capitalism and nationhood, rejecting EC entry, defending the Union and urging repatriation.[2]

THE CHANGING POLITICS OF NATIONHOOD

The national strategies espoused by Heath and Powell did not emerge to replace the traditional Conservative focus on Empire, Union and an integrative state patriotism until the late 1960s, but the years prior to this had seen a gradual disintegration of the Conservative politics of nationhood and Whig imperialism. Central to the changing politics of nationhood was Britain's retreat from Empire. The pattern of decolonization was spasmodic: a late 1940s crisis of imperial rule saw decolonization in India, Burma, Ceylon and Palestine, but both parties backed the development of the African colonies under white rule.[3] Decolonization in Africa began in earnest in the early 1960s as a variety of factors accelerated the process, including nationalist pressures in the colonies, changing trade patterns, Britain's fading world-power status and domestic disillusionment with the imperial idea.

As the party of Empire, the Conservatives' gradual adjustment to the diminution of imperial power and prestige was a painful process for many Tories. Imperial ideas were still prominent in the party in the 1940s and, although primarily reactive and symbolic of another era, retained their emotional appeal for a dwindling band of backbench Conservative MPs and peers (including Lord Salisbury and Julian Amery) until the Rhodesian settlement of 1979. Some support for imperial preference was evident on the Conservative backbenches in the late 1940s and although the 1952 General Agreement on Tariffs and Trade (GATT) effectively ended the prospect of such schemes, concerns about Commonwealth trade were later raised by opponents of EC membership.[4] Imperialist sympathizers supported the political ascendancy of European settlers in the African colonies (using the language of 'kith and kin') and portrayed the colonies as important British interests. Internal dissent was apparent during the Suez Group rebellions in the mid-1950s, but the Tory Right remained a disparate and largely uninfluential grouping.[5] The Monday Club later acted as a focal point of Tory imperialist opposition to government policy, viewing decolonization as an assault on the party's identity and values, rebellions occurring on a number of parliamentary votes on sanctions against Ian Smith's regime.[6]

Decolonization – the 'Winds of Change'

Macmillan's 1960 declaration in South Africa that 'the wind of change is blowing through this continent' and the appointment of Iain Macleod as Colonial Secretary signalled accelerated decolonization.[7] Previous concerns that colonies about to become self-governing should be politically stable, ethnically harmonious and economically viable were downplayed as the government initiated rapid transfers of power to avoid friction and attempt to retain British influence in the newly independent states.[8] The process whereby the imperial idea, once the bedrock of conservative state patriotism and national strategy, disappeared from the leadership's statecraft calculations had been all but completed by the time Heath became leader. Though the leadership paid lip service to the idea of the Commonwealth as a multiracial body linking Britain to her former colonies, the Suez debacle, British isolation in the Commonwealth, changed economic and security considerations, immigration concerns and the EC application meant that the Conservatives did not seriously consider transforming themselves from an imperial to Commonwealth party.

The 'Party of Europe'

In the 1960s the Conservatives instead adopted the mantle of 'party of Europe', but sought to fit this alongside its status as patriotic party and defender of the nation-state. Prior to 1961, successive governments had ruled out full participation in supranational European organizations for a number of reasons: unwillingness to cede national sovereignty; a 'three circles' foreign policy envisaging Britain as a world power with influence in Commonwealth, Atlantic and European spheres; and short-term assessments of the economic implications of membership. In the mid-1950s the Six were determined to establish a customs union, rejecting British plans for a Free Trade Area which would safeguard her preferential trading relations with the Commonwealth and ensure non-discriminatory trade with the continent. Britain was left in the unsatisfactory position of being the leading member of the European Free Trade Association (EFTA).[9]

In 1960 Macmillan began seriously to consider British membership of the EC, but the government adopted a cautious approach, examining its implications and conducting talks with the United States and the Commonwealth before the decision to seek negotiations on membership was taken at a Cabinet meeting in July 1961.[10] Ministers stressed that membership would depend on the negotiations with the Six producing arrangements which took account of the special interests of the UK, including agriculture and Commonwealth ties. The sovereignty implications of membership were also downplayed, Macmillan's 1962 conference speech being one of the first to make a positive endorsement of the EC as a political entity.

The Prime Minister recognized that the application and reorientation of the Conservatives as the 'party of Europe' would be a difficult one.

> It was, after all, asking a great deal of the Conservative Party, so long and so intimately linked with Empire, to accept the changed situation, which might require a new concept by which Britain might serve Commonwealth and world interests more efficiently if she were linked with Europe than if she remained isolated, doomed to a diminishing power in a world in which her relative wealth and strength were bound to shrink.[11]

Macmillan appointed pro-European ministers to key positions, hoping to neutralize ministers such as Rab Butler who were wary of membership. Some 100 Conservative MPs were concerned about the implications of membership, 40 of these convinced opponents, though only 29 abstained on the vote on the application proposal in 1961 with just 1 voting against his party.[12] Backbench concerns often focused on the detailed requirements of entry, particularly agricultural issues and Commonwealth links, but de Gaulle's veto meant that the extent of the constraint on government policy posed by Conservative opposition to concrete membership terms would not be revealed.[13] Forty-nine Tories signed a motion expressing concern about the loss of sovereignty, but Macmillan downplayed the implications of membership.

Accession to the Treaty of Rome would not involve a one-sided surrender of 'sovereignty' on our part, but a pooling of sovereignty by all concerned, mainly in economic and social fields. In renouncing some of our sovereignty we would receive in return a share of the sovereignty renounced by other members. Our obligations would not alter the position of the Crown, nor rob our Parliament of its essential powers, nor deprive our Law Courts of their authority in our domestic life. The talk about loss of sovereignty becomes all the more meaningless when one remembers that practically every nation, including our own, has already been forced by the pressures of the modern world to abandon large areas of sovereignty and to realise that we are now all interdependent.[14]

The Conservative Party's European conversion was a major departure from its imperial and patriotic self-image. In foreign policy terms though, the decision to apply was in many ways a tactical change rather than a fundamental reappraisal of Britain's role in the world. It did not signal an abandonment of pretensions at global influence – rather policy-makers believed that EC entry was essential if Britain were to remain America's leading European partner – although it did mark an acceptance that the Commonwealth would not provide the support system needed for global influence. Fears that the EC might develop a political identity which further isolated Britain and that Britain's relative economic decline would worsen outside the EC also influenced the decision to seek membership. In domestic political terms, Macmillan saw entry as a means of modernizing the Conservative Party, boosting their support among a technocratic middle class at a time when economic and political problems were mounting. It also placed the Labour leadership in a difficult position given that party's internal divisions on the issue, Gaitskell's attempt to seize the patriotic mantle being condemned by pro-Europeans in both main parties.[15]

Ultimately de Gaulle's 1963 veto removed the prospect of entry in the medium-term and left a central plank of the Conservatives' modernization strategy in limbo. Macmillan felt that 'all our policies at home and abroad are in ruins', but this and Wolfram Kaiser's claim that even the failed application had been a diplomatic success appear exaggerated.[16] The party retained the goal of entry but the political benefits of a successful application (though entry on British terms was by no means guaranteed) had been denied.

The application had involved neither fundamental rethinking on the future of the British state, economy or foreign policy, nor the scale of principled opposition from Conservative MPs evident in Heath's successful membership bid. Macmillan had pointed the way towards a post-imperial Conservative politics, one that would be more fully developed in a revised national strategy under Heath's leadership.

Immigration Controls

Another issue to emerge in the Conservative politics of nationhood during Macmillan's premiership was New Commonwealth immigration. A bipartisan consensus existed on immigration issues in the 1950s, neither party willing to confront the issue head on despite their private concerns. Cabinet and departmental papers reveal that the Conservative leadership was concerned about the (still low) numbers of West African, Asian and West Indian immigrants entering the UK, and about unemployment and crime among immigrant communities. However, the problems involved in legislating to control immigration (the prospect of damaging relations with Commonwealth states, of special treatment for Irish immigrants provoking accusations of racial discrimination, and problems in redefining British citizenship) were believed to outweigh the need for change in a system under which citizens of the United Kingdom and colonies enjoyed the right of abode in the UK.[17] Conservative and Labour leaders were also keen to keep the difficult and emotive issues of 'race' and immigration off the political agenda of the centre.[18]

By the early 1960s, the immigration issue was proving more difficult to ignore. Concern among Conservative MPs and activists had been growing, evidenced by Cyril Osborne's parliamentary campaign to introduce immigration control and by debate at the 1961 party conference. This reflected wider discourse on the 'otherness' of the coloured ethnic minorities and associated racial or 'kith and kin' accounts of British identity.[19] Public opinion was moving towards control, especially after the 1958 riots in Nottingham and Notting Hill, while primary immigration rose in 1960, having fallen in the previous two years.[20] Macmillan decided to grasp the nettle, introducing the Commonwealth Immigration Bill in 1961 despite opposition from Labour. This sought to control primary immigration by only permitting Commonwealth citizens possessing Ministry of Labour employment vouchers to enter the UK. Direct dependents of voucher holders and students intending to leave Britain after their studies had finished were excluded from these provisions as, controversially, were Irish citizens. The Bill ended the tradition of *civis Britannicus sum* under which all Commonwealth and colonial peoples were British subjects with right of entry into the UK. But rather than satisfying the demands of the Tory Right, the Bill fuelled demands for further measures.[21]

Immigration hit centre stage in Conservative politics in the 1964 election when, after a racially charged campaign, Peter Griffiths won the Smethwick constituency on a 7.5 per cent swing from Labour, compared to a national swing of 3.2 per cent.[22] His exploitation of 'race' issues was taken as a signal by the Tory Right that a populist platform of strict immigration controls and repatriation could win votes and restore the Conservatives' status as a party determined to protect British identity. Party leader Alec Douglas-Home spoke in favour of voluntary repatriation and Shadow Home Secretary Peter Thorneycroft urged measures to end mass immigration.[23] The Smethwick result also influenced Wilson's decision to maintain then tighten immigration controls, but to do so within a bipartisan consensus on balancing controls with measures to tackle discrimination and improve race relations. As with EC entry, immigration issues would have a significant impact on Conservative politics, fuelling factionalism and a dispute between Heath and Powell which went to the heart of Conservative statecraft and the politics of nationhood.

HEATH'S NATIONAL STRATEGY

Heath's period as party leader and Prime Minister was significant for Conservative statecraft in general and the politics of nationhood in particular. He attempted a modernization of Conservative politics, the British state and economy, but saw this falter in the face of strategic problems and political crisis.[24] Heath sought to adapt the Conservative politics of nationhood to the challenges identified above. EC membership was the centrepiece, viewed as the key to Britain's modernization. In territorial politics, Heath promised Scottish devolution but did not act on this in office, and imposed direct rule over Northern Ireland. The 1971 Immigration Act effectively halted mass immigration, but Heath also wanted to defuse 'race' issues. Heath's national strategy was undone by external and internal problems. Its adaptation to changed circumstances was flawed: the UK entered the EC at an inauspicious moment without fully addressing factors, such as her intergovernmentalist perspective and economic decline, which would make for British 'awkwardness'. The flirtation with devolution was not underpinned by a coherent vision of the British state. Statecraft problems – Powell's challenge, intensified factionalism, plus a failure to achieve issue hegemony, governing competence or successful policy implementation – also bedevilled the Heath Government.

In opposition in the late 1960s, the Conservatives undertook a policy review exercise covering a range of issues. Like Heath's strategy as a whole, this was marked by a managerial and technocratic concern with practical policy details rather than an ideological focus on first principles. Manifesto commitments to reducing inflation and public expenditure and encouraging competitiveness drew on New Right themes but lacked its ideological underpinning. The Heath project could not survive the crisis in the world economy nor overcome the structural weaknesses of the British state and economy, and in 1972 the government reverted to state intervention, a prices and incomes policy and reflation of the economy.

Joining the European Community

EC entry was the centrepiece of Heath's domestic and foreign policy, depicted as the means of revitalizing the economy and redefining Britain's role in an interdependent world. But tensions between its intergovernmental vision of Europe and those of other Member States, plus the difficult adaptation of the British political system and economy to EC membership undermined his European strategy. Christopher Lord's study places Heath's strategy at the juncture of competing perspectives on British foreign policy: a 'traditionalist' approach based on the 'sovereign separateness of the state' versus a 'transformationalist' rejection of state sovereignty as an appropriate reference point for foreign policy goals.[25] Heath's approach was flawed in that it incorporated elements of both accounts, accepting a pooling of national sovereignty in the EC as a means of promoting national interests, but maintaining a pragmatic intergovernmentalist vision of European integration in which 'essential national sovereignty' would remain unscathed.

Heath's European convictions were a blend of idealism and realism, supporting closer cooperation between nation-states as a means of ensuring peace, stability and growth. In 1969 Heath stated that 'the unity of Europe will in the end be achieved by European governments forming the habit of working together', backing an incremental pooling of sovereignty to the extent that 'it is inconceivable to me that the unity of Europe could now be established on any other basis'.[26] Eighteen years later, the analysis was similar:

> the Community was created by the founding fathers as an institution *sui generis*.... So it has developed *sui generis* and the final form of its political organization will be *sui generis*. For this reason we are not using our time to the best purpose if we concentrate our argument around federalism.[27]

Whereas Powell focused on the perceived detrimental effects of EC membership on sovereignty understood as political independence, self-government and the legislative supremacy of parliament, Heath saw sovereignty in terms of capacity (a state's effective international influence) and relative executive autonomy (the government's ability to achieve its economic and political goals).[28] For Heath,

> Sovereignty is not something to be hoarded, sterile and barren, carefully protected by the Right Honourable Member for Down South [Powell] ... Sovereignty is something for us as custodians to use in the interests of our country ... It is a judgement which we have to make, and I answer without hesitation that the sacrifice of sovereignty, if it be put in that extreme form, or the sharing of sovereignty, the transfer of sovereignty or the offering of sovereignty is fully justified. Indeed, were we not to do so in the modern world, I believe that as a Parliament, as a party and as a Government we should be culpable in the eyes of history.[29]

Recognizing the limited effectiveness of independent British action in the light of national decline and interdependence, EC membership was necessary if Britain were to be economically competitive and politically influential. The government accepted the Treaty of Rome framework before embarking on detailed negotiations. Its White Paper depicted membership as having only limited implications for parliamentary sovereignty, stressing unanimity and downplaying the significance of the primacy of Community law, claiming that there would be no 'erosion of essential national sovereignty'. But it also noted the dynamic nature of the Community, talking of a 'sharing and an enlarging of individual national sovereignties' which would allow for more effective action.[30] An internal Conservative Research Document stated that 'member states should be prepared to exercise their sovereignty in common', taking binding decisions in the Council based on consent and reflecting 'truly common' interests.[31]

Though supporting an intergovernmental Community and the retention of the national veto, Heath had an evolutionary view of integration, believing that negative integration (liberalization and the removal of barriers to free trade) could not proceed without a degree of positive integration (an increase in the competences of the EC). Enhanced foreign policy cooperation, a single market and monetary integration thus all featured in his vision of EC development.[32] Heath placed his faith in the 'community method' of interstate bargaining in a cooperative framework in which the Commission acts as broker and Member States promote common interests and consensual decision-making. But the boundaries of integration are nonetheless determined by nation-states who retain veto rights in order to protect their core interests.

Heath stressed the economic benefits of EC entry, claiming that membership would revitalize the British economy and society by forcing companies to adapt their production and management techniques to meet the challenge of European competition.[33] By pooling sovereignty, Britain could achieve domestic goals which had previously proved elusive: through the Community, government effectiveness would increase, sheltering it from domestic pressures. Heath's support for a government role in promoting regional economic growth also had a European dimension: a European Regional Development Fund and EC industrial policy were viewed as European means of achieving national economic development.

This strategy of using the EC as an external support framework for the British state and economy was not unproblematic: estimates in 1970 put the net cost of British membership at up to £750 million, allowing Wilson to paper over the divisions in the Labour Party by arguing that Heath's determination to get Britain into the Common Market had seen him pay too high a price in the negotiations with the Six.[34] The underlying weakness of the British economy and changes in the world economy also meant that EC membership would not be an economic panacea. The 'Barber boom' reflation of the domestic economy was in part dictated by a belief that to gain the full benefits of membership, Britain had to join with a growing economy. Expectations of a growth dividend proved unfounded, sterling was forced out of the 'snake' fixed exchange rate system after just six weeks, while entry occurred at an inauspicious moment given the oil crisis and the underlying weakness of the economy.[35]

Heath's European policy was crucial to the redefinition of Conservative statecraft and the politics of nationhood, moving away from notions of indivisible sovereignty and accepting (to some extent) that effective influence and domestic goals might be achieved by pooling sovereignty. However, Heath's vision of European integration was a managerial rather than ideological one. Tensions between British interests and perspectives – pragmatism, intergovernmentalism, parliamentary sovereignty – and those of the Six were already evident, while factional disputes in both main parties illustrated that the adaptation of the British political system to this new context of European integration would be a slow and difficult one.

In terms of statecraft considerations and the politics of nationhood, Heath pressed ahead with entry despite increased factionalism within the Conservative Party. A majority of the party inside and outside Parliament supported entry, but the parliamentary arithmetic was a real concern. Powell was the key figure among some 50 anti-Common Market Tories whose case against entry ranged from the loss of sovereignty and the abdication of the Conservative's status as the patriotic party to opposition to the membership terms.[36] Two members of the government resigned, junior minister Teddy Taylor and Jasper Moore from the Whips office, the 1971 motion supporting the entry application being passed thanks to pro-Community Labour rebels and Pym's decision to allow Conservative MPs a free vote. Thirty-nine Conservatives voted against entry. The 1972 European Communities Bill endured a difficult passage through Parliament, the government again relying on Labour rebels to secure a majority of eight on its Second Reading.[37]

Heath presented EC membership not as an end in itself or a dramatic departure from British foreign policy goals, but as the optimal means of achieving key Conservative aims (stable economic growth, relative autonomy for the party leadership in office and the defence of British interests), given the failings of Britain's postwar political settlement and the limits of national sovereignty. Heath's statecraft though ultimately failed, undermined by deep-rooted problems of the British economy, problematic assumptions within his domestic strategy and vision of Britain's role within the Community, and heightened factionalism within the Conservative Party. The relationship between the Conservative's status as the party of Europe and as the defender of the nation-state and national identity remained problematic and would again be at the heart of Conservative factionalism in the 1990s.

Immigration and Race Relations

Immigration was a major issue in this period, Heath hoping to depoliticize the politics of 'race' and backing Wilson's attempts to forge a consensus on linking stricter immigration controls with action to counter racial discrimination and encourage integration.[38] The Conservative leadership followed a 'dual approach', backing the limited measures in the 1965 Race Relations Act after a compromise on conciliation rather than criminal sanctions.[39] But as the influence of the populist Right increased, the leadership expended more energy on demands for immigration controls, depicting this as the key to successful integration and good race relations. Heath's personal determination that the Conservative Party would not be blighted by a Smethwick-style exploitation of 'race' issues helped ensure that immigration did not feature prominently in the 1966 general election.

By 1967–8 the bipartisan approach was becoming more difficult to sustain. Populist Conservatives expressed their dissatisfaction with Roy Jenkins's 'liberal hour' formula which envisaged an integrated plural (that is, multicultural) society of equal opportunity, cultural diversity and mutual tolerance.[40] Progressives in the party supported immigration controls but tempered this with an emphasis on equality before the law, race relations legislation and an integrated, multicultural society. They were prepared to defy the Whips when they felt party policy was too harsh and urged Heath to sack Powell from the Shadow Cabinet following his 1968 'rivers of blood' speech.[41] Populists, with Powell the key figure, sought an end to immigration, backed repatriation and expressed unease at the prospect of a multicultural society, equating it with social disorder and a weakening of national identity.[42]

In the face of backbench and constituency pressure, the leadership refused to support the 1968 Race Relations Bill which extended anti-discrimination laws to housing and employment and established a Community Relations Commission to take over some of the functions of the Race Relations Board. Forty-five Conservatives defied the party Whips and voted against the Bill. Labour's 1968 Commonwealth Immigrants Act, a quickfire reaction to the migration of Kenyan Asians, established the ascendancy of those stressing tough immigration controls. The Act established the principle, subsequently developed by the Heath Government, that any citizen of the UK or colonies would be subject to immigration control unless they had close connection with the UK, that is if they, a parent or grandparent had been born, adopted or naturalized in the UK, or had earlier been registered as a citizen of the UK or colonies.[43]

Powell's Birmingham speech dealt a further blow to the hopes of maintaining an elite consensus. Heath called the speech 'racialist in tone and liable to exacerbate racial tension' and dismissed Powell from the Shadow Cabinet, thereby signalling his determination to prevent Conservatives from playing the 'race card' for electoral advantage.[44] But the influence of the populists in the party increased and Heath toughened party policy on immigration control, moving further away from the principle of common citizenship by stating that immigrants should not have the automatic right to bring their dependents to Britain. The leadership supported state assistance for immigrants wanting to return to their countries of origin, but refused to press them to leave and wanted a more tolerant society.[45] In the 1970 general election campaign, Heath again urged Conservative candidates to steer clear of immigration issues, but Powell's intervention is viewed by some commentators as a significant factor in the narrow Conservative victory.[46]

When the Conservatives were in office, the 1971 Immigration Act introduced the principle of 'patriality' under which only persons with a close connection with the UK ('patrials') would be free from immigration controls. It also replaced the system of employment vouchers with work permits which did not entail either permanent residence or rights of entry for dependents.[47] Legislation to ensure that Pakistani citizens in Britain retained their voting rights despite Pakistan's withdrawal from the Commonwealth and the government's decision to allow some 57 000 Ugandan Asians to enter the UK following their expulsion by Idi Amin signalled Heath's desire to promote good race relations and his humanitarian concerns, but the latter decision met with a hostile reaction from the Tory Right. Dissent over EC entry and immigration reached its peak on a vote on EC free movement and immigration rules when 56 Conservatives either abstained or voted against the government.[48]

As Conservative leader, Heath tried to defuse the immigration issue by balancing controls with a concern with harmonious race relations, rejecting Powell's warnings about the dangers of integration and his demands for repatriation, and refusing to exploit concerns about immigration for electoral advantage.[49] However, striking a balance between race relations and immigration control became more difficult to sustain, pressure from the populist wing of his party pushing Heath to focus more on immigration measures than tackling racial discrimination or disadvantage.

Devolution and Direct Rule

Territorial politics was the third area of the Conservative politics of nationhood to be reshaped under Heath's leadership, the party adopting a policy of limited legislative devolution despite its traditional support for parliamentary sovereignty and the Union. Defence of the Union had historically been a central feature of the Conservative politics of nationhood. Scottish Conservatives presented themselves as the party of the Union and British state patriotism as well as a Scottish national party defending Scottish interests and identity.[50] Their electoral support reached a pinnacle of 50.1 per cent of the vote in the 1955 election, benefiting from a broad electoral coalition, its popular One Nation politics, support for the Union and administrative devolution in Scotland, plus UK economic success.

By the mid-1960s the Scottish party was running into problems, its share of the vote falling to 12.4 per cent (16 MPs) at the 1966 general election. Heath attributed the decline to the growth of Scottish nationalism and the Scottish National Party (SNP), believing that 'nationalism is the biggest single factor in our politics today'.[51] Concern about the level of dissatisfaction with existing governmental arrangements among the Scottish electorate and the perceived shortcomings of the Conservative message were also being raised by elements of the Scottish party. Organizational changes had followed the 1964 election defeat, but the Thistle Group advocated policy change including legislative devolution.[52] Sir William McEwan Younger's internal party committee advocated an elected Scottish Assembly with powers to initiate and consider legislation, though ultimate legislative authority would be retained at Westminster. Heath welcomed the proposals and in his 'Declaration of Perth' at the 1968 Scottish party conference surprised his audience by committing the Conservatives to legislative devolution.[53]

A committee chaired by Douglas-Home was set up to find a solution which preserved 'the essential principle of the sovereignty of parliament' but provided a devolution scheme which improved the machinery of government in Scotland. The Convention proposed in the committee's 1970 report *Scotland's Government* would have 125 directly elected members, but its powers would be limited to those performed by the Scottish Grand Committee and Scottish Standing Committees. Federalism and independence were rejected. Though backing limited legislative devolution, the Convention proposals were designed with a commitment to the sovereignty of Westminster as paramount: it would not be able to initiate legislation and although the Second Reading, Committee and Report stages of Scottish Bills would be dealt with by the Convention, the Third Reading and Lords stages would stay with Westminster. Little attention was paid to wider constitutional issues such as the relationship between the Convention and local government, though there was to be no reduction in the number of Scottish MPs at Westminster.[54]

Although the Scottish party approved the Douglas-Home proposals and the 1970 manifesto included a commitment to establish a Convention, the Heath Government made no move towards legislative devolution. Various reasons have been given for this failure to act: the Royal Commission on the Constitution set up by Wilson in 1969 would not report until 1973 and Heath did not want to pre-empt it by pressing ahead with his own devolution scheme; the Government's attempted modernization of the state focused its energy on local government reform and regional policy rather than devolution, the two-tier proposals sitting uneasily with the Convention blueprint; support for devolution in the Scottish party had never been deep rooted, and during the early 1970s opposition grew though English MPs took little interest in the debate. Perhaps most significantly, the issue of devolution had (briefly) lost some of its potency in British and Scottish politics, with the fortunes of the SNP in decline until its gains in the 1974 general elections.[55] Following election defeat in February 1974, Heath was again concerned by the nationalist revival, promising an indirectly elected assembly with spending powers.[56] But Conservative opposition to devolution gathered pace and under Thatcher's leadership the party soon returned to an anti-devolution stance.

The Heath Government faced a worsening situation in Northern Ireland, the difficult decisions taken during that period on direct rule, the Irish dimension and the search for a settlement built around consociational power-sharing devolution, forming the basis of government policy for at least the next 25 years.[57] Heath treated Northern Ireland as a 'place apart', the divisions between the unionist and nationalist communities and mounting security problems requiring special treatment. He sought an elite consensus on handling the Northern Ireland situation, insulating the principle of its status within the UK and the details of its government after the introduction of direct rule from partisan high politics. The Government inherited a deteriorating situation, pressing the Stormont regime to introduce further civil rights legislation against a backdrop of escalating violence, but the situation was worsened by internment in 1971 and the deaths of 13 unarmed protesters at the hands of British paratroopers on 'Bloody Sunday' in 1972.

The worsening security situation was a key factor in the Government's decision to prorogue the Stormont regime (a Unionist hegemony practising institutional discrimination) in 1972 and establish direct rule from London with Northern Ireland affairs coming under the remit of a new Secretary of State and Northern Ireland Office. Direct rule was not viewed as an ideal solution, the Prime Minister claiming that it was a temporary measure to take security issues out of Ulster politics and allay international concern.[58] The 1973 Northern Ireland Constitution Act formalized the new arrangements, setting out the formula that a united Ireland could only come about with the consent of the majority of people living in Northern Ireland, confirmation that a majority wanted to remain in the UK subsequently coming in a referendum. The Act also confirmed that Secretary of State William Whitelaw would play a brokering role in the search for a devolved power-sharing assembly.[59] This brokering appeared to have reached a successful conclusion with the December 1973 agreement to establish the power-sharing Sunningdale executive in which the official Unionists, Social Democratic and Labour Party (SDLP) and Alliance parties would form a coalition government, with a cross-border Council of Ireland with minor consultative powers also being created. But opposition in the Unionist community led to the 1974 Ulster Workers' Council strike which brought about the executive's collapse.[60]

The Heath Government's commitment to power-sharing and rejection of Unionist majority rule, its talks with the Republic and claims to be playing the role of honest broker, plus short-lived discussions between Whitelaw and the Irish Republican Army (IRA), brought about a break between the official Unionists and the Conservative Party. Unionists had traditionally taken the Conservative whip but the official Unionists resigned the whip in 1974 in protest at the Sunningdale agreement. Powell was again Heath's major critic, but Conservative dissent on policy towards Northern Ireland was limited.[61]

POWELL'S NATIONALIST STRATEGY

Conservative opposition to Heath's political strategy found its most significant and coherent expression in the speeches and writings of Enoch Powell, in which the politics of nationhood had a central, unifying role. For Powell, the Conservative Party was 'the nationalist party *par exellence*', 'a Conservative Party which cannot present itself to the country as a national party suffers under a severe handicap'.[62] Powellism constructed an alternative post-imperial nationalist strategy which redefined the conservative nation and constructed a political strategy built around monetarist economics, repatriation and an end to New Commonwealth immigration, plus the defence of the nation-state and parliamentary sovereignty through opposition to membership of the EC and support for the Union with Northern Ireland. This commitment to a strong nation-state was combined with a commitment to neo-liberal economics, Powell claiming that the Conservatives must be 'the party of free choice, free competition and free enterprise... the party of capitalism'.[63] Powellism broke with the prevailing elite consensus and directly challenged Heath's strategy, but it was his campaign on immigration which accounted for much of its populist appeal.[64]

At the heart of Powellism was the quest for a renewed national identity and a strong nation-state, redirecting the Conservative Party towards its role as the hegemonic party of British state patriotism. This was not a nostalgic longing for past imperial glories, but a search for a 'realistic' understanding of Britain's identity and status as a 'parliamentary nation', with English history and values of particular significance.[65] Powell's idea of the nation drew on familiar Conservative themes but presented them in a new configuration, adapted to changed circumstances. He stressed the organic nature of British constitutional evolution and its parliamentary political culture, central to which was the doctrine of parliamentary sovereignty. The nation is the key form of community: 'a nation is not a rational thing. There is no rational basis for nationhood. What a nation is, is what it feels itself to be, instinctively and emotionally.'[66] Powell thus defined nationhood in subjective terms, looking to its history, the homogeneity and unity of its people and their shared experiences – 'the life of nations, no less than that of men, is lived largely in the imagination'.[67] National consciousness is built around the corporate imagination of a nation's past, expressed in the form of myth.

A nation lives by its myths... my particular thesis is that some of the British people's most important myths in this period of time are bad myths, harmful myths, and that they need urgently to be replaced by better.[68]

Powell's redefinition of British nationhood thus rejected nineteenth-century myths of empire and industrial strength as damaging fictions: the nation must learn to know itself again. Empire was a 'political mythology' created to mask Britain's decline by offering illusions of racial union and prosperity.[69] Also contributing to the country's 'psychosomatic illness' was the myth of Britain as the 'workshop of the world' which had fostered the false belief that economic weakness was a new phenomenon indicating national decline. Powell's 'realistic' national identity was, however, also built around myth. He saw the essence of British identity in 'the magic of the free Parliament of a united nation', the continuity of its history and the homogeneity of its people.[70] The Westminster parliament was treated as central to Britain's constitutional development and represented national homogeneity in the sense of common allegiance to a single sovereign. This emphasis on sovereignty, allegiance and homogeneity underpinned Powell's campaign against immigration and EC entry plus his defence of the Union.

The essence of a nation is that it is... homogeneous, that it accepts a single sovereign system, yes, but above all that every part of it thinks that the whole is more important than the parts. Inside the nation you cannot contain elements that are foreign to it in the sense that they cannot share that devotion to the whole against its parts.[71]

The EC and Parliamentary Sovereignty

Powell's key concern was the effect of EC membership on parliamentary sovereignty and British nationhood. He turned against membership in the late 1960s believing that the EC's ultimate goal was political and economic union. The inevitable consequence of EC membership was the loss of sovereignty, understood as 'political independence and self-government' which were also the essence of British nationhood. 'Parliament ... would no longer be the body which took the principle decisions which govern the economic and social life of the people of this country and which determines its safety and even its existence.'[72] Powell recognized that no nation was free to do entirely as it wished, that nations are mutually dependent and that defence or trade treaties were an expression of national sovereignty rather than its denial.

> A nation may enter into contract or associations or agreements and thereby voluntarily limit its freedom, as does any individual who signs a contract. But this is totally different from deliberately giving up for all time the freedom in future to take a decision ... In a political and economic union of Europe it would be contradictory to speak or think of national sovereignty in the sense in which it exists at present.[73]

Community membership bound the government to the future decisions of others, entailing a loss of political independence. Under the Treaty of Rome, Parliament would lose its legislative supremacy and its exclusive control over taxation; judicial independence would also be given up to an external authority.[74] Claims that sovereignty could be pooled or shared in the EC were rejected.

> Though XYZ may be formed from a combination of X and Y and Z, it is not the same as any of those three and none of them enjoys independence or possesses sovereignty if it accepts the overriding authority of XYZ; they are not governed by themselves but by others.[75]

Powell was critical of the Heath Government for the manner in which membership occurred: in the 1970 election campaign Heath had promised that membership would only come about 'with the full consent of parliament and people' and the Conservative manifesto had committed the party only to negotiation. Subsequently, however, the Government accepted the Treaty of Rome before negotiations began, Powell accusing the Prime Minister of breaking the 'compact between parliament and people' and of shattering the Conservative Party's status as the national and patriotic party by effectively conceding that 'the nation-state as exemplified

by an independent and self-governing United Kingdom was obsolete'.[76] In the February 1974 election Powell encouraged people to vote Labour as its commitment to holding a referendum offered a way of leaving the Community. Powell also spoke of Britain's political distinctiveness from continental Europe, but this again primarily rested on its parliamentary tradition.[77]
Britain would prosper if it pursued an independent foreign policy outside of the EC and was free of special ties with the Commonwealth which encouraged misplaced paternalism and unrealistic expectations of a world role. Only a move away from past imperial commitments could prevent national humiliation and further damage to the national interest (Powell thus arguing when Shadow Defence Secretary that Britain should withdraw from her commitments in the Far East).[78] An independent foreign policy would also free Britain from the unwelcome influence of the United States – especially on Northern Ireland.

Ulster Unionism

Powell's defence of Northern Ireland's place in the Union was also constructed in terms of British nationhood and parliamentary sovereignty. As noted above, Powell viewed nationhood as a subjective status, a nation existing when its people demonstrate their unity and see themselves as part of a wider community with a common idea of itself. For him, the Ulster issue was a crucial one for British nationhood, 'to decide who we are, to establish or re-establish our identity as a nation' in the face of a direct threat to national integrity and identity which symbolized a loss of confidence in being British.[79] Northern Ireland was British because the majority of the people living there regarded themselves as such and were historically distinct from the rest of the island of Ireland, feeling that they should be treated as an integral part of the UK. Ulster Unionism was thus different from nationalism as it demanded full recognition that the people of Northern Ireland were part of the UK.

Following the abolition of the Stormont Parliament and during his spell as Ulster Unionist MP for Down South from October 1974 to 1987, Powell urged the further integration of Northern Ireland into the UK political system.[80] He criticized the Heath Government for treating Northern Ireland as a conditional part of the UK, for denying the people of Ulster their nationhood, for curtailing their democratic rights under direct rule, for looking towards power-sharing and an Irish dimension and for meeting with IRA terrorists. He demanded that the Republic of Ireland be treated as a foreign state, being critical of special citizenship rules and travel arrangements, and claimed that EC membership would further erode the border. Given his perception that the government had failed the people of Ulster, Powell also welcomed the Ulster Unionist's split from the Conservative Party.

Powell demanded that Northern Ireland be treated as an equal part of the UK – Ulster's representation at Westminster should be increased to a level appropriate to its population, Northern Ireland legislation should not have to follow the Orders in Council route and elected local government should be restored. But his support for integration sat uneasily with the Ulster Unionist Party's policy of backing legislative devolution, Powell arguing that devolution weakened the Union and undermined parliamentary sovereignty. He opposed a return to the Stormont regime, but was prepared to accept that, if Scotland and Wales were granted devolution, then Ulster had to be treated in the same way. In the 1980s he accused the Conservatives of reneging on their national and unionist role by signing the Anglo-Irish Agreement, which he depicted as foisted upon the government by American pressure.[81]

Powell also regarded the prospect of legislative devolution as damaging for the territorial integrity of the UK and for the sovereignty of parliament. The essence of the British constitution was parliament's exclusive power to make laws covering the whole country: this would be undermined by devolution. However, he argued that, should Scottish and Welsh nationalism become irresistible, London could not stand in their way. In the 1976–7 parliamentary debates, Powell pointed to the anomalies of the devolution proposals, rejecting Wilson's description of Scotland and Wales as 'political nations' which had the right to levy their own taxes, claiming that true nations had a right to self-government.[82]

Immigration and National Identity

For Powell, nationhood was determined by subjective feelings of what sort of people the British were but also by reference to threats to national identity by non-nationals, illustrating the nature of Britishness by identifying those alien to the national community. Chief among the perceived threats to British nationhood were the 'alien wedge' of New Commonwealth immigrants. Powell's assault on immigration established him as a populist politician, broke with the liberal consensus on 'race' issues and signalled the emergence of a New Right ethnic-ideological account of British national identity. Powellism was instrumental in fostering a climate in which ethnic minorities were seen as a problem, the prejudices of the white population were legitimized and concepts of 'race', culture and nation were fused in a populist account which spoke of a 'common sense' desire to live with 'people of one's own kind'. Only in a homogeneous nation could common allegiance to a single sovereign, shared identity and a common idea of the national community be secured. Although Powell himself was careful to avoid using the terms 'race' and 'culture', and was concerned with national identity rather than racial superiority, his populist nationalism marked a racialization of the Conservative concept of the nation and of British politics in general.

Powell's 20 April 1968 Birmingham speech was his most significant on immigration and was also representative of his 'race' discourse. He began the speech by stating that 'the supreme function of statesmanship is to provide against preventable evils', before claiming that Britain was 'a nation busily engaged in heaping up its own funeral pyre' given the growth of immigrant communities. He ended the speech by proclaiming 'as I look ahead, I am filled with foreboding. Like the Roman, I seem to see "the River Tiber foaming with much blood" . . . to see, and not to speak, would be the great betrayal'.[83] Here, Powell claims to be speaking on behalf of those people whose fears about immigration were being ignored by the political elite thus opening up a gulf between governed and government. His populism and emotive language was further demonstrated in the Birmingham speech when he referred to the race relations situation in Wolverhampton as illustrative of 'the sense of being a persecuted minority which is growing among ordinary English people' which resulted from the growth of ethnic minority communities in the inner cities. Powell used projections of the birth rate of the existing New Commonwealth ethnic population to legitimize popular prejudices and argued that in the near future parts of the inner cities would become black ghettos, subsequently urging the government to act on people's fears by introducing a programme of voluntary repatriation.[84]

Integration was a flawed concept, multiculturalism a threat to the homogeneous national community. Nationhood is a subjective feeling which develops from immersion in the traditions and values of the national community. Immigrants are alien to the British way of life and the subjective experiences at its core, Powell thus suggesting that integration is unachievable if immigrants cannot share the allegiance to the nation, culture and sovereign present in the indigenous population. Separate identities mean separate loyalties, and these are deep rooted. Allegiance to, and belonging in, the nation cannot be fully experienced by those New Commonwealth immigrants who have different values, traditions and loyalties. 'The West Indian or Indian does not, by being born in England, become an Englishman. In law he becomes a United Kingdom citizen by birth; in fact he is a West Indian or an Asian still.'[85]

A homogeneous national community requires a strong sense of patriotism and common allegiance to the sovereign authority. 'Inside the nation you cannot contain elements which are foreign to it in the sense that they cannot share that devotion to the whole as against the parts.'[86] Membership of the nation is a matter of shared political values in this ethnic-ideological account of nationhood which stresses allegiance and loyalty, claiming that these are only strongly felt by the indigenous population. But implicit in Powellism's political definition of the nation is a myth of cultural homogeneity and perception that groups alien to the British way of life are a threat to national identity and unity. The attributes of nationhood are joined by 'difference' as a means of distinguishing that which is integral to Britishness from that which is alien.

Bhikhu Parekh contends that Powellism fused nationalist and assimilationist themes, claiming that Powell believed that New Commonwealth immigrants could only be part of the national community if they abandoned those elements of their identity which are incompatible with Britishness.[87] Patrick Cosgrave similarly states that Powell 'argued the virtues of assimilation, provided the immigrant sedulously sought to assimilate himself to the habits, laws and traditions of the host country, to become in effect a coloured Britain'.[88] This fits with the analysis of New Right thinking on 'race' as nation discussed earlier and in Chapter 6, but it should also be noted that Powell doubted that immigrants could become members of a subjectively defined national community and favoured repatriation.

British Citizenship

Powell's concern with the revitalization of national identity coupled opposition to immigration with demands for a reform of British citizenship laws. The failure to produce a coherent concept of British citizenship in the 1940s was presented as a root cause of the immigration and nationality problems which emerged in the 1960s.[89] The legal status of British citizen did not automatically confer membership of the national community on a person, for nationhood is a complex of subjective feelings of loyalty and identity which Powell suggested are only found in the historical ethnic community (that is, in the white population of Britain).

Before 1948, according to Powell, British nationality was based on allegiance to the Crown: 'allegiance is the very essence of nationhood ... Nationhood means that a man stands to one nation, to one loyalty, above all others'.[90] However, the 1948 British Nationality Act established nine separate citizenships plus a citizenship of the United Kingdom and its Colonies, a fictional entity which failed to base the rights and duties of nationality upon membership of one sovereign nation-state. Powell criticized the citizenship implications of the 1971 Immigration Act, the 1972 Pakistan Act and the 1981 British Nationality Act, claiming that the latter maintained the 'rag-bag principles' of citizenship and nationality while ignoring concepts of rights, duty and allegiance which had formed the basis of British subject status.

CONCLUSIONS

The Conservative political strategy based around state patriotism, social cohesion, Union and Empire gradually unravelled in the postwar era as consensus politics, decolonization, relations with the EC, immigration and devolution demands posed new challenges to Conservative statecraft and its status as the patriotic party. These developments first affected the Conservative politics of nationhood in the 1950s and 1960s but were met by pragmatic adaptation by the party leadership and defensiveness by the Tory Right. Moves towards a realignment of the politics of nationhood based on a post-imperial reappraisal of nationhood and the nation-state took shape in the late 1960s, tentatively in Heath's national strategy and more fundamentally in the populist nationalist strategy developed by Powell. These were different conceptions of the nature of Conservatism, the ends and means of Conservative governance and the future of the nation-state.

Heath's strategy was one of flawed and frustrated modernization:

a European vision which accepted a limited pooling of sovereignty to modernize the British state and economy, but which clung to 'essential national sovereignty' and was undermined by economic and political turbulence; a confused approach to devolution and the Union, governed by short-termism in the case of Scotland and facing seemingly intractable problems in Northern Ireland; and a commitment to a tolerant multicultural society which became a secondary concern in the face of pressure for strict immigration controls. Heath's national strategy imploded given its conceptual inconsistencies and statecraft shortcomings.

Powell offered a coherent post-imperial reassessment of the place of the politics of nationhood within British Conservatism, based on a trenchant defence of the nation-state from perceived enemies within and without and a populist reassertion of a British national identity defined in ethnic-ideological terms. Powell's supporters believed that he pointed the Conservatives back towards their true volition as the patriotic party and defender of the nation-state at a time when 'the Conservative Party lost its sense of nationhood'.[91] However, Powellism's nationalist strategy was an oppositional form of politics, driven by ideology, removed from and unsuited to the demands on party statecraft imposed by the realities of government. The measures proposed by Powell were inappropriate to governing a plural society and his defence of parliamentary sovereignty and preference for an independent foreign policy unsuited to an interdependent world. Powellism recognized the need for a redefined sense of national identity to reflect Britain's changed world role and changes in British society, but in seeking this promoted myths of national homogeneity and indivisible parliamentary sovereignty which were obstacles to modernization. His forecasts about the social consequences of the inevitable failure of integration also proved erroneous.

Although Powellism was fundamentally flawed both as a redefinition of the Conservative concept of the nation and as a political strategy, its influence on Conservative politics was considerable. Powell's mix of free economy and strong state themes plus his populist patriotic discourse were picked up by Thatcherism. However, Thatcherism had to react to the constraints and demands of governing and differed from Powellite solutions in a number of policy areas central to the politics of nationhood, notably repatriation, citizenship, Ulster and EC membership. Powell was himself critical of Thatcher for not developing her nationalist instincts into a coherent political project and for claiming to defend national sovereignty while agreeing to further European integration and signing the Anglo-Irish Agreement. But although significant differences of policy exist between the two, the origins of the Thatcherite politics of nationhood can be traced to Powell's populist nationalism.

3 Thatcherism and the Politics of Nationhood

Thatcherism prompted renewed interest in the role of the politics of nationhood in Conservative statecraft and conservative thought, a relationship which became still more significant given the problems encountered by the Major Governments in EU and territorial politics. In the 1980s populist themes of national sovereignty and identity evident in Conservative policy towards the EC, in the politics of 'race' and during the Falklands War were cited as evidence that the defence of nation and nation-state was again central to the Conservative project. Thatcher's instinctive patriotism, the emphasis on the national community in some New Right thought and the centrality of a strong nation-state to the Thatcherite political project were cited as evidence of this. But an examination of the politics of nationhood in the Thatcher and Major period requires careful navigation through the literature on Thatcherism and an examination of key policy areas.

Many studies of the Thatcher period make some reference to nationhood and the nation-state – looking for example at Thatcherite nationalist discourse, ideas of the nation in New Right ideology or the Thatcher Governments' policy on European integration, territorial politics and immigration. But few studies have drawn these themes together in an integrated study of the Conservative politics of nationhood. This chapter examines some of the key accounts of Thatcherism, grouping them into explanations which focus primarily on Thatcher herself, on New Right ideology and Thatcherite discourse, on the political project of the Thatcher Governments, and on their policy limitations, noting the usefulness and shortcomings of these accounts. None of the broad approaches covered can by themselves fully explain the multidimensional nature of the Thatcherite project, though each offers important insights. Subsequent case study chapters examine the policies of the Thatcher and Major Governments in the areas of European integration, territorial politics and 'race' and immigration, drawing on these approaches and providing further analysis of the significance, complexity and problems of the Thatcherite politics of nationhood.

Thatcherism and the Politics of Nationhood 49

Although Thatcherism used a populist patriotic language, it did not produce a coherent national strategy, that is a clearly defined view of the nation and the Conservative politics of nationhood which underpinned government policy in areas affecting issues of national identity (immigration and race relations), national independence (sovereignty and European integration) and national integrity (the territorial management of the UK). Indeed, during this period developments within and beyond the nation-state worked against the development of an effective Conservative statecraft in which the politics of nationhood would bring political argument hegemony, governing competence and relative autonomy for the centre. Interdependence and the ensuing erosion of government autonomy, plus the challenges to an inclusive national identity posed by regionalism and ethnic pluralism thus underlay some of the policy problems faced by the Thatcher and Major Governments.

A One Nation political strategy had established the Conservatives as the party of nation, Empire and Union, the authentic voice of a state patriotism built around British identity and institutions. Also significant in this One Nation national strategy had been the Conservative appropriation of the language and symbols of nationhood, underpinned by a distinctive Conservative concept of the nation, rhetoric of social unity and the defence of the Union through a British state patriotism and administrative devolution. Although Conservative predominance in the politics of nationhood brought the party considerable political and electoral advantages, it also provoked factional disputes about the party's role and core values. By the late 1960s, the Conservative national strategy had been weakened by British decline, the end of Empire, peripheral reassertion and a developing multiculturalism. Powellism was a Tory nationalist reaction to this, an authoritarian individualist approach which recast elite autonomy, populist patriotism and the defence of the nation-state in the light of new challenges, but replaced imperial myths with those of national homogeneity and unfettered parliamentary sovereignty.

Thatcherism was also a reaction to these challenges to the nation-state and Conservative statecraft, rejecting One Nation politics, looking to restore government authority and a populist patriotism and seeking to modernize British identity through an emphasis on enterprise and individualism. Though influenced by New Right thinking, it did not produce a coherent account of the nation, while as a political project Thatcherism defended some of the traditional elements of the Conservative politics of nationhood rather than adapting them to changed circumstances. Doctrinal and statecraft problems weakened the Thatcherite project: its defence of the nation-state often rested on problematic assumptions about national sovereignty and elite autonomy, territorial management or the management of a multicultural society. Far from achieving hegemony or being natural territory, the politics of nationhood again proved a difficult area for the Conservatives, raising conceptual, statecraft and policy problems across a range of key issues.

THATCHERISM AND THATCHER

From a political science perspective, explanations of Thatcherism which attribute much of the distinctiveness of the Thatcher Governments to the character, convictions or leadership style of Margaret Thatcher are superficial and unsatisfactory. Although memoirs and 'insider' narratives offer some important insights into Conservative politics in the 1980s, works of this type tend to lack theoretical underpinning, overstate the impact of individuals and ignore the complexity of the Thatcherite project and policy-making process.

Anthony King described the Thatcher Governments as unusually personalized, reflecting Thatcher's 'conviction politics' and stretching the boundaries of prime-ministerial power.[1] In the politics of nationhood, Thatcher's personal agenda and activist approach was evident in her defence of British sovereignty in the EC and during the Falklands conflict.[2] But although EC 'high' politics afforded significant scope for heads of government to influence European integration, domestic and external constraints were also significant. In the late 1980s, the EC moved in directions which the Prime Minister opposed but over which she had a decreasing and negative influence. Cabinet disputes over membership of the Exchange Rate Mechanism (ERM) and the optimal response to proposals for Economic and Monetary Union (EMU) also revealed the limits of prime-ministerial power.[3]

Thatcher was not a leading intellectual force on the New Right, its leading exponents in the Conservative Party being Powell and Keith Joseph, but her personal beliefs and values do have some significance for the politics of nationhood. For Peter Riddell, 'Thatcherism is essentially an instinct, a series of moral values and an approach to leadership rather than an ideology', an expression of Thatcher's experiences and values, including her English patriotism.[4] Compared to that of Powell or de Gaulle, Thatcher's was an instinctive patriotism rather than a coherent account of nationhood and the nation-state. She emphasized individualism, enterprise and respect for state authority as attributes of English identity, but this English cultural nationalism often sat uneasily alongside her unionism. Thatcher defended national sovereignty but spoke variously of parliamentary sovereignty, executive autonomy and national self-determination, acting pragmatically when signing the Single European Act and the Anglo-Irish Agreement, both of which modified national sovereignty. The 1988 Bruges speech highlighted the Prime Minister's commitment to the nation-state but departed from established policy towards the EC in tone rather than substance. Her populist patriotic discourse was significant in the Falklands conflict and on immigration, Thatcher claiming in 1978 that 'people are rather afraid that this country might be swamped by people with a different culture', thereby politicizing 'race' issues.[5]

IDEOLOGY, IDEAS AND THATCHERITE DISCOURSE

Rather than focusing on Thatcher's personal values, a number of influential studies of Thatcherism depict it as a coherent and distinctive ideological project informed by the neo-liberal and cultural conservative branches of New Right thought. Such accounts assume that government policy drew significantly upon New Right ideology and was consistent over time but, as will be noted below, this is problematic. Thatcherism has been viewed as an ideological project by theorists on the Left and politicians on the Right. Supporters presented Thatcherism as coherent and distinctive, whereas 'Wets' like Ian Gilmour depicted it as a dogma alien to the Conservative tradition, a neo-liberal ideological experiment which overturned the party's One Nation and pragmatic ethos.[6] Gilmour's claims are over stated: although the collectivist tradition was dominant for much of the twentieth century, liberal-conservative themes also have a long tradition in Conservative politics.[7] Thatcherism was, though, tangential to post-war Conservatism in many respects, including the politics of nationhood where its rejection of One Nation ideals, its post-imperial outlook and its management of the Union were distinctive.

New Right thought fractured the civic-ethnic blend found in the conservative concept of the nation, its neo-liberal and authoritarian wings emphasizing the political and cultural bases of the nation respectively. Political and cultural accounts of nationhood are both evident in conservative thought, but the Burkean account outlined in Chapter 1 fused the two, looking towards a political culture of ordered liberty which reflected national character and fostered patriotic allegiance to state institutions. The political account finds expression in liberal-conservative thought with its emphasis on limited politics, civil association and individualism, whereas the cultural account emphasizes the pre-political basis of the national community plus the importance of common culture to national identity. They also presented differing accounts of British and English national identity.

The Political Nation

The political account of the nation espoused by liberal-conservative thinkers such as Michael Oakeshott and Shirley Letwin focuses on the civic or constitutional basis of political association. The political community is based on impersonal law and legitimate state authority, so British political culture combines traditional authority and individualism, while shared political values and citizenship provide a sense of commonality. The concept of community is a minimal one, based on legal rights and obligations plus patriotic attachment to traditional rules and institutions. The civic elements of the conservative nation are highlighted, ideas of a pre-political national community and a deterministic national identity viewed as threatening to individual freedom and the rule of law.

Neo-liberals promote a limited politics of constitutionalism, the free market and negative liberty, being critical of activist or end-state politics which rely on guiding principles to structure social and political relations. Concepts of overarching national unity, the common good or cultural homogeneity are dangerous abstractions which undermine individual liberty and civil association. The political account looks to the state-based and civic elements of political association, but develops at tangents to the paradigmatic conservative nation, as it downplays themes of national community.

Hayek criticized conservatism's proneness to nationalism and economic protectionism, these conflicting with his vision of a rule-based, free market 'Great Society'.[8] Nationalism and communal solidarity are 'primitive' or 'tribal' feelings inappropriate to the international and impersonal Great Society in which the key groupings are small, voluntary associations. The evolution of the free society and market order will ultimately erode communal loyalties, but Hayek accepted the continued existence of nation-states and the relevance of shared identities.

While I look forward as an ultimate ideal to a state of affairs in which national boundaries have ceased to be obstacles to the free movement of men, I believe that within any period with which we can now be concerned, any attempt to realise it would lead to a revival of strong nationalist sentiments and a retreat from positions already achieved. However far modern man accepts in principle the ideal that the same rules should apply to all men, in fact he does concede it only to those whom he regards as similar to himself, and only slowly learns to extend the range of those he does accept as his own.[9]

Hayek also regarded immigration controls as an essential function of the state for so long as 'certain differences in national or ethnic traditions (especially in the rate of propagation) exist'.[10] His account of political association is conservative in its emphasis on tradition and the evolution of rules: humans are not self-determining beings using abstract rules to order society, but work within a 'spontaneous order' in which the optimal social rules evolve as traditions. Freedom is optimally expressed in an ordered society where traditional rules and institutions act as 'knowledge bearers'. Hayek's idea of community is thus a limited one: society is a collection of strangers meeting in the market place to make mutually beneficial exchanges, linked only by allegiance to shared rules.

Oakeshott emphasized the legal-political basis of social relations and restricted the idea of community to those human relations governed by constitutionalism and traditional rules of association.[11] The optimal set of arrangements is found in a 'civil association' organized around authoritative, traditional rules. This compares favourably with 'enterprise association' based on the pursuit of common interest and which extend the scope of the political, threatening ordered liberty. Oakeshott rejected the *universitas* or corporate mode in which the state seeks to bond people through a common purpose such as national homogeneity. Quests for community as a basis of social solidarity are rationalist projects: the political nation based around limited politics and allegiance to established rules is the proper basis of association.

Oakeshott noted the virtues of the British political community with its emphasis on rule of law and individual freedom. Important New Right authoritarian individualist accounts of the development of British, or more frequently English, nationhood are, though, more fully developed in the work of Letwin, Jonathan Clark and Alan Macfarlane. Letwin depicts Thatcherism as a coherent expression of a distinctive English individualist morality which rejects the Whig focus on integrative British statecraft, looking instead to the restoration of the English 'vigorous virtues' of enterprise and independence to bring national revival.

The Cultural Nation

The second sub-category of the New Right view of the nation is the cultural or social authoritarian account, emphasizing the pre-political, group-based elements of identity. It claims that legitimacy rests upon the pre-political elements of society, namely nationhood and culture. Membership of the national community is prior to the contractual citizenship fostered by liberalism: nationhood encompasses common identity and is expressed through a common culture which links state and civil society. The pre-political nature of these ties gives the cultural concept a greater ethnic flavour than is found in the Burkean nation.

The major vehicles of cultural conservative thought have been 'The Salisbury Review' and the work of its editor, Roger Scruton. Scruton focuses on state authority and common culture, rejecting the 'first person perspective' of liberal thought.[12] His conservatism adopts a 'third person perspective' in which human beings are viewed as social animals immersed in the shared culture of the national community. A common culture, made up of shared traditions and values, develops communal solidarity and should be fostered and protected by the state. As a community, the nation is more than the sum of its constituent parts, uniting state and civil society through shared values and authority.[13] Scruton is critical of liberal accounts of nationhood for neglecting social unity and community. The nation is instead a pre-political entity, membership of which is prior to citizenship and provides the identity and unity lacking in the liberal separation of state and society. The individual is not an autonomous being but becomes conscious of his or her identity through rootedness in cultural practices. These themes are taken up by Graham Dawson:

What makes a nation the nation that it is, is the congeries of customs and traditions which it has inherited. And so it is these customs and traditions that constitute at least in part its people as the people they are. It follows that a person would not be the person he is if it were not for the customs and traditions which have given him his passions and his prejudices, his instincts and institutions. Without what he owes the nation in which he was born, the individual is less than fully human being.[14]

John Casey also espoused a cultural account of the nation claiming that nationhood is the true state of man and the national community the source of morality.[15] Rules of the common life make sense only within the framework of a shared culture and through the special bonds between co-nationals, and between subjects and the nation-state. English cultural identity revolves around 'piety' or man's capacity for respect and loyalty to place, traditional authority and national institutions.

Membership of the nation is ostensibly based on subjective feelings of belonging, but in the cultural conservative account these are intrinsically linked to ethnic and cultural factors. Cultural homogeneity is desirable, for in plural societies the bonds afforded by common culture are irrevocably loosened. Political loyalty and membership of the national community should go hand-in-hand: legitimate authority is rooted in the shared morality of the national culture and the state must protect this against diverse and threatening ways of life. The authoritarian New Right moved towards an ethnic-ideological account in which immigrant communities are seen as alien. Cultural integration is viewed as undesirable or impossible, while ethnic minority groups have to pay a high price to enjoy citizenship, namely the acceptance of the primacy of British values over their own cultural traditions.

Although the political and cultural concepts of nationhood found in New Right thought include some familiar conservative themes, they move away from the paradigmatic conservative idea of the nation which attempts to marry individualist and communitarian themes. Both accounts develop at tangents to the conservative nation. The political nation downplays the claims of community and identity, while the cultural nation relies on myths of national homogeneity and threatens to relegate individual interests to those of the whole. Proponents of the political account offer only a minimal account of the national community, while in the cultural nation the individual cannot be abstracted from the culture, traditions and loyalties which shape one's identity.

Underpinning the Conservative politics of nationhood has historically been a relatively consistent concept of the nation. Thatcherism, though, left an unstable hybrid of individualist and communitarian themes, plus a defensive attachment to national sovereignty and a common national culture. Whereas the Burkean nation sought to marry the civic and ethnic bases of identity in a vision of state patriotism, authoritarian individualism is less conciliatory and more willing to present itself as an expression of English identity rather than Britishness.

Thatcherism and Hegemony

The most influential account of the ideological basis of Thatcherism has been Stuart Hall's 'authoritarian populism' thesis.[16] Hall depicts Thatcherism as a hegemonic project which sought to displace social democratic hegemony, reconstituting the state, economy, civil society and basic social and political values by mobilizing discontent around a populist right-wing platform. Neo-liberal and social authoritarian themes in New Right ideology are important elements of this, but Thatcherite discourse also responds to 'moral panics' such as immigration, disorder and permissiveness by espousing authoritarian populist values such as patriotism, racism and a reactionary 'common sense' as part of its national-populist programme.[17] Hall depicts Thatcherism as a successful hegemonic project achieving political leadership, redefining core social and political values, imposing a new trajectory on the state and economy, and forging a broad cross-class social base for its accumulation strategy.

O'Shea also treats Thatcherism as a hegemonic project seeking to 'rework the totality of popular experience', looking in particular at themes of 'national-popular' identity within its discursive strategy.[18] Thatcherism departs from earlier Conservative discourse on nationhood by citing collectivism as a cause of national malaise and individual enterprise as the key to renewal. But Hall and O'Shea also claim that Thatcherism 'resurrects the traditional patriotism kept alive in political circles by the old right', directing patriotic discourse against enemies within and without.[19] Studies of Thatcherite discourse and nationalism have focused on its populist fusing of themes of 'race', nation and culture in a 'new racism' (examined in Chapter 6) and on the Falklands conflict.

The Falklands War

During the conflict which followed the 1982 Argentinian invasion of the Falkland Islands, Thatcherism made effective use of the language of nationhood to establish its national-popular credentials. The 1981 British Nationality Act had denied the Falkland Islanders British citizenship, but during the conflict Thatcher used the language of kith and kin: 'the people of the Falkland Islands, like the people of the United Kingdom, are an island race. Their way of life is British; their allegiance is to the Crown'.[20] Thatcherite discourse also espoused notions of Britishness, allegiance, territorial sovereignty and the right of the islanders to choose to remain under British rule, although they had enjoyed little democratic input into decision-making or earlier attempts to reach a diplomatic settlement on the disputed status of the Falklands.[21]

The Prime Minister talked of the British victory in the conflict with nostalgia for a time when Britain 'built an Empire and ruled a quarter of the world' – 'the lesson of the Falklands is that Britain has not changed and that this nation still has those sterling qualities which shine through its history'.[22] But Thatcher also saw the conflict as inaugurating a period of national renewal after political and economic decline. She claimed that 'the nation has begun to assert itself. Things are not going to be the same again... We have ceased to be a nation in retreat', identifying Thatcherite economic policies as a key element of this renewal and berating its 'enemies within' (namely, striking trade unions).[23] On the Left, Eric Hobsbawm and Robert Gray noted how Thatcherism exploited jingoistic patriotism for domestic political purposes, treating this as evidence of the continued political potential of patriotism and strength of the historical links between the Right and concepts of the nation.[24] Anthony Barnett depicted Thatcherite discourse as an extreme variant of 'Churchillism' which during the Second World War had used patriotic language to urge national unity, but which was rooted in One Nation patrician Conservatism. Thatcherism by contrast had a capitalist ideological zeal, mixing nostalgia for Empire with themes of national renewal, national identity (with an English flavour) and sovereignty. However, the imperialist trappings of Conservative patriotic discourse which Barnett saw during the Falklands conflict were absent in other areas of the Thatcherite politics of nationhood. In similar vein to Powellism, Thatcherism sought economic renewal and a revived national identity free from myths of Empire.

The Falklands conflict helped the Thatcher Government restore the pre-eminent position of the Conservative politics of nationhood and achieve the statecraft goals of issue hegemony, governing competence and electoral success, despite making policy errors prior to the Argentinian invasion. But the conflict is best viewed as providing the circumstances for a short-term expression of Thatcherite nationalism rather than as a key stage in the realization of a hegemonic national or nationalist strategy. The conflict neither ensured the predominance of the Tory Right nor inaugurated a new Conservative nationalist strategy, though it did illustrate the continuing resonance of the Conservative populist patriotic rhetoric.

Beyond Ideology

Explanations which grant primary status to New Right ideology are useful for our understanding of the significance and distinctiveness of the Thatcherite politics of nationhood in that they explore the differences between Thatcherite values and those of One Nation Conservatism and recognize the political significance of its national-popular discourse. But overall such accounts are unsatisfactory, offering at best partial and at worst faulty analysis. Ideological accounts fail to examine adequately the policies of the Thatcher Governments, over-stating the coherence of the Conservative project; they fail to explore the political significance of tensions between neo-liberal and cultural conservative thought, and problematic notions of sovereignty and national identity; they exaggerate the extent to which ideology rather than pragmatic political considerations informed government policy; and they underestimate the impact of wider political and economic factors. A political party's ideological commitments are inevitably tempered by political efficacy, pragmatic management and constraints on government autonomy.

Letwin's analysis treats ideas as important in British politics but rejects ideologism, claiming that Thatcherism was constructed from a coherent set of values which formed the basis of policy themes. It had a sense of purpose and a concern with 'doing the right thing' without being an ideology or theory.[25] It was a practical form of politics addressing issues in a specific time and space: 'Thatcherism is non-exportable' and is 'British by essence not accident', its roots in British history and experiences being particularly evident in the government's response to European integration.[26] As noted above, Letwin argues that Thatcherism marked a restoration of a traditional English morality (though she talks of Britishness) which has a distinctive conception of the individual and his role in society, seeking to reassert self-sufficiency, enterprise, loyalty and patriotism. But as well as the authoritarian individualist language of enterprise and sovereignty, Thatcher also used the language of Whig history, notably when talking of Magna Carta and the Glorious Revolution at the French Revolution bicentenial celebrations or when pressing for the teaching of national history, though the tendency was still to conflate English with British history.[27]

THATCHERISM – A POLITICAL PROJECT

Explanations which treat Thatcherism as a political project give priority to broad political factors such as achieving governing competence, promoting the interests of the party and its key supporters, winning the battle of ideas and ensuring electoral success. Ideology is a tool used by the Thatcher Governments to pursue these political interests rather than a blueprint informing policy.

Jim Bulpitt analyses Thatcherism in terms of Conservative statecraft, that is 'winning elections and achieving some necessary degree of governing competence', a desire to gain relative autonomy for the centre in matters of high politics being 'the principle rule of Conservative statecraft'.[28] The focus is on the actions of rational actor political elites at the centre, namely party leaders in office or the 'Court'. Statecraft has a number of dimensions: (1) effective party management; (2) a winning electoral strategy; (3) political argument hegemony, that is achieving predominance in elite political debate; (4) governing competence, including rejecting policy options which may create implementation problems; and (5) another winning election.

In a number of works Bulpitt has examined European integration, territorial politics and the politics of 'race'. He applies the statecraft thesis to British policy on Europe, focusing on the Conservative defence of relative autonomy in domestic politics and the challenges further integration posed for this.[29] In territorial politics, he contends that the Conservatives' governing code has seen its leaders in office protecting their relative autonomy in high politics by granting local elites autonomy in areas of low politics, producing a 'dual polity' in which separate institutional arrangements existed in the component nations of the UK.[30] In the politics of 'race', the pre-1976 Conservative leadership supported a bipartisan consensus on depoliticizing 'race' issues and insulating the centre from demands for repatriation or a key coordinating role in tackling racial inequality.[31]

Andrew Gamble's analysis of Thatcherism emphasizes political factors but also notes the influence of New Right ideology and the context of political and economic crisis: Thatcherism was 'a political project developed by the Conservative leadership... to re-establish the conditions – electoral, ideological, economic and political – for the Conservative Party to resume its leading role in British politics'.[32] The key objectives of the Thatcher Governments were to revive the fortunes of the Conservative Party, to restore free market ideas to political predominance and to reassert the authority of the nation-state. Ideology was largely a tool used by the government to pursue its political interests rather than a blueprint dictating policy. Gamble analyses Conservative statecraft in terms of the politics of support (electoral success, creating a populist platform) and the politics of power (governing competence, coping with structural constraints). He argues that Thatcherism was an attempt to clear the way for a new hegemony (that is, political and moral leadership) but, though undermining social democratic hegemony, it failed to establish a new hegemony itself, undermined by contradictory goals, flawed economic policies and a failure to modernize adequately the state.

Gamble has also examined the place of the nation-state and national identity in the Thatcherite project, characterizing it as 'the latest religion of little England' with its electoral support and values rooted in southern England, and as 'a political project which sought to reassert the importance of a strong nation'.[33] He explores the differing conceptions of national identity offered by Gilmour and Letwin. Gilmour's is depicted as a 'British nationalist' view in which Conservative statecraft is concerned with the management of the multinational UK state and has its roots in the One Nation politics of Empire, Union and state patriotism. Letwin's is a post-imperialist authoritarian individualism which looks to rejuvenate the individualist morality at the heart of English national identity, finding practical expression in Thatcherism.[34] In similar vein, David Marquand notes how a Thatcherite view of the nation-state, characterized by a post-imperial English individualism, replaced a Whig imperialist outlook, with the doctrine of parliamentary sovereignty being a central element of both.[35] Though by instinct, disposition and geography, the Conservative Party came to look more like an English national party in the Thatcher period, claims that the Conservatives had become or were in the process of becoming an English nationalist party need to be treated with some caution. Thatcher was committed to the Union and to a British state patriotism, though the primacy of England and English cultural values were pronounced.

Bob Jessop's work explores the relationship between Thatcherism and the state and economy, criticizing Hall's authoritarian populism thesis for concentrating on ideology.[36] Jessop locates the emergence of Thatcherism in the 1970s' 'dual crisis of the state' when economic and political crises fatally damaged the Keynesian Welfare State, creating the space for Thatcherite solutions. Thatcherism aimed to create a new hegemony and construct a new accumulation strategy, but was a 'two nations project' dividing society into favoured productive groups and a marginalized 'undeserving' underclass. But Jessop recognizes that Thatcherism was not a coherent project, noting for example that its nationalist rhetoric sat uneasily with the international outlook of its accumulation strategy, while extensive state intervention was required to free the economy. Thatcherism evolved over time, was marked by permanent improvization in its attempts to modernize the state and experienced problems mobilizing consent. Colin Hay develops and amends Jessop's analysis, exploring Thatcherism's strategic concerns and the profound structural changes to the state and economy it brought about.[37]

The political project explanation is a fruitful one for the study of the Conservative politics of nationhood and is developed and amended in this book. It is argued here that a defence of the nation-state (and relative executive autonomy) and national identity has historically been a core concern of Conservative statecraft. The politics of nationhood has brought electoral and political benefits for the Conservative Party, but its defence of the nation-state and role as the patriotic party also reflect deeper strategic concerns and have been central to the party's values and self-image.

A COHERENT PROJECT? SCEPTICAL VIEWS

Claims that Thatcherism was a coherent political project have been questioned by a number of sceptics who variously point to its pragmatism and inconsistency, policy failures and areas of minimal change, plus the importance of external factors such as changes in the world economy which limit government autonomy. David Marsh regards 'unidimensional' explanations of Thatcherism as flawed and superficial, looking instead towards explanations which explore the relative importance of political, economic and ideological factors.[38] Among the variables he highlights are: Britain's relative economic decline and the restructuring of the world economy; the relationship between structure and agency, namely the relative autonomy of the Thatcher and Major Governments in the face of structural constraints; the strategic political and electoral (rather than purely ideological) decisions made by leading politicians; and the problems associated with top-down policy implementation.

Marsh and Rod Rhodes accept much of Gamble's analysis, but, having disaggregated government policy, conclude that, although the Thatcher Governments pursued radical policies in some areas, they were often frustrated by implementation gaps or unintended consequences, while in other areas there was significant policy continuity.[39] Policy was often shaped by pragmatic rather than ideological concerns, with policy implementation hindered by a lack of consultation with established policy communities. Elsewhere, Ivor Crewe concluded that there was no widespread acceptance of Thatcherite values among the electorate in the 1980s, while Philip Norton noted that the Conservatives did not become an ideologically Thatcherite party, Thatcherites making up only 20 per cent of MPs in the late 1980s.[40] Support from the 'party loyalists' for Mrs Thatcher was not unconditional and was gradually withdrawn when she became viewed as an electoral liability and an obstacle to party unity.

These sceptical accounts importantly warn against exaggerating the distinctiveness and coherence of the Thatcherite project. Accordingly, statecraft problems in the politics of nationhood will be examined in subsequent chapters, including constraints on Conservative European policy, a failure to carry out manifesto commitments on immigration, continued pragmatism in race relations and on Northern Ireland, plus problems in Conservative unionism in Scotland. However, an overly-sceptical approach also leads to unsatisfactory conclusions, underestimating Thatcherism's political significance. Thus the significance of changes in elite discourse, strategic learning during a long spell in office, the Conservative's broader strategic motivations and statecraft goals, plus the cumulative effects of policy on the state and economy are recognized in a number of works.[41]

CONCLUSIONS

The analysis of the Thatcherite politics of nationhood employed in this book highlights the importance of political factors, particularly the defence of the nation-state, national identity and executive autonomy in Conservative statecraft. Alongside political factors, the distinctiveness and potency of Thatcherite ideas and ideology, plus the tensions between its political and cultural views of the nation, are also recognized. It is also important to identify and assess policy shortcomings, inconsistency and constraints on the autonomy of the Thatcher and Major Governments. Strong state and national sovereignty themes assumed a high level of elite or state autonomy, but this often proved illusory given policy failings, statecraft problems and changes in the political and economic environment.

Thatcherism altered the basis of Conservative statecraft, aiming to free the economy, strengthen the nation-state, revitalize national identity and restore the leading position of the Conservative Party. Utilizing the explanations of Thatcherism outlined above in relation to the politics of nationhood, this and subsequent chapters argue that:

1. Thatcherism departed from key elements of One Nation statecraft, reacting to the challenges to this national strategy posed by economic decline, the end of Empire, EC membership, problems of territorial management and the development of a multicultural society.

2. Thatcherism was influenced by, and drew upon, the new directions in the Conservative politics of nationhood signalled by Powellism and New Right thinking, but did not treat these as a blueprint for government policy. Indeed, the tensions between neo-liberal and cultural conservative views of the nation worked against the development of a coherent Thatcherite idea of the nation, while Conservative concepts of sovereignty and identity were problematic in an interdependent world and plural society.

3. Thatcherite statecraft in the politics of nationhood was significantly shaped by political factors, including (relatively) short-term concerns such as achieving governing competence and electoral success, plus longer-term concerns such as reviving the Conservatives' status as the patriotic party and defending the relative autonomy of its leaders in office. Thatcherism sought to defend the

nation-state (that is, executive autonomy, national sovereignty and the Union) and revitalize national identity (through economic renewal, the promotion of English cultural values and defence of state patriotism, plus the development of a populist patriotic discourse). However, the Thatcher Governments did not develop or pursue a coherent and consistent national or nationalist strategy, often acting pragmatically, facing constraints on their autonomy and contradictions within the Thatcherite political project. The latter include: the defence of national sovereignty and support for the Single European Market; a staunch unionism in Scotland but support for devolution and intergovernmentalism in Northern Ireland; the imperialist echoes in Conservative discourse during the Falklands conflict but the general post-imperialist orientation of the Thatcherite politics of nationhood; and its mix of liberal individualist and cultural conservative approaches to race relations.

4. The Thatcher Governments thus did not achieve hegemony over the politics of nationhood. Instead, European integration, the management of the Union and of a multicultural society raised important problems for Conservative statecraft which became more apparent under the Major Governments and contributed to the 1997 election defeat. Thatcherism's English cultural outlook and the eroded legitimacy of the 'Westminster model' constitutional settlement (such as the monarchy and Parliament) during the Thatcher and Major period also undermined conservative state patriotism.

Before exploring key areas of the politics of nationhood in more detail, it is first worth briefly examining the relationship between the Major Governments and Thatcherism. Major's leadership style was more consensual than Thatcher's and his personal convictions on 'race' and Europe differed from hers, though he saw the defence of the nation-state and national identity as key tasks for the Conservatives. The Major Governments retained core elements of the Thatcherite socio-economic project not because of the difficulties of over-turning the Thatcherite inheritance, but through a desire to extend and develop those changes to the central state and modes of governance which emerged in the final term of the Thatcher Government.[42] Hay depicts the Major Governments as a further stage in the Thatcherite project, one concerned with consolidating structural transformation and characterized by political managerialism.[43] But, as Gamble notes, successful statecraft or political management proved more problematic in the 1990s as Thatcherism had undermined the pillars of traditional Conservative hegemony, namely defence of the constitution and Union, defence of property interests and a successful foreign economic policy.[44]

Some of the key problems enveloping the Conservatives in the 1990s thus fell within the sphere of the politics of nationhood, where both continuities with, and departures from, the Thatcherite approach are apparent. At its outset the Major Government sought a more constructive relationship with the EC, but became progressively more hostile to further integration and found the Government's room for manoeuvre increasingly constrained by internal and external factors. Major did not share Thatcher's dogmatic attachment to a maximalist reading of sovereignty but nonetheless was determined to defend the UK nation-state, declaring that this was the 'highest cause this party knows'.[45] But in the final days of his premiership, Major was admitting a dichotomy between the national interest and the short-term interests of the Conservative Party. Major restated the Conservative commitment to Scotland's place in the Union but introduced limited reforms to the system of administrative devolution, while taking important steps in the search for a peaceful settlement in Northern Ireland. The Major Governments pursued tighter asylum rules but maintained a managerial approach to race relations.

The following chapters examine the politics and policies of the Thatcher and Major Governments in three areas central to the politics of nationhood – European integration, territorial politics and the politics of 'race' and immigration. These case studies will assess the relative importance of ideological and political factors, noting the policy and statecraft problems encountered by the Conservatives in the politics of nationhood. Each chapter takes account of the specific features and problems of those policy areas, including issues of sovereignty and identity plus various constraints on executive autonomy.

4 European Integration

Since the mid-1980s Britain's role in a European Community and then European Union intent for the most part on 'ever closer union' has been a central issue in Conservative politics, posing a number of significant challenges for party statecraft. Following EC entry in 1973 and the self-imposed exile of its chief opponent Enoch Powell, the Conservatives appeared largely at ease with the twin mantles of 'party of Europe' and national party, but membership had not brought about a major reordering of the politics of nationhood. By the 1990s many in the party believed that support for European integration was incompatible with its commitment to the nation-state and national identity.

This chapter outlines Conservative policy in the EC/EU under the Thatcher and Major Governments, particularly since 1988, noting policy continuities and changes. The relationship between domestic and EU politics – the domestic making of British European policy plus the EU's impact on the British state and political system – is a central concern. The characterization of EU decision-making as a 'two-level game' of domestic policy-making on European issues and inter-state bargaining within the EU lends itself to this type of study.[1] But it is also important to take account of the special circumstances which have made this two-level game an especially fraught one for the UK, namely British 'semi-detachment' or 'awkwardness' in the EU and the nature of Conservative politics.[2]

An analysis of party statecraft, linking the politics of support (electoral strategy, party management and ideology) and the politics of power (executive autonomy, policy coherence and effective management of foreign affairs) is employed to assess Conservative politics and European integration.[3] At the heart of Conservative statecraft is the defence of executive autonomy, that is the authority and capacity of party leaders in office to take decisions in areas of high politics, such as European policy, while relatively insulated from domestic and external pressures. It will be argued that key elements of Britain's relations with the EC/EU in this period – for example, opposition to and limited influence over key aspects of the EU agenda, disputes in the Cabinet and parliamentary party over European issues, the 'Europeanization' of many policy areas

– curtailed executive autonomy and made it difficult for Conservative leaders to produce a coherent, agreed European policy and exercise significant influence in the EU. National sovereignty is also of real and symbolic importance to the Conservative politics of nationhood, bound up with the statecraft goal of executive autonomy and the Conservatives' self-image as the patriotic party defending the nation-state.

'Europe' is the prime example of the contemporary importance of, but difficulties inherent in, the Conservative politics of nationhood. In terms of the politics of support, it raises problems in party management, electoral fortunes and ideology, and in the politics of power, the defence of the nation-state (as the context for executive autonomy), policy-making and an effective UK foreign economic policy.

CONSERVATIVE POLICY AND EUROPEAN INTEGRATION, 1979–97

1. 1979–84: The British Budgetary Question

During the first term of the Thatcher Government, British policy in the EC was structured around familiar themes of intergovernmentalism, free trade, Atlanticism and a concern to maximize the benefits of membership and minimize its costs. However, the Prime Minister's tone was notably abrasive and her approach informed by a personal commitment to national sovereignty and the restoration of British influence.[4] The government focused its energies on reform of the Community budget and the Common Agricultural Policy. Thatcher's determination to hold out for a budget deal based on an automatic rebate formula, plus her refusal to accept a number of proposed compromises, dismayed other leaders and some of her own ministers, but contributed to her 'Iron Lady' image. Agreement was finally reached at the 1984 Fontainebleau summit when Thatcher accepted a formula giving Britain a rebate of 66 per cent of the gap between the amount it paid to the Community and the amount received from it, though VAT revenues paid to the EC would be increased from 1 per cent to 1.4 per cent.

Though presented as a triumph for Thatcher's determined stance, the deal was not substantially better than those previously rejected

– 'in every negotiation there comes a time to settle: this was it'.[5] Aware of French plans to inject new momentum into the Community, and Mitterrand's suggestion that Britain be relegated to a second tier, Thatcher felt that a deal would allow her Government to press its free trade agenda more effectively.

2. 1984–8: Towards a Single European Market

The budget settlement and submission of the 'Europe – The Future' paper at Fontainebleau marked a more positive phase. Though intergovernmental in tone, the paper's emphasis on fulfilling the Single European Market (SEM) indicated that Britain could play a constructive, perhaps leading role.[6] The Single Market agenda mirrored Thatcherism's domestic liberalization programme and accorded with its vision of a free trade Community of nation-states. The administration of neo-liberal medicine was the favoured antidote to European uncompetitiveness, and British economic interests were identified with an open international economy and Community-wide deregulation. Cockfield's 1985 White Paper *Completing the Internal Market* provided a detailed legislative blueprint for the removal of barriers to the free movement of goods, services, persons and capital. The government had to compromise to achieve its objectives: Thatcher was prepared to seek alliances to strengthen the free trade agenda, being persuaded that an extension of Qualified Majority Voting (QMV) to Single Market legislation was necessary to prevent *dirigiste* states blocking progress.[7]

The launch of the Single Market programme marked a high point of British enthusiasm for the EC, but also sowed the seeds of future discontent. Ministers claimed that, despite its supranational elements, the Single European Act (SEA) was closer to the British vision than that of a federal Europe.[8] By employing the principle of mutual recognition of national standards and limiting harmonization to essential health and safety measures, opening up public procurement, reducing state aid and liberalizing protected sectors, the SEM would be constructed using methods approved of in Downing Street. Thatcher felt the project marked the realization of the Treaty of Rome's status as a 'charter for economic liberty' and a logical conclusion to the European project.[9]

But other Member States and the Commission, under the activist Presidency of Jacques Delors, did not share the government's outlook. For them, the SEM was part of a dynamic process including institutional reform, a social dimension, enhanced regional policy and EMU. This approach gathered pace after 1988 but was signposted in the SEA where the goal of EMU was included in the preamble to the Treaty. Its significance was downplayed by British negotiators who dismissed it as a meaningless reference to a goal tainted by failure.[10] On European Political Cooperation (EPC), key states viewed SEA arrangements not as the finished version, but as a platform from which steps towards EC competence in foreign policy could be made.

The government resisted important elements of the Single Market project as tensions between its neo-liberal emphasis on the free economy and attachment to national sovereignty revealed themselves.[11] It opposed harmonization of indirect taxes and refused to remove border controls on EU citizens. Thatcher's view that Cockfield 'tended to disregard the larger questions of politics – constitutional sovereignty, national sentiment and the promptings of liberty' is revealing.[12] Where realization of the SEM implied harmonization or a significant erosion of autonomy, the government often reverted to a defence of national sovereignty. Divergent views on the relationship between the Thatcherite economic project and European integration were also emerging in Cabinet, notably in the Westland Affair and disputes over entry into the Exchange Rate Mechanism.

3. 1988–90: 'No. No. No.' to 'Ever Closer Union'

This third period was dominated by the construction of the Delors Model of 'ever closer union' – in the Social Charter, the Delors Report on EMU and pressure for political union – and Thatcher's increasingly dogmatic opposition to it. The Prime Minister's hostility to further integration and distrust of Community methods provoked intensified disputes within Cabinet, particularly over ERM membership and Britain's response to EMU. For her, 'there was no option but to stake out a radically different position from the direction in which most of the Community seemed intent on going, to raise the flag of national sovereignty, free trade, free enterprise – and fight'.[13]

France, Germany and the Commission stepped up their campaign for further integration, effectively isolating the UK on key issues. The government was unable to slow the momentum towards EMU or influence the deliberations of the Delors Committee of central bank governors, whose 1989 report recommended a three-stage transition to EMU, participation by all Member States in the ERM and the creation of a European Central Bank (ECB). Britain was also in a minority of one opposing the Social Charter which confirmed the SEM's 'social dimension'. The widening gulf between Thatcher and the Delors–Kohl–Mitterrand axis was vividly illustrated in her Bruges speech of September 1988. Thatcher presented five 'guiding principles' for the development of the EC: 'willing and active cooperation between independent sovereign states'; a practical approach to policy-making; the promotion of free enterprise in the Community; EC support for global free trade; and the continued primacy of NATO in the defence of Europe.[14] These were familiar themes in British policy, but the speech sent out an uncompromising and abrasive message.

Meanwhile the government was divided over the optimal strategy for reconciling British interests with the planned further development of the EC. Lawson had become convinced that sterling's participation in the ERM would secure low inflation but Thatcher vetoed membership in 1985. Government policy remained that sterling would enter the ERM when the 'time was right' (or 'ripe'), but Lawson 'shadowed' the Deutschmark in 1987–8, conducting policy as if the central aim was to maintain the pound's value at DM 3.00. Thatcher halted this in March 1988, later blaming Lawson's actions for the high inflation which followed.[15]

Moves towards EMU raised the stakes further. Thatcher's attitude was uncompromising – for ideological reasons (floating exchange rates and national sovereignty) she would not accept EMU and was prepared to block progress. Lawson and Howe felt that through engagement in EC negotiations, the government could delay or water down EMU.[16] ERM membership was an essential part of this strategy: by joining, Britain would gain the credibility needed to have real influence over EMU, a view Thatcher rejected. Divisions escalated as Lawson and Howe executed the 1989 'Madrid Ambush', threatening to resign unless the Prime Minister agreed to set out the conditions under which Britain would enter the ERM.[17] Thatcher duly outlined vague conditions at the Madrid summit, including lower UK inflation and interest rates plus progress on the removal of exchange controls, believing that these would make British participation more remote. Howe was subsequently demoted and Lawson resigned in October 1989 over the influence of Thatcher's anti-ERM economic adviser Alan Walters.

The Delors Report was accepted at the Madrid summit, Thatcher surprisingly promising a British alternative based on a non-binding, market-led approach. A short-lived idea on competing currencies was superseded by the Treasury's 'hard Ecu' plan under which the European Currency Unit (Ecu) would become a common currency and could eventually become a single European currency.[18] Chancellor John Major presented the 'hard Ecu' as a workable alternative to the Delors route, whereas Thatcher viewed it as a political tactic to derail or delay EMU. This ambiguity of purpose did not help its cause and the plan won minimal support in the Community. Recognizing the commitment of many states to the Delors plan, Major suggested that the government work for a full definition of EMU in a treaty which included an opting-in mechanism. But Thatcher rejected any deal which would see the Delors definition of EMU included in a new treaty, believing that 'it was psychologically wrong to put ourselves in a frame of mind in which we accepted the inevitability of moves towards EMU rather than attacking the whole concept'.[19]

Isolation in Europe, a worsening economic situation and Nicholas Ridley's resignation left the Prime Minister vulnerable, enabling Major and Foreign Secretary Douglas Hurd to finally persuade her to agree to ERM membership. This duly occurred in October 1990 at a rate of DM 2.95 within 6 per cent bands, Thatcher insisting on a contemporaneous reduction of interest rates.[20] The following month, Britain was the lone dissenter when the starting date for the second stage of EMU was set at 1 January 1994. Returning to the Commons after the Rome summit, Thatcher's declaration that the 'hard Ecu' would not be widely used and her 'No. No. No.' to political union set in motion a chain of events which resulted in her downfall.[21]

4. 1990–2: At the Heart of Europe? Major and Maastricht

Having been convinced as Chancellor that British concerns would be received more favourably if the government sought constructive engagement in the EC, Major set about restoring British credibility. His 1991 declaration in Bonn that 'I want us to be where we belong – at the very heart of Europe, working with our partners in building the future', marked a change of tone and an acceptance that Britain had to be actively involved in negotiations to exercise effective influence.[22] Being at 'the heart of Europe' did not, though, signal a departure from the main objectives of British policy:

opposition to political union and the social dimension remained, though Major spoke of his opposition to the imposition of EMU on the UK rather than EMU as a Community project.

Major and Hurd presented British concerns in more *communautaire* language, but viewed subsidiarity as a means of countering excessive EC regulation and restating the primacy of the nation-state. In the twin Intergovernmental Conferences (IGCs) and at the Maastricht summit ministers sought alliances, making concessions on lesser issues (new EC competences, the codecision procedure and more QMV in existing policy areas) to win ground on its core concerns, on which it refused to bow to pressure. Major claimed that the Maastricht Treaty – properly, the Treaty on European Union (TEU) – vindicated this strategy, his aides citing the IGC outcome as 'game, set and match' for Britain.[23] The 'hard Ecu' plan hardly figured in the EMU IGC, but the government refused to commit itself to EMU membership. Requests for an opting-in mechanism for Stage III were rejected, but ministers accepted a specific British 'opt-out' in the form of a Treaty Protocol stating that the UK was not committed to joining Stage III (in which national currencies are replaced by a single currency and the European Central Bank [ECB] has responsibility for interest rate policy), any future decision on entry being taken by the Westminster parliament. But Major signed a Treaty which proclaimed that EMU was an irreversible goal of the Community and would happen by 1999 for states meeting the convergence criteria. Britain had only limited influence on the EMU negotiations, the opt-out confirming that on this issue the UK was far from the 'heart of Europe'. But by keeping options open Major hoped to protect British interests and shape subsequent negotiations.

Aware that Howard was likely to resign if he accepted an extension of QMV in social policy, the Prime Minister resisted pressure from other states to accept even much-weakened late proposals. In an eleventh hour deal, the other Member States signed a separate Social Agreement outside the Treaty proper, backed by a Social Protocol allowing them to use Community institutions and excluding Britain from policies agreed using this route. Ministers heralded the outcome (often inaccurately referred to as an 'opt-out' from the Social Chapter) claiming it secured UK competitiveness and inward investment. Ministers also welcomed the three-pillar architecture of the EU in which Common Foreign and Security Policy (CFSP) and Justice and Home Affairs (JHA) matters were dealt with in intergovernmental 'separate pillars' where unanimity would be the norm. On foreign and defence affairs the British position was intergovernmental and Atlanticist, stressing unanimity and the leading role of NATO, but accepting a European defence identity through the Western European Union (WEU). British influence on CFSP negotiations was more pronounced than over EMU, aided by the UK's importance in this area and more successful alliance-building. Elsewhere, subsidiarity and removal of reference to a 'federal vocation' were cited as evidence that centralizing pressures had been successfully resisted. At this stage, Conservative reaction was largely favourable, though Thatcher was critical of the EMU provisions and called for a referendum.

5. 1992–6: A British Alternative – Critics at Home and Abroad

Major's post-Maastricht honeymoon period proved short-lived as events in 1992 changed the domestic and EU environment. Firstly, the Conservatives won the general election but had their majority reduced to 21. Secondly, uncertainty in the EC following the Danish referendum 'No' to Maastricht persuaded the government that new opportunities existed to promote its vision of a Europe of nation-states with the Maastricht Treaty a means to that end, but convinced domestic Euro-sceptic opponents of the Treaty that its ratification could be blocked. Thirdly, sterling's withdrawal from the ERM in September 1992 confirmed that Britain remained 'semi-detached' in the EC.

Believing that Maastricht was a good deal for Britain, Major was determined to ratify the Treaty but the European Communities (Amendment) Bill endured a tortuous progression through Parliament.[24] Following defeat on a vote on the Social Agreement, the government won a vote of confidence in July 1993 but dissent had not been extinguished.[25] In June 1995, Major resigned the party leadership, challenging his Euro-sceptic critics to 'put up or shut up'. John Redwood duly resigned from the Cabinet to stand against him on a Thatcherite platform including opposition to the single currency. Major was re-elected with 218 votes but Redwood won 89 votes and 20 MPs abstained, confirming the growth of Euro-sceptic feeling.

The September 1992 crisis in the ERM emboldened the Euro-sceptics, cast a shadow over claims that Britain was at the 'heart of Europe', necessitated a redirection of government economic policy and seriously damaged its electoral fortunes. High German interest rates and an overvalued pound pushed sterling towards the bottom of its ERM band, leaving ministers with unattractive options of interest rate rises or devaluation.[26] When two interest rate rises and massive intervention failed to prop up sterling, it was unilaterally withdrawn from the mechanism by the government on 16 September. The exit was an acrimonious one. Lamont criticized the Bundesbank and Major spoke of serious 'faultlines' in the ERM, ruling out re-entry in the medium term. Ministers felt that their views were confirmed by the 1993 crisis which resulted in ERM bands being extended to 15 per cent for all but the DM and guilder.

The Danish 'No' and the ERM crisis pushed Major towards a more (albeit moderate) sceptical view of European integration and the single currency, though he recognized the importance of British involvement in the EU and was scornful of the Euro-sceptic rebels in his party.[27] The Danish referendum indicated to Major that the federalist agenda was obsolete, lacking legitimacy and unable to meet the challenges of enlargement and economic downturn. Problems in the ERM showed that successful EMU was unrealistic in the foreseeable future. A British approach stressing decentralization and liberalization in an intergovernmental EU was promoted with added gusto.[28] Ministers developed the case for a partnership of nation-states, claiming that support for a 'nation-state in balance with strong international institutions' was 'not a hangover from a more nationalist era, but a tradition rooted in the experience and culture of the British people'.[29] Britain was committed to a European identity but whereas people 'feel part of a European culture, they do not feel themselves to be part of a single European nation'. As legitimacy and democracy are rooted in the nation-state, national governments must play the leading role in the EU.[30]

Rejecting tighter political integration and centralization, the British approach looked to economic cooperation, liberalization and deregulation. The Single Market requires common rules, but 'economic integration is essentially a natural, organic, market-led process. It is also a process of decentralization. Removing national controls and subsidies leaves the decision-making to the many different individuals who run the productive sector of the economy'.[31] The government urged the completion of the SEM and reduced non-wage labour costs to promote enterprise, claiming that the Social Agreement destroyed jobs and competitiveness.[32] But evidence for British claims that this agenda was winning support in Europe was mixed. EU social policy activism waned and the 1993 Commission White Paper *Growth, Competitiveness and Employment* proposed some deregulation, but its general ethos supported EU intervention and high levels of social protection. The government also challenged the introduction of the Working Time Directive under the health and safety provisions of Article 118a in the European Court of Justice (ECJ), which ruled against Britain in 1996.

Tensions surfaced on other issues: as domestic Euro-scepticism gathered pace, the government opposed a reweighting of QMV in March 1994, before accepting the Ioannina compromise which increased the votes required for a blocking minority to 27 (reduced to 26 after the Norwegian referendum opposed entry) following the 1995 enlargement but provided a breathing space if the dissenting minority numbered between 23 and 25. Major then vetoed Dehane's candidacy for Commission President at the Corfu summit but subsequently supported Santer's nomination. The government was also critical of 'quota-hopping', the registering of boats as British by citizens of other Member States in order to qualify for the UK's Common Fisheries Policy quota. The most serious crisis in UK/EU relations arose in May 1996 when the government adopted a strategy of non-cooperation having failed to persuade a majority of states to relax the EU's world-wide ban on the export of British beef products. Britain blocked over one hundred EU measures before a phased lifting of the ban, subject to a large-scale cull of British cattle, was agreed at the June 1996 Florence summit, though little progress was then made within the proposed timetable.[33]

A key plank of the British approach was added when Major spoke of flexibility in a 'multi-track, multi-speed, multi-layered' Europe.[34] Flexibility was presented as essential in an enlarged EU of diverse national interests, objectives and traditions. But the government opposed the prospect of a vanguard of states moving towards further integration, Major seeing

> real danger in talk of a 'hard core', inner and outer circles, a two-tier Europe. I recoil from ideas for a Union in which some would be more equal than others. There is not, and should never be, an exclusive hard core either of countries or of policies.[35]

Any arrangement which allowed a small group of states to use Community institutions would have to be agreed by all states, open to all, and must not force reluctant states into further integration.

All would be bound by Single Market rules, but would be free to opt-out of other policy areas or pursue closer cooperation if all Member States agree. But this recipe for flexibility was condemned as one for an *à la carte* Europe by other states.

The 1996 White Paper, *A Partnership of Nations* confirmed that the UK would enter the 1996–7 IGC largely defending the *status quo* and uncompromising in its defence of national interests.[36] It sought reinforced intergovernmentalism, a streamlined legislative process and a greater role for national parliaments. It opposed the extension of Community competence and any further extension to the scope of QMV, supporting proposals to reweight voting to take account of population. A subsequent memorandum proposed limits on the role of the ECJ including limitation of retrospective effect and damages, introducing an appeal procedure and allowing the Council to amend legislation which the ECJ interpreted in a manner contrary to its original intentions.[37] Alongside proposals for Treaty amendments overturning the ECJ's Working Time Directive judgement and on 'quota-hopping', this amounted to demands for a limited renegotiation of existing commitments. The government opposed communitarization of the CFSP and JHA pillars, favouring improved policy co-ordination within the existing framework. The leading role of NATO and the right to maintain British border controls were again highlighted. As the IGC progressed, it became evident that Britain was in a minority, often of one, on a number of areas with Major reiterating his threat to veto significant constitutional change and prevent agreement unless British demands were met.

Throughout this period, the Prime Minister stood by the Maastricht opt-out on EMU, refusing to state whether he would in time support or oppose British membership. Major treated the matter pragmatically, arguing that a decision based on the national interest could only be made when economic evidence about the effects of EMU was available. But EMU was not just an economic matter. He was 'wary of a single currency for economic reasons, wary of its economic impact and of the serious political and constitutional implications', but refused to rule out participation in advance claiming that this would reduce British influence in continued negotiations on the details of EMU.[38] Whether or not Britain joined, a single currency would have important consequences for the UK so it was in the national interest to ensure that EMU was not fudged – without adequate convergence, EMU would 'tear the Union apart'. He also wanted to ensure that the UK would not be penalized by decisions on the workings of EMU. The government agreed in principle to a new ERM2 for the 'pre-ins' but ensured that membership was voluntary, effectively ruling out British involvement, and sought assurances that fines imposed under the Stability and Growth Pact would not apply to non-euro states.

In April 1996, the Cabinet amended its policy by agreeing that should a Conservative government recommend joining the single currency in the next parliament, a referendum would be held. In the 1997 election campaign Major indicated that if re-elected his government would also allow Conservative MPs a free vote on EMU entry. In January 1997, the government's position on EMU hardened as, having examined progress towards convergence in the EU, the Cabinet concluded

> that it is very unlikely, although not impossible, that a single currency will be able to proceed safely on 1 January 1999. I am talking not just about Britain's participation, but about the single currency itself. If it did proceed without reliable convergence, we would not, of course, be part of it.[39]

In the face of an EMU revolt by Conservative candidates in the 1997 election campaign, Major re-iterated that 'we would negotiate until we knew what was involved and then we would decide having negotiated the very best deal for the UK'.[40] Although the Conservatives retained the 'wait and see' or 'negotiate and decide' policy, participation in the first wave of EMU already seemed highly unlikely, given the level of opposition to EMU entry in the party and the government's unwillingness to introduce the requisite legislation.

NATIONHOOD AND EUROPE

Over the last decade, many Conservative MPs have come to see European integration as incompatible with the Conservative politics of nationhood. Developments in the EU sit uneasily alongside the primacy of the nation-state and a conservative state patriotism organized around the British constitution and English cultural values, all of which are defended by the Conservative Party and important to its self-image. Euro-sceptics urged the leadership to defend the nation-state against European integration more vigorously, while pro-Europeans sought a rethinking of British identity to take account of EU membership. For Macmillan and Heath, membership complemented the Conservative's patriotic message, offering economic modernization and renewed purpose without requiring a major restructuring of the state. Imperial discourse gradually waned, but the party did not reposition its defence of nationhood within a European context, instead downplaying the implications of membership by claiming that it would not adversely affect 'essential national sovereignty' and that the core attributes of British identity would endure.

A number of states have added a European dimension to their official nationalisms, adapting their political systems and national identity so that regional, national and European identities coexist. They maintain their identity as nation-states, viewing the EU as an arena in which sovereignty is pooled and where national interests can be effectively pursued.[41] A 'Europeanization' of national identity and national interest has not occurred to the same extent in Britain where political elites at the centre felt that neither a modernization of the state nor a fundamental rethinking of national identity were a requisite for British success in the EU. Critics argue that this failure to adapt to her European status, plus the continued attachment to parliamentary sovereignty, Anglo-Saxon distinctiveness and an outdated sense of nationhood undermine British foreign policy.[42]

Powellism advocated a post-imperial reordering of Britishness which spurned European integration. Echoes of this were evident in Thatcherism, but whereas Powellism placed the politics of nationhood at the centre of a coherent ideology, Thatcherism was more a reflection of instinctive patriotism and an attachment to English individualism and national sovereignty. Thatcherism cannot be fully appreciated in terms of Thatcher's personal values, but a brief examination of these is useful given her role in British European policy and status as a leading Euro-sceptic. In her Bruges speech, Thatcher claimed that Britain's destiny was in Europe, but stressed the distinctiveness of Anglo-Saxon culture and British nationhood, plus Britain's close links with the USA. References to the unique early development of parliamentary government in England, Britain's historical role as a bastion and guarantor of liberty in Europe, traditions of free trade and individual liberty, and her island status featured in the speech.[43]

The Thatcherite view of British nationhood is an 'authoritarian individualist' one focusing on state authority and individual liberty. It seeks to restore values of individual liberty and free enterprise, while protecting a constitutional settlement built upon the sovereignty of parliament. At Bruges, Thatcher criticized abstract notions of an 'identikit European personality' or a 'European superstate'. A federal Europe would not have the legitimacy or enduring appeal of the nation-state; nationhood is the glue that holds the nation-state together, linking political institutions and civil society. Only a Europe of sovereign nation-states is compatible with expressions of nationhood. Indeed, 'Europe will be stronger precisely because it has France as France, Spain as Spain, Britain as Britain, each with its own customs, traditions and identity.'[44] A denial of nationhood risks producing extreme nationalism rather than the benign state patriotism of the mature liberal democratic nation-state.

Thatcher also set much store by notions of national character, advising her successor, in 1991, to take account of it when determining the national interest.

> It has rightly been said that it is the character of a people which determines the institutions which govern them, and not the institutions which give people their character. Yes, it is about being British and it is about what we feel for our country, our Parliament, our traditions and our liberties. Because of our history that feeling is perhaps stronger here than elsewhere in Europe, and it must determine the way in which our government approach such fundamental matters.[45]

At a Chequers seminar on German national character in 1990, Germany was depicted as a country veering between self-doubt and aggression. Ridley also wrote of a German desire to dominate Europe, but rhetoric of this type was likely to be counter-productive, alienating potential allies in the EU and distracting attention from the virtues of the British approach.[46] Not all opponents of further integration resorted to crude stereotypes: Lawson, a staunch defender of British nationhood, criticized Thatcher's 'saloon-bar xenophobia'.[47]

For Euro-sceptics, EMU is incompatible with national self-government for 'the ability to run monetary, economic and fiscal policy lies at the very heart of what constitutes a sovereign state'. EMU would diminish the nation-state, reducing its status to that of a rate-capped local authority while sterling is also 'an expression of our sovereignty' and an important symbol of independent British nationhood.[48]

In his biography of Major, Anthony Seldon notes that 'Major did not have any deep beliefs about Europe. It did not arouse the gut feelings in him about identity, national pride and sovereignty that it stirred in more traditional Tories like Mrs Thatcher'.[49] But Major defended the nation-state and opposed a federal Europe, claiming that his government 'would not do anything that would damage the nation-state. If I thought it would damage the nation-state, I would choose the nation-state. That is the position of the Conservative Party.'[50] Though recognizing this historic role of his party, he saw EU membership as in the national interest and characterized Euro-scepticism as

> frustration that nowhere is the nation-state fully sovereign, free to conduct its policies without concerting with ruddy foreigners. There is frustration that some of the fixed and treasured aspects of our national life are subject to seemingly relentless change... I understand these feelings but I cannot share them.[51]

SOVEREIGNTY AND AUTONOMY

The defence of national sovereignty is a central theme of the Conservative politics of nationhood and its discourse on Europe. However, the meaning of the concept is disputed and has provoked serious divisions within the party. Euro-sceptics often define sovereignty in maximalist terms, as the ultimate decision-making authority of parliament, but also relate it to national self-government and British identity. Thatcher variously equated sovereignty with the constitutional supremacy of Parliament, the independent policy-making capacity of the executive, the expression of democratic consent through election or referendum and with nationhood and self-governance. Helen Thompson quotes an unnamed colleague of Thatcher on her veto of ERM membership in 1985: 'she stood out on grounds of sovereignty, a concept she had read about somewhere but could never tell you where'.[52] Euro-enthusiasts point to the limitations of state sovereignty in an interdependent world, supporting its pooling within the EU as a way of enhancing the state's capacity for effective action.

Given the normative and empirical difficulties of establishing a single authoritative and verifiable definition of sovereignty, it is more productive to unpack the concept, noting three broad but intertwined facets – state, constitutional and popular sovereignty – which inform Conservative discourse and on which European integration has had a significant impact.[53] The state dimension of sovereignty locates the concept in the era of the nation-state. State sovereignty has a territorial element which sets out the physical limits of state authority, a functional element, which delineates the state's economic, social and administrative role, and an external or international element. The latter concerns recognition that the sovereign authority within the state has exclusive rights of jurisdiction over its citizens and that states are the dominant forms of political organization in international affairs. Within Conservative discourse, state sovereignty is also linked to nationhood as the nation is seen as the supreme form of self-governing political community.

The constitutional dimension concerns the location of sovereign authority within the state and its constitutional standing. The supremacy of Parliament is a cornerstone of the British constitution, establishing that Parliament has 'the right to make or unmake any law whatever; and further that no person or body is recognized by the law of England as having a right to override or set aside the legislation of Parliament'.[54] The gap between the doctrine of parliamentary sovereignty and political reality is considerable, but it remains a potent force in Conservative discourse. Finally, the popular dimension of sovereignty concerns the relationship between state and society, claiming that state authority derives its legitimacy from the consent of the political community, that is the nation.

The state, constitutional and popular dimensions of sovereignty are all evident in Conservative Euro-sceptic thought. Sceptics defend the primacy of the nation-state, focus on the erosion of parliamentary sovereignty resulting from membership and are concerned by its implications for self-government. Noel Malcom defines sovereignty in terms of constitutional independence and the exclusive exercise of political authority within the nation-state, rejecting definitions which focus on power or influence.[55] While sovereign authority may be delegated to international bodies, it is not divisible and cannot be shared or pooled. In this perspective, the delegation of authority to the EU has had profound and unwelcome sovereignty implications. The supremacy of Community law subordinates the British constitution to an external authority which does not have organic links with the political community.

The implications of the supremacy of Community law were illustrated in the *Factortame* case in which the 1988 Merchant Shipping

Act was overturned when it was deemed contrary to Community law. The Act had altered the rules on the registration of fishing boats to prevent non-British citizens registering boats as British in order to qualify for the UK's Common Fisheries Policy quota. A number of Spanish fishermen challenged the Act under Community law and applied for interim relief. The House of Lords referred the case to the ECJ for a preliminary ruling and in 1990 ruled that to comply with Community law, the Act had to be disapplied and interim relief granted.[56] This disapplication of an Act of Parliament provoked a hostile response from Thatcher. Lord Bridge, however, noted that the overriding of national legislation and granting of interim relief in protection of rights under Community law was a reaffirmation of the supremacy of Community law rather than a 'novel attack' on parliamentary sovereignty.[57] The European Communities Act 1972 gave present and future Community law legal force and required UK courts to defer to it. Although the Act avoided an explicit statement of the supremacy of Community law, it denied effectiveness to national legislation which conflicts with it.

The constitutionalist Euro-sceptic critique draws on an absolutist account of *de jure* sovereignty, yet Euro-sceptics do not view parliamentary sovereignty as a dry, legal matter but as an essential component of national self-government and identity. The transfer of policy competences to the EU fractures the bond between government and electorate, the consequences of which cannot be rectified by empowering the European Parliament, as democracy and authority are rooted in the nation-state. The tradition of democratic self-government exercized within the nation-state is said to be particularly strong in the UK where parliamentary sovereignty is central to state patriotism.

Euro-sceptic thought combines state, constitutional and popular dimensions of sovereignty, but offers a narrow perspective on the concept and on the impact of European integration on the nation-state. An alternative approach distinguishes between authority and power. David Held thus contrasts *de jure* sovereignty (the supreme legal authority to take decisions) and *de facto* sovereignty (the practical exercize of sovereign authority) while William Wallace contrasts sovereignty with autonomy, that is a state's capacity to achieve its desired results and control its destiny.[58] This broader perspective places the sovereignty implications of EU membership in a wider political, economic and security context, noting the constraints on independent state action arising from globalization and 'informal integration'. The global economy (multinational companies, international finance markets), technological change (nuclear weapons, global communications), global or regional problems which cross national borders (migration, terrorism), all limit the autonomy and *de facto* sovereignty of the nation-state.[59]

Conservative pro-Europeans reject absolutist accounts of sovereignty and adopt this broader perspective, treating it as a flexible rather than zero-sum concept. For Howe, 'sovereignty is not some pre-defined absolute, but a flexible, adaptable, organic notion that evolves and adjusts with circumstances'.[60] The doctrine of parliamentary sovereignty is an idealized one; within the modern state, political authority is dispersed, sovereignty is divisible and attempts to locate a single sovereign authority flawed. The notion of state sovereignty is also problematic because in an interdependent world nation-states are 'porous', their autonomy constrained by developments which do not respect national boundaries. Howe thus defines sovereignty as 'a nation's practical capacity to maximize its influence in the world'.[61] States can increase their sovereignty (their capacity for effective action and influence) by playing an active role in international organizations such as the EU, an association of nation-states retaining distinctive identities but enjoying 'sovereignty in partnership'. The nation-state remains the leading international actor and a focus for democratic consent, but must manage interdependence by sharing its sovereign authority.

Despite the rhetoric and symbolic importance, the defence of sovereignty has not been an absolute in Conservative European policy, rather a matter of degree. The Thatcher and Major Governments resisted the erosion of 'essential' national sovereignty, but in other respects treated sovereignty as negotiable. Thus an erosion of the national veto was accepted as necessary for the completion of the Single Market, an example of sovereignty being treated as a resource to be used to promote the national interest. The SEM exposed latent tensions in the Conservative project between, on the one hand, the identification of British interests with free trade and open EC markets, and on the other, with the defence of national sovereignty.[62] The government favoured a market-led approach to the single market and EMU, but both processes led to increased supranational authority. David Willetts recognized the tensions between markets and communities, questioning whether the classic nation-state is 'the ultimate supply-side constraint'.[63] The

SEM is an example of 'deep' free trade, requiring mutual recognition and supranational regulation, eroding national authority. Willetts argued that EMU would not mean a massive erosion of sovereignty, for 'sovereignty which has been voluntarily renounced and can be regained has never been truly lost'. But, reflecting the government's tendency to speak of nationhood and national self-government, he believed it would 'be a significant erosion of independent nationhood'.[64] Defending national sovereignty, or disguising its erosion, had both symbolic and concrete elements under the Major Governments (for example, the removal of references to a 'federal goal' in the TEU, the Ioannina compromise and its challenge to the Working Time Directive) given the Prime Minister's concern with party management.

Executive Autonomy

Effective analysis of Britain's relations with the EU requires then a cautious treatment of the concept of sovereignty plus an examination of the effects of European integration on the British state and political system. As noted earlier, analysis of government policy and the effects of European integration in terms of executive autonomy offers a clearer assessment than an exclusive focus on sovereignty. Relative executive autonomy is also central to Conservative statecraft, the Thatcher and Major Governments seeking to defend the authority and policy-making effectiveness of central government, insulating it from domestic and external pressures in matters of high politics.

Intergovernmentalist studies of the EU treat nation-states as the dominant actors, pursuing their national interests: integration has strengthened the nation-state rather than brought about its demise.[65] States pool their individual sovereignties in order to achieve domestic socio-economic objectives, which are shaped in part by interest group pressure, and pursue collective trade and economic goals. They make only limited surrenders of sovereignty, doing so for narrowly defined purposes, and preserve a balance of power favouring national governments by insisting on unanimity for 'sovereignty-related reforms' and using intergovernmental institutions rather than granting open-ended authority to supranational bodies.[66]

Though national governments pursue domestic policy objectives through European integration, states should not be treated as unitary actors. What constitutes the 'national interest' is contested within the domestic arena, a state's European policy emerging from a process of bargaining between a range of domestic actors. Andrew Moravcsik contends that cooperation in the EU tends to redistribute domestic political influence in ways that reinforce the power of national executives. EU decision-making offers the executive greater policy initiative and enhanced control of the domestic agenda, alters institutional arrangements, restricting opportunities for meaningful opposition to the executive's European policy, gives it access to information unavailable to other domestic actors and provides additional justification for its policies.[67] Ministers can 'cut slack' during inter-state bargaining, loosening the constraints imposed by domestic pressures.

Two problems with this perspective will be outlined, the first concerning the application of the thesis of enhanced executive autonomy to the British case, the second reflecting shortcomings of liberal intergovernmentalism as a theory of domestic policy preference formation and EU decision-making. The claim that the EU enhances executive autonomy is problematic in the British case for a number of reasons. Firstly, the drive for further integration since the late 1980s directly challenged central elements of the Conservative project. Secondly, Britain's relative isolation and limited success in EU inter-state bargaining hampered the government's prospects of winning support for its position. At a domestic level, European integration caused serious strategic and ideological divisions within the Cabinet and Conservative Party, limiting the government's room for manoeuvre and affecting its negotiating position. Finally, the 'Europeanization' of many policy areas means a range of domestic actors are involved in EU policy formation and implementation. These challenges to executive autonomy will be examined in turn.

The support of a majority of Member States for the social dimension, institutional reform and EMU left the British government in a difficult strategic position, divided over the optimal means of reacting to a series of proposals of which it largely disapproved and over which it was likely to have limited influence. It favoured a Europe of nation-states and viewed integration as an economic project concerned with the removal of trade barriers, not a political process with a federal vocation. Differences of outlook strengthened the perception that Britain is an 'awkward partner'. British governments have often taken a pragmatic stance on EU policy proposals, focusing on short-term problem solving, maximizing the national interest and minimizing the costs of membership. Policy responses tend to be reactive, constructed on an issue-by-issue basis and determined foremost by considerations of short-term national interest and party management rather than by a long-term vision of the UK's role.

British prospects of winning support in the EU have also been hampered by limited success in working the 'rules of the game' of EU negotiations.[68] Thatcher's critics claimed that her confrontational approach and nationalist rhetoric alienated other heads of government, making them less amenable to compromise. Major's negotiating skills at the Maastricht summit were praised but the policy of non-cooperation during the beef crisis was a costly failure. But an over-emphasis on negative factors can produce a distorted picture, given the UK's good implementation record and support of much SEM legislation. United Kingdom Personal Representation to the European Communities (UKREP) officials in Brussels are also respected for the coherence and clarity of their negotiating positions, although the negative tone of government policy in the mid-1990s left officials little leeway in negotiations.

Although the thrust of key parts of the EC/EU agenda ran counter to the preferred direction of British European policy in this period, the government had some success in shaping the SEA and TEU. Moravcsik characterized the SEA as a lowest common denominator deal, with Britain the most satisfied state given the Treaty's minimalist position on institutional reform and broad neo-liberal thrust.[69] Significantly though, neither the SEA nor TEU held up the momentum for 'ever closer union' or decisively steered the EC towards the British agenda. Thatcher's neo-liberal perspective on the Single Market and Major's proposals on flexibility proved too limited in scope to win support from states committed to further integration.

While able to steer Treaty outcomes away from maximalist positions and win some support on individual policy issues, the government was unable to build durable coalitions of interest across a range of key issues or win support for its policy packages as a whole. In the 1990–1 twin IGCs, domestic considerations, negotiating concerns and the scope for compromise differed from issue to issue. Meanwhile, the extension of QMV to a range of policy areas has altered practices in the Council as opponents of policy proposals are no longer able to veto them unilaterally but have to think in terms of extracting concessions or constructing blocking minorities on an issue-by-issue basis.

The assertion that EU policy cooperation increases central government control over the policy agenda also encounters problems in the British case. In terms of executive-legislative relations, the SEA and TEU further eroded parliamentary influence over European issues as decisions formerly taken exclusively at a national level now fall within the remit of EU decision-making over which national parliaments have limited influence. The rhetoric of parliamentary sovereignty has disguised this increased executive dominance of the legislative process and government determination to protect executive autonomy. However, the House of Commons remains the main arena for debating British policy in Europe and one where dissent has revealed itself. Conservative Whips found management of the parliamentary party and the legislative process particularly difficult during the ratification of the Maastricht Treaty, while parliamentary committees on EU matters have periodically raised awkward issues for the government.[70]

British European policy-making is centralized in that it is focused within the core executive, reflecting the political and institutional culture of British government, though sectorization and disputes within the core executive itself are significant.[71] The European Secretariat in the Cabinet Office seeks policy coordination in Whitehall and provides UKREP with detailed, tightly defined guidelines. But centralization does not ensure coherence. Policy often appears reactive and negative and where there is disagreement in the core executive – EU matters being considered in a range of Cabinet committees – policy is often based on compromise. The Prime Minister can exercize considerable control over government European policy, but the limits of prime-ministerial authority were evident in disputes over ERM and EMU within the Thatcher and Major Governments.

British semi-detachment and the complex impact of Europe on executive autonomy are illustrated in the case of the ERM and EMU which offered alternative macro-economic and governing codes, departing from a monetarist strategy of domestic control of inflation towards externalized control through exchange rate management in the ERM or by the ECB under EMU.[72] Both meant significant constraints on executive autonomy. Thompson depicts decision-making on ERM entry as characterized by the 'dominance of personalized, non-institutional leadership influences', confrontation within the core executive shaping policy decisions and preventing a consistent or coherent approach.[73] Differences between the central actors were multi-layered, Lawson's frustration with monetary targets and attraction to exchange rate management leading him to advocate ERM membership, while Thatcher favoured domestic means of controlling inflation and believed that to focus on the exchange rate subordinated domestic goals to external ones. EMU complicated the picture as Lawson urged British engagement, including ERM entry, to slow momentum towards EMU, whereas Thatcher was prepared to veto EMU rather than compromise. When sterling did join the mechanism, careful examination of the proposed rate and implications of entry at a time of recession and German unification was largely absent. This together with British opposition to EMU (the ERM having become a stepping-stone to EMU for many states) and a reluctance to accept the costs or norms of membership contributed to the decision to withdraw from the mechanism and return to a revized domesticist macro-economic strategy in 1992.

British policy on EMU was also characterized by Cabinet divisions over the optimal response to proposals for which it was unprepared, which it did not support and over which it had limited influence. The 'hard Ecu' plan originated in the City and Treasury but was undermined by strategic disputes in Cabinet and imprecise policy goals – Major presented it as a genuine alternative to the Delors blueprint, but Thatcher treated it as a spoiling tactic – emerging too late in the day to have any real impact. The Maastricht opt-out did not ensure executive autonomy or ease the government's problems. Domestically, Euro-sceptic dissent intensified and key supporters in the City and the Confederation of British Industry (CBI) expressed concern over government policy. In the EU, political will to launch the euro in 1999 remained despite difficulties *en route*, raising the prospect of a radical change in Britain's relations with Europe.

Core executive control over decision-making is most pronounced in macro-economic and foreign policy, but a range of domestic actors exercise influence in other areas of British European policy and play an important role in policy implementation. This is particularly true for technical and administrative matters, decided away from the political spotlight, in which policy networks have important inputs.[74] Recent studies of EU policy-making have challenged state-centric accounts, recognizing the plurality of factors affecting European integration and depicting the EU as a system of 'multi-level governance' in which interest groups, national bureaucracies, sub-national authorities and supranational institutions play a role in shaping and implementing policy.[75] Whereas state-centric accounts contend that the state is strengthened and executive autonomy enhanced in the EU, the multi-level governance perspective claims that although nation-states are still the key actors, they do not enjoy a policy-making monopoly, as sub-national and supranational institutions play an important role in a number of policy areas. John Peterson notes that although national governments are important actors, particularly in 'history-making decisions' (including Treaty amendments and European Council decisions), they are less well-placed to control 'policy-setting' decisions (where supranational institutions play an agenda-setting role) and 'policy-shaping decisions' (where policy networks are active).[76]

The complexity of EU decision-making is most apparent in policy areas affected by the Single Market project with the EU expanding its regulatory role as states delegate sovereignty to ensure compliance with credible, uniform SEM rules. Policy-making involves a complex web of actors: the Commission has a key role initiating regulatory policies, though national agencies deal with their implementation.[77] The effects of the EC's regulatory role on the British state and politics are also complex. The Conservative government was a key supporter of market liberalization and mutual recognition, using the SEM to export domestic policy objectives. But EC activism in these areas had important, sometimes unwelcome, consequences for the executive as policy-making becomes more difficult to control, given the additional influence of supranational institutions and sectoral interests.

The 'Europeanization' of many domestic policy areas and the multi-layered nature of EU decision-making have impacted upon the British state in other ways. Local government plays a greater role in EU regional policy, encouraged by the Commission to play a pro-active role and charged with implementing a variety of directives, though central government retains significant policy-making and administrative control over structural funding. British courts have, meanwhile, often proved willing to interpret national legislation in line with Community law.

EUROPEAN INTEGRATION AND CONSERVATIVE POLITICS

'Europe' does not easily fit into the normal British models of party competition and electoral mobilization given intra-party divisions, the difficulties of exploiting European issues for partisan advantage and the mixed messages emanating from the electorate. With the EU moving in a direction at odds with the Conservative's free market–national sovereignty ethos, its identity as the patriotic but pro-European party was further strained. In the early 1980s Conservatives exploited Labour's opposition to membership, but Labour's conversion to a pro-European stance later in the decade further complicated the Conservative politics of support.

In the 1988 European elections, the Conservatives fought a largely negative campaign warning of a 'diet of Brussels' which left many in the party uneasy and failed to enthuse voters. Concerned by damaging internal divisions on European issues, the leadership opted for an adversarial campaign in the 1994 European elections. This focused attention on a left–right economic divide between Labour's support for the European social model and the Conservative vision of competition and deregulation, plus Labour's support for a limited extension of QMV. Direct Euro-sceptic influence over the manifesto was minimal, but the campaign's emphasis on liberalization, the national veto and flexibility provided a semblance of party unity.[78] Europe figured more prominently in the 1997 general election campaign. Major called European issues 'the heart and guts of the election', but large numbers of Conservative candidates veered from the official 'wait and see' position by indicating their principled opposition to joining the single currency. He appealed to his party not to bind his hands in Europe as this would weaken his negotiating position and nobody could yet be certain of the outcome or details of EMU.[79] Major also stated that he would 'negotiate in the interests of the United Kingdom as a whole, not in the convenient party political interests of the Conservative Party', an admission which contrasted with the ethos of the Conservatives as the national party.

Opinion polls have not offered clear messages for Conservative campaign managers on European issues. Despite Thatcher's hostility to the EC, the percentage of the electorate saying that membership was a good thing increased over the decade.[80] Concerns about EMU and political union increased after 1992, swayed by the negative images presented by a Euro-sceptic press, but there has been little evidence of popular support for withdrawal. The direct impact of European issues on the heavy Conservative defeats in the 1989 and 1994 elections was limited. A quarter of voters mentioned Europe as a 'very important' issue in the 1997 election, but a Gallup post-election survey found that 44 per cent of voters felt Labour would best handle Britain's relations with the EU, only 32 per cent naming the Conservatives.[81] The 1997 BBC/NOP general election exit poll found that 47 per cent of all voters approved of the 'wait and see' approach to EMU, including 51 per cent of those voting Conservative, though 41 per cent of Conservative voters thought Britain should say that it would never join the single currency.[82] But disunity on Europe and particularly the exit from the ERM had significant electoral repercussions for the Conservatives, severely damaging their claims to governing competence and effective economic management.[83]

Though differences on European policy narrowed, the two main parties nonetheless employed Europe as a partisan issue. But substantive policy differences were limited: both parties favoured an intergovernmental Europe, preserving unanimity on issues of vital national interest.[84] The Conservatives portrayed Labour's willingness to accept a limited extension of QMV as an abdication of sovereignty and its support for the European social model as economically damaging. Although Labour hardened its position on EMU and integration in 1996–7, Conservatives continued to claim that Blair's inexperience meant he would 'surrender' British decision-making powers, an election poster depicting the Labour leader as Chancellor Kohl's ventriloquist dummy.

Labour's move to a pro-European stance and the hostility towards further integration within Tory ranks pushed the Conservative leadership away from a mainstream pro-European outlook towards a cautious Euro-scepticism. While insisting that Britain must remain a member of the EU, the tone of recent Conservative election campaigns has been notably hostile to key elements of the EU agenda. The 1997 general election produced a further complicating factor for Conservative electoral strategy in the form of high profile anti-European parties. Sir James Goldsmith's Referendum Party stood candidates against all but a hard core of Tory Eurosceptics and attracted support from a small number of former Conservative politicians, including de-selected MP Sir George Gardiner and former party treasurer Lord McAlpine. It increased the Euro-sceptic profile in the run-up to the election but offered a confused message to voters, proposing a complex referendum question and adopting an anti-EU tone without the clear commitment to withdrawal offered by the UK Independence Party, while the main parties offered a referendum on EMU. The Referendum Party won over 800 000 votes, its best results coming in English coastal constituencies, and the UK Independence Party over 100 000 votes, together totalling some 3 per cent of the vote. The impact of the Referendum Party on the Conservative vote is unclear: in 19 constituencies its vote was larger than the notional majority achieved by the Conservatives in the 1992 general election, but 1 exit poll found that only half of the votes won by the Referendum Party came from people who had voted Conservative in 1992.[85]

The prospect of anti-European parties tapping into sceptical public opinion contributed to the decision of many Conservative candidates to state their opposition to a single currency during the 1997 election campaign, including two junior ministers, John Horam and James Paice, and Conservative Party Vice-Chairman Angela Rumbold. Conservative candidates declaring their opposition to a single currency received campaign funds from Euro-sceptic businessman Paul Sykes. Much of the Conservative press took a Euro-sceptic line during the campaign, *The Times* urging its readers to vote for Euro-sceptic candidates and listing over two hundred and fifty Conservative Euro-sceptics, although the number who explicitly stated their opposition to EMU was lower. Senior ministers also stressed their Euro-sceptic credentials during the campaign, Michael Howard claiming that the conclusion of the IGC at the Amsterdam summit was 'so far reaching that it would indeed put our survival as a nation-state in question'.[86] But Euro-sceptic rhetoric had little electoral impact: the Conservative candidates who made apparent their opposition to EMU fared no better than their pro-European counterparts in the 1997 election.

The reverberations of divisions within the parliamentary party were felt to a lesser extent in the voluntary party. A study of Conservative Party members in the early 1990s revealed that a majority opposed further integration and EMU, but one-third of those questioned had pro-European attitudes.[87] A Central Office survey of party members in 1994 indicated grassroots support for government policy but avoided questions on EMU or a referendum; a 1996 consultation exercise showed a majority of activists opposing the single currency. Euro-sceptic feeling at grassroots level made itself felt in constituency support for dissenting Euro-sceptic MPs, the increased number of annual conference motions hostile to integration and the enthusiastic reception Euro-sceptic speeches received at conference.[88]

A final difficulty 'Europe' poses for the politics of support concerns the Conservative Party's claims to represent the interests of British business and financial interests, strong supporters of EU membership. The CBI backed the Conservative commitment to completing the Single Market, competitiveness and deregulation, but its members were concerned by the negative images of the EU presented by Euro-sceptics and the implications of government obstructionism.[89] A 1996 CBI survey found that 73 per cent of companies supported non-participation in the Social Agreement, though some established works councils in their British outlets despite the opt-out.[90] There is little consensus within the business community over whether Britain should adopt the euro – larger companies in the CBI appear more favourable to British participation than small and medium-sized enterprises. In the CBI survey, 58 per cent of companies favoured adopting the euro, though many were worried about the conditions and timing of entry. The Institute of Directors warned that Britain had 'nothing to gain and much to lose' from EMU. A 1997 survey of companies found that although 64 per cent opposed entry in the first wave, 73 per cent believed that the UK should join at some stage and 58 per cent felt the euro would be good for their companies.[91] Messages emanating from the City and Bank of England on the potential costs of non-participation in EMU were also mixed, but fears of exclusion from key negotiations were again apparent. Relations between the party and agricultural interests were damaged by failure to lift the EU's world-wide ban on British beef exports.

Party Management

One of the most visible manifestations of the difficulties the politics of nationhood has raised for British Conservatism is factionalism in the Conservative Party. Europe has become the main fault-line in the party, accounting for much of the dissent experienced by the Major Government. David Baker, Andrew Gamble and Steve Ludlam note that the most serious divisions in the Conservative Party – on the repeal of the Corn Laws in 1846, tariff reform in 1903 and European integration in the 1990s – have occurred over major strategic choices about Britain's place in the world political economy.[92] But serious divisions in the party, particularly tariff reform and Europe, have also tended to reflect differing conceptions of the Conservative politics of nationhood (that is, questions of national sovereignty and identity, plus the Conservative's self-image as the defender of the nation-state).

Euro-sceptic opposition to government European policy increased quantitatively (the scale of dissent) and qualitatively (the intensity of disputes) in the 1990s.[93] Thatcher's Bruges speech provided a rallying cry, but dissent did not reach critical levels until a June 1992 Early Day Motion urging a 'fresh start' on Europe was signed by 84 Conservative MPs. The parliamentary ratification of the TEU proved difficult. To win a Paving Motion debate in November 1992 the government delayed the Bill until after the second Danish referendum but was defeated on an amendment on the Committee of the Regions and on the Social Chapter vote when 23 Tory Euro-sceptics voted with Labour in the hope that Major would abandon the Treaty. Instead he called and won a confidence vote. A total of 45 Conservative MPs voted against the government on the Bill on at least one occasion.

Emboldened by their campaign against the Maastricht Treaty, sterling's exit from the ERM and tacit support for their views from some Cabinet ministers, Euro-sceptic dissent continued. From 1992, the centre of gravity in the Conservative parliamentary party moved in a Euro-sceptic direction during Major's leadership, a majority of MPs exhibiting some degree of scepticism. Having made the 1994 European Communities (Finance) Bill a vote of confidence, Major removed the party whip from the 8 MPs who abstained (another MP resigned it). But this backfired as the whipless MPs became a more homogeneous and rebellious group before having the whip unconditionally restored. In the face of further dissent, Major resigned the party leadership in 1995 challenging the Euro-sceptics to 'put up or shut up'. Redwood stood against him on a platform of opposition to EMU and won 89 votes.

Adding to the difficulties of party management and policy-making were Cabinet divisions over European policy. The resignations of several Cabinet ministers – Michael Heseltine, Lawson, Ridley and Howe under Thatcher; Lamont and Redwood under Major – owed at least something to disputes over European issues. The imbalance between a pro-European Cabinet and sceptical parliamentary party concerned Major's backbench critics in the early 1990s. But when the shifting centre of gravity in the party was, to some extent, matched in Cabinet as pragmatic ministers took more hostile positions on European issues, disputes within the Cabinet intensified. Kenneth Clarke's determination to hold firm against pressure to rule out participation in the first wave of EMU and signals that he would resign if the policy were changed limited Major's room for manoeuvre.[94]

Conservative Euro-sceptic MPs have a range of concerns, favoured outcomes and preferred tactics. Different perspectives on economic integration existed within the ranks of the sceptics in the 1980s. Thatcherites opposed further integration for both neo-liberal and sovereignty reasons, but were divided between those supporting floating exchange rates and others, such as Lawson, who supported ERM membership as a means of entrenching anti-inflationary discipline. Arguments for economic integration were presented by free marketeers, welcoming the monetary discipline imposed by an independent bank, and interventionists, supporting a greater level of social protection and industrial support than exists in the UK.[95]

Michael Spicer identified four broad groupings within the Euro-sceptic ranks: diehard 'veteran anti-marketeers' who opposed EC entry in the 1970s; 'marketeers' or neo-liberals primarily concerned about the EC's economic interventionism; 'constitutionalists' who focus on the legal and institutional implications of the continued transfer of legislative competence from Westminster to the EU institutions; and finally 'patriots' or populists whom Spicer feels reflect the instinctive nationalism of the British people.[96] The most significant organized Euro-sceptic groups within the Conservative Party were the Bruges Group and the European Foundation (set up by Cash), while broader Thatcherite groupings such as the No Turning Back Group and Conservative Way Forward were also Euro-sceptic in outlook. No classification of Euro-sceptic positions can be perfect given the variety of arguments used by sceptics, differences in tactics and across issues and changes over time.[97] Thus Lawson supported ERM membership but opposed EMU while Norman Tebbit's scepticism links constitutionalist themes of national self-government with populist rhetoric about British identity.[98] Euro-sceptics may also change their positions over time and from issue to issue, supporting QMV on SEM legislation to achieve neo-liberal goals, but opposing its further extension on sovereignty grounds. The significance of the Maastricht Treaty was that it brought together neo-liberal, constitutionalist and populist sceptics in an organized backbench campaign, providing a sense of common purpose which masked differences in their ranks. Despite contrasting views and favoured options, plus differences in how far MPs were prepared to go in their attempts to scupper the Treaty, a number of broad themes of the Conservative Euro-sceptic critique can be identified.

The Euro-sceptic Critique

The defence of national sovereignty is a guiding Euro-sceptic theme, understood in constitutionalist terms as the ultimate decision-making authority of parliament, in neo-liberal terms as the leading role of national governments in economic policy and in populist terms as national self-determination. For most sceptics, the EU should ideally be little more than an association of sovereign states cooperating for free trade purposes in a Single Market. Further transfers of sovereignty are resisted and a 'repatriation' of policies, that is the transfer of policy competences such as agriculture and fisheries back to the nation-state, is favoured. Sceptics also want to redress the institutional balance of the EU in favour of national governments. Typical demands include: limiting the role of the Commission to that of a civil service carrying out the will of the Council, which would gain the right to initiate legislation; downgrading the legislative role of the European Parliament; giving national parliaments greater input; and curtailing the 'policy-making' powers of the ECJ.[99]

Maastricht was a 'treaty too far' for the Euro-sceptics, its provisions taking the EU further down the road towards a federal Europe and away from the Common Market model. Clarke's claim that EMU does not require political union was firmly rejected. The centralizing ambitions of the Commission and a dominant Franco-German axis are presented as driving the EU inexorably towards a 'European superstate'. Sceptics distrust EU decision-making procedures, viewing them as a 'conveyor-belt to federalism' which works against British interests. Thatcher saw Maastricht as a bad deal for Britain. Her critique is worth quoting at length:

> The problem with John Major's alternative approach was that although it initially won plaudits, it left the fundamental issues unresolved. Under it we would effectively abandon our attempts to win support for our alternative vision of the Community, going along with a new European framework which did not suit us, while relying on special exemptions which ultimately depended on the goodwill and fair dealing of people and institutions whose purposes were radically different from ours. Arguably, the changed

approach actually made our position worse by accepting important points of principle about the Union's future direction... which will make it more difficult for Britain to argue its own conception of Europe in the future.[100]

The opt-out from Stage III of EMU did not appease the Eurosceptics. Instead they were critical of Major for accepting EMU as the EU's goal, believing that once the euro was introduced, additional pressure to sign up to the single currency would be brought to bear on Britain. Compromise sent out the wrong signals, leading others to believe that Britain would eventually back down. The opt-out did not neutralize EMU as a divisive issue in the Conservative Party, instead it remained a live issue as sceptics demanded an early statement of non-participation. Thatcher's warning about relying on the fair dealing of other Member States reflected her experiences over an SEA reference to EMU – 'vague declarations which we assumed at the time had no practical implications are subsequently cited to justify the extension of Community powers into fresh areas of national life' – and her belief that the SEA included a legally watertight clause on retaining border controls.[101]

Given their conviction that the EU is moving towards a federal vocation, sceptics rejected the government's post-1992 claims that the debate in the Union was moving Britain's way. Lamont claimed that 'there is not a shred of evidence at Maastricht or since then that anyone accepts our view of Europe'.[102] Writing in 1992, Bulpitt suggested that the only available strategy for Conservative Eurosceptics was to wait for the difficulties which EMU and enlargement would raise to undermine the Maastricht model.[103] But this option was not an attractive one for those determined to resist further integration at the IGC and stay outside EMU.

A number of sceptics thus began to explore alternative strategies. Thatcher felt that 'we must be prepared to exercise our veto and resolutely use all avenues of non-cooperation open to us' in order to win special arrangements for Britain. The IGC gave the government an opportunity to extricate itself from disadvantageous Treaty provisions and negotiate special status in a flexible Europe in return for its assent to some Member States forming a 'hard core' pursuing further integration. Lamont suggested that leaving the EU could not be discounted in the medium-term but negotiating an outer tier membership in which Britain would only be bound by the free trade parts of the Treaty of Rome was more realistic.[104]

Aside perhaps from the Single Market, sceptics argue that membership of the EU has not produced tangible economic or political benefits but has had clear costs (for example, budget contributions and the Common Agricultural Policy [CAP]).[105] Few in the mid-1990s supported withdrawal from the Union, but many felt that making Europe the primary focus of foreign economic policy had been damaging, particularly given the EU's collectivist ethos. Lamont claimed that Britain was economically over-reliant on the EU and should devote more attention to free trade arrangements with the North American Free Trade Agreement (NAFTA) states, the 'Tiger economies' of South Asia and developing markets such as China.[106] Teresa Gorman's ideal is of Britain as 'an offshore island like Hong Kong, a free trade area with the minimum of government intervention and the maximum of business activity'.[107] In Euro-sceptic thought, an internationalist free trade outlook often sits alongside a defence of the nation-state and national identity.

Major responded by stressing the benefits of membership and rejecting Euro-sceptic scenarios: 'the idea that if we were outside the EU we could somehow become a trading haven on the edge of Europe ... while others fix the rules without any regard at all to our national self-interest, is cloud cuckoo land.'[108] Other Member States may also prove reluctant to grant special arrangements, especially if these give the UK a competitive advantage. Separating those areas which make up a core of policies binding on all Member States from peripheral policies which states can opt-out of would also be a difficult task. Disputes over Value Added Tax (VAT) harmonization, border controls and social policy illustrate that even the boundaries of Single Market policy are far from settled.

The problems withdrawal from the EU would raise should not be under-estimated, but a number of steps to reordering Britain's relations with the EU have been suggested. Constitutionalist Euro-sceptics point to Lord Denning's view that the supremacy of Community law is not limitless:

> if the time should come when our Parliament deliberately passes an Act – with the intention of repudiating the Treaty or any provision of it – or intentionally of acting inconsistently with it – and says so in express terms – then I should have thought that it would be the duty of our courts to follow the statute of our Parliament.[109]

Although the 1972 Act gave legal force to future Community legislation, it did not prevent a future Parliament from repealing the European Communities Act. Following the German Constitutional Court's verdict on the TEU, sceptics sought a restatement of the legislative supremacy of parliament, 66 Tory MPs supporting a failed 1996 Ten Minute Rule Bill giving the Commons the authority to disapply ECJ rulings.[110] Seventy-eight Conservatives backed Cash's Referendum Bill in 1996, believing that a referendum vote against a federal Europe would strengthen the hands of a government seeking to negotiate a special position for the UK.

Divisions on European issues made the Conservatives a difficult party to lead, many commentators depicting Major as a weak leader unwilling or unable to provide clear leadership, his actions shaped by pressure from both Euro-sceptics and pro-European Cabinet ministers.[111] Major decided against pushing ahead with the ratification of the Maastricht Treaty after the close Paving Motion vote in 1992, but was determined to ratify the Treaty thereafter. He appeared at different stages to support both the pro-European case (calling Euro-sceptic ministers 'bastards') and moderate Euro-scepticism (claiming to be the 'biggest Euro-sceptic in the Cabinet'). Major's drift towards moderate Euro-scepticism and some ill-judged actions in the EU, notably the beef crisis non-cooperation policy, undermined British influence in the Union. But simply viewing Major as a weak leader is simplistic: it underestimates the difficulty of uniting the Conservative Party across the range of European issues, does not adequately assess the influence of the Euro-sceptics over government policy and fails to appreciate the extent to which Major's balancing act for the most part held the party together. Baker, Gamble and Ludlam depict the European issues dividing the Conservative Party along a sovereignty–interdependence axis (between those eager to prevent further transfers of sovereignty and those who see a pooling of sovereignty as beneficial) but also along a limited state–extended state axis.[112] The latter cuts across the sceptic/enthusiast divide, notably in disputes about currency management (ERM membership, central bank independence) and the role of QMV and the ECJ in the Single Market project.

Major became Conservative leader in part because he was deemed to be the candidate most likely to unite (most of) the party on European issues once a sufficient number of MPs had decided that Thatcher's hostility to developments in the Community prevented her from achieving this central element of party statecraft. Major sought to lead the party from the pragmatic centre, constructing an alternative British approach to European integration and maintaining the 'wait and see' stance on EMU around which he believed much of the Conservative Party could unite, albeit with varying degrees of enthusiasm. In addition he responded to changing dynamics within the party and the EU by conducting a balancing act over European policy, couching his policy in language which promised something (but often delivered little) to both Euro-sceptics and Euro-enthusiasts, while reacting to dissent with a mix of limited conciliation with tough sanctions. However, the influence of Euro-sceptic rebels over government policy was limited, Clarke proving a significant bulwark against encroaching scepticism. Though recanting on his opposition to a referendum on EMU and making sceptical noises about a single currency, Major refused to abandon his 'negotiate and decide' stance or adhere to the sceptics' main demand by ruling out British participation and claimed that the national interest took priority over party political considerations.

In the 1995 leadership contest Major again presented himself as the person best able to unite the Conservatives. Given the balance of opinion in the party, a leader constructing an alliance around an intergovernmental, 'wait and see' platform would be backed by the loyalist, pragmatic European majority of the party and win some support from both wings of the Euro-divide. His leadership rivals in 1990, the pro-European, interventionist Heseltine and Hurd may well have proved less able to appease moderate Euro-sceptics, while a Redwood victory in 1995 would have alienated the hitherto relatively passive pro-European MPs.

The perception that the rebel Euro-sceptics, a voluble but minority group in the Commons, were having undue influence over the tone if not substance of government policy, prompted pro-European Conservatives to raise their profile. Senior figures like Howe and Hurd presented a positive case for membership and the pooling of sovereignty; the Positive European Group had the support of some 90 Tory MPs; and key party figures were prominently placed in the Action Centre for Europe. Howe championed constructive engagement, concerned that the national interest was taking second place to short-term considerations of party management, resulting in Britain's 'semi-detachment' from the EU. Ahead of the IGC, the government's 'strident rhetoric of national independence' undermined the British position while Major's attitude on flexibility raised the prospect of permanent British isolation which would be a 'national defeat of significant proportions'.[113] Pro-Europeans also claimed that EMU would bring economic and political benefits for the UK, a position Clarke appeared close to until he, publicly at least, concluded that fudging the convergence criteria to ensure a 1999 start date for EMU would prevent British entry.[114]

CONCLUSIONS

'Europe' is a difficult issue for British political parties. The domestic rewards integration may offer other Member States are not available to the UK to the same extent. The 'two-level game' of defending national interests in the EU while ensuring executive control over British European policy in the domestic arena is frequently a fraught one for British governments working in a domestic environment where transfers of sovereignty often bring political costs rather than benefits, and in an EU environment in which their opposition to further integration frequently leaves them in a minority position with limited influence over policy outcomes.

These problems are particularly acute for the Conservative Party as European integration poses multiple challenges to party statecraft and identity, the politics of nationhood being a central aspect of both of these. 'Europe' has provoked fundamental divisions in the party over how to react to a dynamic agenda for European integration which few Conservatives actively support, as well as over the self-image and strategy of the Conservative Party itself. Identifying Conservatism with free market economics, limited government and the defence of national self-government, Thatcher suggested that support for further political union and EMU was antithetical to Conservatism as it spelled the end of the sovereign nation-state, an erosion of self-government and an assault on national identity. She branded the policies favoured by some pro-Europeans in the party as 'No Nation Conservatism'.[115] Euro-enthusiasts argue that their desire for Britain to be at the heart of Europe is consistent with patriotic Conservatism. Tristan Garel-Jones recognized that patriotism and sovereignty are central to Conservative politics, the party having a 'tribal instinct for nationhood', claiming that 'it is impossible to think of oneself as Conservative unless one is animated by a deep, almost atavistic, sense of belonging to one's nation'. However, he believed that sovereignty is 'a moving target', and that the 'patriotic choice' for Conservatives was to support an active British role in a confederal Europe of nation-states. 'To argue against the European Union is to argue against Britain's profoundest self-interest, against her place in the world, and flies in the face of that patriotic instinct that is one of the defining elements of Conservatism.'[116] Given the dynamism of the EU agenda and the intensity of these disputes, Conservative divisions on Europe are unlikely to be healed or contained.

5 Territorial Politics

The Conservative Party has historically sought to manage the multinational United Kingdom state and defend the autonomy of the centre by providing limited administrative devolution (but rejecting, for much of its history, legislative devolution) and developing a discourse of integrative state patriotism. For Bulpitt, the Conservative Party's governing code involved its leaders in office protecting their relative autonomy in high politics by granting local elites autonomy in areas of low politics, producing a 'dual polity' in which different institutional arrangements existed in the component nations of the UK.[1] As noted in Chapter 1, the Conservative national strategy was built around British state patriotism and its discourse of constitutional stability, Unionism, imperialism and national cohesion. But by the 1960s, Conservative statecraft was facing a number of challenges: in territorial politics these included the growth of sub-state nationalism, the end of the imperial basis of conservative state patriotism and economic decline. This chapter examines how the Thatcher and Major Governments sought to reassert the autonomy of the centre, assessing their territorial management and changes in Conservative unionism.

The component nations of the UK have retained their own identities, plus varying degrees of political, cultural and institutional distinctiveness. James Kellas claims that Scotland is a 'political system' but, given its limited autonomy and the susceptibility of Scottish institutions to a determined and centralizing government, it is more appropriate to refer to a Scottish dimension of the British system of government mediated through a system of administrative devolution.[2] Administrative devolution refers to the role of the territorial ministries for Scotland (established in 1885) and Wales (1964), created to give a greater voice for their respective nations in central government, and headed by Secretaries of State who sit in Cabinet. The ministries have a dual role, defending territorial interests and distinctiveness at the centre whilst also implementing a range of centrally determined policies in their respective nations.[3] However, this should not disguise the concentration of power at the centre of the British state, characterized by the doctrine of parliamentary sovereignty and centralized decision-making in the core

103

executive. The Secretaries of State for Scotland and Wales are relatively junior members of Cabinet; they and the territorial ministries have largely defensive and reactive rather than innovative roles in policy-making. Administrative devolution does not imply that territorial elites are able to take authoritative decisions, rather that some administrative functions of the centre are organized on a territorial basis to ensure the relative autonomy of the centre and accommodate local elites. Legislative devolution, by contrast, refers to the creation of separate parliaments with legislative and perhaps tax-raising powers.

Northern Ireland remains a 'place apart' in UK politics, political elites in Westminster and Whitehall believing that the conflict between the Unionist and Nationalist communities necessitates different arrangements.[4] The 1973 Northern Ireland Constitution Act confirmed that Northern Ireland is part of the UK on a conditional basis, remaining part of the UK for so long as this remains the wish of a majority of people in Northern Ireland. Successive governments have accepted that the Republic of Ireland has a legitimate interest in the affairs of Northern Ireland. Bipartisan consensus exists too on the main goals of policy in Northern Ireland, namely security, stability and the search for a political settlement which would satisfy the minimum demands of the two communities. The Conservative and Labour parties have also shared a desire to exclude Northern Ireland issues from mainstream British politics and party competition.

Aside from the ill-fated Sunningdale executive, Northern Ireland has been under direct rule from Westminster since the abolition of the Stormont Parliament in 1972. Though viewed as a temporary measure and recognized as flawed by successive governments, the apparatus of direct rule has remained largely unchanged.[5] With the abolition of Stormont, legislative powers were transferred to Westminster where legislation takes the form of Orders in Council, while the Northern Ireland Office has a key coordinating role in a range of (depoliticized) policy areas. The Secretary of State for Northern Ireland, drawn from the UK's governing party, has greater autonomy and a wider range of responsibilities than the Secretaries of State for Scotland and Wales.

SCOTLAND

On becoming Conservative leader in 1975, Mrs Thatcher inherited a long-term decline in the electoral fortunes of the Scottish Conservatives and some confusion over the party's devolution policy. Since Heath's 1968 'Perth Declaration', the party had officially supported legislative devolution but had not acted upon this in government, and internal dissent was evident. Under Thatcher, who had been sceptical of Heath's pro-devolution line, the Conservatives reverted to a unionist position, campaigning for a 'No' vote in the 1979 referendum and regarding the devolution issue as effectively dead after its 'Yes' vote failed to reach the required threshold of 40 per cent of the electorate.[6] In the 1979 election, the Conservatives won 31.4 per cent of the vote in Scotland, an increase of 6.7 per cent since October 1974, and 22 seats, a gain of 6. However, the optimism generated by the rejection of devolution and improved electoral performance would prove a false dawn.

Since 1955, when the party reached its peak performance of 50.1 per cent of the vote, there has been a largely consistent trend away from the Conservatives in Scotland. The partial recovery of 1979 could not mask the growing gap between levels of Conservative support in England and Scotland. This long-term decline was exacerbated in the Thatcher and Major period when the party scored still poorer shares of the vote, culminating in the 1997 election which left it without an MP in Scotland. Deep-seated factors contributed to the decline, but it was hastened by the Thatcher Governments' determination to pursue a Britain-wide implementation of neo-liberal economic policies and restore the authority of the centre. The Conservative's Scottish electoral coalition unravelled in the post-war era. The party's identification with unionism and British state patriotism had helped it secure relatively high levels of support from the Protestant working class, but by the 1960s the potency of the Orange vote was declining.[7] Its support was also affected by the eroded autonomy of the Scottish Conservative and Unionist Party.[8] In terms of socio-economic structure, Scotland seemed unfavourable electoral territory for the Conservatives. In the 1980s, the Scottish working class was proportionally larger than its English counterpart, was more likely to live in public housing, rely on the welfare state and be employed in heavy industry. The proportion of the middle class employed in the public sector was also higher than in England, underpinning a social democratic culture supportive of state intervention and welfarism.[9]

The Scottish Conservative and Unionist Party had espoused a unionism that respected Scottish distinctiveness and supported state involvement in socio-economic management, increasing its cross-class appeal. Thatcherism did not share these values, the Thatcher Governments being determined to roll back the state through monetarism, privatization, reduced regional aid, the sale of council housing and cuts in public spending. In the early 1980s, Secretaries of State for Scotland George Younger and Malcom Rifkind, both sympathetic to One Nation Conservatism, sought to defend Scottish interests and soften the effects of Thatcherite economics, but with only limited success (like delaying the closure of the Ravenscraig steelworks) as macro-economic policies were implemented with only limited deviation from the English norm.[10] Scottish resistance to Thatcherism irritated the Prime Minister. In her memoirs, she states that the transformation of Scotland had been difficult to achieve because 'the conditions of dependency were strongly present. And the conditions of dependency are conditions for socialism'.[11]

The third Thatcher Government embarked upon radical policies in education, local government and health, with Thatcherite minister Michael Forsyth moved to the Scottish Office. Though by-passing much policy community resistance, popular opposition to government policy grew, notably in the case of the poll tax.[12] Ironically the poll tax had come onto the agenda in part as a response to the rates revaluation exercise in Scotland. Scottish Conservatives largely welcomed the new tax but it ultimately proved highly unpopular, especially as it was introduced in Scotland a year earlier than in England and as the government mishandled its implementation by failing to take sufficient account of the Scottish dimension when acting to reduce bills in England.[13]

Thatcher claimed that 'the balance sheet of Thatcherism in Scotland is a lopsided one: economically positive, but politically negative'. Scotland's social and economic structure, Labour patronage and a Scottish Office which viewed Scottish interests as synonymous with high public spending were identified as obstacles to Thatcherism's advance. She also bemoaned the absence of a 'Tartan Thatcherite revolution', criticizing Younger and Rifkind's paternalism and their search for preferential treatment for Scotland. Forsyth was the key Thatcherite in the Scottish Party, but was a controversial figure whose short-lived period as Scottish Party Chairman was resented by One Nation Conservatives and viewed as an unwelcome example of London's dominance.[14] The Prime Minister took the Thatcherite message to Scotland herself in 1988 but won few converts when claiming that thinkers such as Adam Smith and entrepreneurs like James Watt had 'invented Thatcherism' by stressing 'hard work, self-reliance, thrift, enterprise'.[15]

Government economic policy fuelled a Scottish economic nationalism which denounced Thatcherite policies deemed alien to Scottish political culture. Following the Conservatives' poor performance in the 1987 election, when they scored 24 per cent of the vote and won only 10 seats, critics claimed that the government lacked a mandate in Scotland. The election also prompted renewed interest in legislative devolution resulting in Labour, the Alliance and key figures in the Scottish Establishment setting up a Constitutional Convention which made a 'Claim of Right' for Scotland and ultimately drew up a blueprint for a Scottish Parliament.[16]

Changes in Conservative Unionism

The Thatcher and Major Governments were staunch defenders of the Union between England and Scotland but employed different approaches to territorial management. For Thatcher, Scotland had no right to insist upon its own terms for remaining in the Union or 'claim devolution as a right of nationhood inside the Union'.[17] Devolution did not figure prominently in the political agenda during the first and second terms of the Thatcher Governments, but significant changes in the Conservative's pro-Union approach were underway which ultimately weakened the unionist cause and prompted high profile demands for a Scottish Parliament. Having abandoned their short-lived support for legislative devolution, the Conservatives under Thatcher returned to a defence of the existing system of administrative devolution as the best means of accounting for Scottish distinctiveness within the British political system. But, employing Stein Rokkan and Derek Urwin's typology, James Mitchell importantly contends that Thatcherism departed from traditional Conservative statecraft by treating Scotland as just one part of a unitary state rather than a distinctive unit within a union state.[18] Though administrative standardization prevails across much of the territory of a union state, the centre permits regions to retain some degree of autonomy and differential governing arrangements, whereas in a unitary state the dominance of the centre is more pronounced and it pursues 'a more or less undeviating policy of administrative standardization'.[19]

Conservative unionism had traditionally upheld the distinctiveness of Scottish institutional arrangements and interests, granting a degree of relative autonomy to Scottish elites and to the Scottish Conservatives who depicted themselves as the defenders of Scottish identity and British state patriotism. Crucially, this claim to be contemporaneously the party of the union state and the Scottish nation, representing Scottish interests and identity alongside British ones, was weakened by Thatcherism. The imposition of Britain-wide policies with limited reference to the Scottish dimension, poor electoral performances in Scotland, centralization of power and trenchant opposition to legislative devolution also combined to weaken Conservative unionism.

Rather than blending unionism with a sympathy towards Scottish distinctiveness, the Conservatives in the 1980s became widely perceived as an English party with a pronounced anti-Scottish bias.[20] Thatcherite authoritarian individualism was viewed as distinctly English in heritage and outlook, its emphasis on parliamentary sovereignty contrasting with a Scottish tradition of popular sovereignty and suggesting a unitary state conception of the UK. An increasingly assertive English nationalist section of the party did not disguise its belief that Scotland was a thorn in the side of the government. A number of English MPs on the Tory Right thus began to take a more active role in Scottish parliamentary business on the floor of the House, criticizing the Scottish Office and transfer payments from England to Scotland.[21]

Defending the Union

Thatcher's fall from power and the replacement of the poll tax removed two elements of Conservative unpopularity in Scotland but John Major's Governments remained resolute in their opposition to legislative devolution and pressed ahead with Thatcherite changes in local government, the welfare state and the civil service. They did, however, spell out a principled case for the Union which accepted limited reform of the arrangements for administrative devolution. While believing that the Union was good for both England and Scotland, Major also recognized the significance of Scottish distinctiveness.[22] After some speculation about a change in policy, Major and Scottish Secretary Ian Lang determined to present the Conservative case for the Union more forcefully believing that, coupled with economic success, defence of the Union and constitution could prove a vote winner. The Conservatives claimed that they were the only true defenders of the Union, attacking Labour and Liberal Democrat proposals for a tax-raising Scottish Parliament as economically damaging and leading irrevocably to the break-up of Britain. Major and Lang did, though, promise to 'take stock' of arrangements for the government of Scotland. Late in the 1992 election campaign, Major placed defence of the Union at the top of his agenda: 'if I could summon upon all the authority of this office, I would put it into a single warning – the UK is in danger. Wake up. Wake up now before it is too late.'[23] The Conservatives won 25.6 per cent of the vote in Scotland, an increase of just 1.6 per cent (though Conservative support fell in southern England and had been predicted to fall in Scotland) and 11 seats, a gain of 1. The leadership claimed their high-profile defence of the Union had paid dividends, though the evidence is disputed. Andrew Marr suggests that the anti-devolution campaign 'scared more Tory unionists into turning out' and may have contributed to an increase in Conservative support in pro-Union areas.[24] But John Curtice and David Seawright claim its effects were neutral and focus instead on economic factors. They note that the gap between the Conservative vote in England and Scotland narrowed in just two elections in recent years, namely February 1974 and 1992: on both occasions the Scottish economy was outperforming the rest of the UK.[25]

The 1993 White Paper *Scotland in the Union: A Partnership for Good* (Cm 2225) was the outcome of Major's pre-election 'taking stock' pledge, but proposed only limited changes to the apparatus of administrative devolution. The Scottish Office was thus given increased responsibility for training, industrial support, European Social Fund spending, arts policy and for the Highlands and Islands; and the arrangements for dealing with Scottish matters at Westminster were reformed, including a greater role for the Scottish Grand Committee. The language of the White Paper departed from Thatcher's unionism, stressing that Scotland's willingness to stay in the Union should not be taken for granted and recognizing its distinctive identity. Government policy should be tailored according to Scottish circumstances: 'the Union must permeate every area of government. Account must be taken of the Union by all government departments at all times.' The Prime Minister stated that 'Scotland is voluntarily part of the Union, and as part of the Union we must continue to recognize its distinctiveness, its own nationhood, its own sovereignty, if you want to use that word.'[26]

In 1995, new Secretary of State Forsyth responded to the Constitutional Convention's final report by announcing further changes. The role of the Scottish Grand Committee was enhanced: it was to hold Second Reading debates on Scottish legislation, question the Prime Minister and other Cabinet ministers and meet on a regular basis at various locations in Scotland. Forsyth claimed that Conservative plans to empower local communities and individuals were a real devolution of power. 'The ultimate units of devolution are the family and the individual. That is our idea of devolution – a great liberation of talent and individuality through choice and personal empowerment.'[27] Some policy responsibilities, over housing and crofting for example, were transferred from the Scottish Office to local authorities. Wider changes in local governance such as compulsory competitive tendering, the transfer of local authority housing stock to housing associations, the creation of Scottish Enterprise, the Citizen's Charter and changes in health and education were also presented as decentralizing measures. But the growth in indirect government and the appointment of Conservatives to these quangos was badly received in Scotland, as was water commercialization.

Plans for the restructuring of Scottish local government were already in place by 1995 with the two-tier system to be replaced by 29 unitary authorities which were said to offer greater accountability and efficiency, lower costs and more effective services.[28] However, the measures were controversial: the new authorities and boundaries were imposed without reference to local opinion, and rate capping still applied. The changes were also designed to complicate Labour's plans to establish a Scottish Parliament which would take over some of the responsibilities of the unitary authorities.

Conservative unionism in this period was expressed in both a positive case for existing constitutional arrangements and a critique of the principles and details of legislative devolution. The case for the Union drew upon traditional Conservative principles and values rather than short-term political considerations. Thus, ahead of the 1992 election Major noted: 'We are a Unionist party. We should fight for the Union . . . It is our party that supports the Union, not because it has always been good for us, but because it has always seemed right to us.'[29] He and Lang accepted that Thatcher's confrontational approach had damaged Conservative unionism, and so placed renewed emphasis on Scottish distinctiveness and developed a coherent case for the Union, while continuing to implement Thatcherite socio-economic policies.[30]

This Conservative unionism stressed the proved worth of the Union and constitutional settlement, echoing Conservative beliefs in tradition, prescriptive authority and the organic evolution of institutions which reflect and shape political culture. The Union has historically provided stability and strength alongside diversity and flexibility: Scotland enjoys the economic and political benefits of Union with England while retaining, even enhancing, its distinctive identity and institutions.[31] The Union is greater than the sum of its parts: outside the Union the UK's component nations would be diminished. Conservatives argued that Scotland receives tangible economic and political benefits in the Union, pointing to the greater public spending per head in Scotland and its over-representation at Westminster – though some English MPs were clearly uneasy with these.

While noting the benefits of Union, the Major Government sought 'new ways of building on the existing strengths of the Union' to ensure responsive government, reflecting Conservatism's willingness to accept reform which runs with the grain of existing arrangements where the case for change is proven.[32] The case for the Union espoused by the leadership denied that legislative devolution had a legitimate place in Conservative politics, even though it was party policy 20 years earlier and was viewed by its adherents within the party as an extension of a Conservative commitment to decentralization.[33]

A 1996 report by the Conservative Political Centre's National Policy Group on the Constitution, made up of Conservative MPs, activists and academics, set out a coherent defence of the Union. It argued that the Union 'reconciles order with personal liberty and national differences with common citizenship', promoting a constitutional citizenship and integrative identity which allow cultural diversity to flourish, preventing national separatism and imposed cultural hegemony.[34] Scottish identity is protected but, existing alongside a British state or constitutional patriotism, does not degenerate into separatism. Nationalism, in the sense of the ethnic assertiveness of a 'sovereign people', is presented as alien to British constitutionalism which preserves 'nationality' (understood as patriotic allegiance). British identity is based upon constitutional patriotism, an attachment to common institutions and shared historical development.

To be British is to denote an allegiance to the Crown and constitution rather than a national identity. As such, it does not denote the suppression of other identities but rather the expansion of identity, allowing the individual the opportunity to be part both of a national entity and a wider, liberating constitutional entity.[35]

Opposing Legislative Devolution

In tandem with a principled case for the Union, Conservatives developed a detailed critique of legislative devolution, attacking both the concept of a Scottish Parliament and the details of Labour's devolution proposals. Ministers claimed that, rather than revitalizing the Union, legislative devolution would bring about the breakup of Britain. There could be no workable middle way between the Conservative agenda of a reformed model of administrative devolution and full independence for Scotland. The constitutional and political problems which would bedevil a Scottish Parliament would render it unworkable, propelling public opinion towards independence as the logical conclusion to changes in UK territorial politics. Conservatives claimed that the non-uniform pattern of territorial government envisaged by Labour, with a tax-raising parliament in Scotland, a weaker Welsh Assembly and appointed regional assemblies in England (with the possibility of directly elected assemblies should local demand prove strong enough), was incoherent, would damage relations between the component nations of the UK and unhinge the constitutional balance. But such arguments are problematic: Conservative unionism had traditionally accepted that the distinctive characteristics of the nations of the UK are recognized through administrative devolution.

The Constitutional Convention's final report favoured transferring the functions of the Scottish Office to an elected Scottish Parliament (and a Scottish Executive), which would take responsibility for key 'domestic' policy areas such as health, education, local government, the environment and agriculture. The Parliament would also have the power to vary income tax by 3 per cent, though it would be primarily funded through a block grant from Westminster. Its members would be elected partly on an additional member system mixing first-past-the-post and proportional representation. These recommendations subsequently formed the basis of the Labour Government's 1997 White Paper, *Scotland's Parliament*.[36]

Conservative critics of legislative devolution pointed to the likelihood of constitutional conflict between a Scottish Parliament and the Westminster Parliament.[37] The principle of parliamentary sovereignty would be challenged should a parliament in Edinburgh seek to vote itself greater powers or expressly contradict the will of Westminster. The West Lothian Question – whether Scottish MPs at Westminster should still be permitted to vote on English matters while their English counterparts are unable to vote on matters falling within the remit of the Scottish Parliament – continued to figure in devolution debates, even though the UK does not have a uniform system of territorial government. Some demanded a reduction in the disproportionately high number of Scottish seats at Westminster, though the influence of those remaining Scottish MPs would nonetheless be emasculated as they would have no say in key Scottish matters. Other constitutional questions raised by Conservative critics included: the consequences for the office of Secretary of State for Scotland; the impact of the Scottish Parliament on local government; Scotland's relations with the EU; and the use of proportional representation and gender quotas for the Edinburgh Parliament and the absence of a revising chamber.

Forsyth's most telling line of attack was on the 'Tartan Tax', namely the proposal to give the Scottish Parliament the power to alter the level of income tax by 3 pence in the pound, with its potential to make Scotland the highest taxed part of the UK. Given Scotland's narrower tax base and higher levels of public spending, the Parliament might well seek to raise taxes, thereby reducing inward investment and prompting business migration. Conservatives also warned that, post-devolution, English public opinion would be less likely to tolerate transfer payments to Scotland and that the rump of Scottish MPs left at Westminster would have little influence over financial arrangements.[38] Finally, ministers warned that setting up a Scottish Parliament would itself be a costly and bureaucratic move.

Forsyth's campaign against the 'Tartan Tax' appeared to concern Labour strategists. Seeking to bury Labour's image as a high-spending, tax-raising party and draw the sting from the anti-devolution campaign, Blair forced a reworking of Labour's devolution plans in 1996. He committed the party to holding a two-question referendum asking Scottish voters whether they supported a Scottish Parliament and whether they backed tax-raising powers for the new body. This marked a retreat from the previous position that a strong showing for Labour and the Liberal Democrats in the general election would be sufficient proof of popular support.

The Failings of Conservative Unionism

The Conservative campaign against a Scottish Parliament made some limited inroads into popular support for change (devolution or independence) in Scotland, but only 43 per cent of those supporting the *status quo* intended to vote Conservative according to an opinion poll conducted shortly before the 1997 election.[39] Warnings about the implications of Scottish devolution for the rest of the UK failed to impress English voters who showed little concern about, and some support for, a Scottish Parliament.[40] Thus the Conservatives fought the 1997 election on an unpopular unionist platform, albeit having made limited reforms to the apparatus of administrative devolution, hoping that warnings about the break-up of Britain would rally pro-Union voters behind the party. Their campaign was also beset by problems and the election result proved devastating: the Conservative vote slipped to 17.5 per cent (down 8.2 per cent) and the party lost all its seats in Scotland, including those of three Cabinet ministers.[41]

In 1997, the Major Government's attempts to rebuild Conservative unionism by reforming the apparatus of administrative devolution failed their most important electoral test. Major had taken some half-hearted steps to reassert the Conservatives as the party of the union state and move away from Thatcherism's unitary state outlook.[42] But reverting to traditional Conservative unionism, even if this is what the Major Government intended (and given its commitment to key features of the Thatcherite project, this is unlikely), would be difficult to achieve given that some of its core elements had been removed or fundamentally altered. Administrative devolution was unpopular. The Scottish Office was viewed not as an effective defender of Scottish interests but as an agent of an assertive centre and was itself affected by changes in governance.[43] Scottish elites and policy communities had been alienated by Thatcherism, local government had been undermined and the creation of a plethora of quangos added to the legitimacy problems of administrative devolution. Neither was the gulf between Conservative unionism and public opinion bridged by the reforms. This, plus the gap between the Conservatives' electoral performance in England and Scotland made it more difficult for the party to reassert its identity as a unionist party which would represent and defend Scottish interests. Opinion poll evidence suggested that although a majority of people in Scotland, viewing themselves as 'British more than

Scottish', wanted no change to the government of Scotland, a majority of those feeling 'equally Scottish and British' and even 'British not Scottish' supported legislative devolution.[44]

The scale of the Conservative defeat in Scotland in the 1997 general election raised a number of problems for party leaders. Having featured the defence of administrative devolution prominently in the campaign, the result represented a significant defeat for Conservative unionism, but abandoning a policy so central to the party's message also has political costs. Intra-party dissent on devolution was limited in the 1990s: there was some Cabinet support for a Tory version of legislative devolution in the early 1990s but, apart from a claim by Stephen Dorrell that a future Conservative government would abolish a Scottish Parliament, key figures upheld the official line.[45] But personal and political animosities were still evident in the Scottish Conservative Party in this period and, following election defeat, critics of the leadership expressed unease at the anti-devolution stance and the limited autonomy of the Scottish Conservative Party.

WALES

Whereas many commentaries on Scottish issues in the 1980s noted the lack of attention paid to Scottish distinctiveness by the Thatcher Governments, those on Welsh affairs often painted a different picture, claiming that under Secretary of State Peter Walker, Wales had avoided both the assimilationist thrust of Thatcherism and elements of Thatcherite socio-economic policy.[46] Walker himself claimed that he enjoyed significant leeway to adopt and implement economic policies which differed from those pursued in England and Scotland, taking account of Welsh distinctiveness. 'The big attraction of the Welsh Secretary's job was that I was told [by Thatcher] that I could do it my way... with a range of interventionist policies and I always had her backing.'[47] Walker pointed to increased public spending, inward investment and regional development, claiming that achievements in Wales were the result of 'close government cooperation with industry, councils and trade unions'.[48] His successor David Hunt also cited 'willingness to cooperate' and a 'special Welsh partnership' as the foundations of Conservative economic success in the Principality.[49]

However, 'Welsh exceptionalism' can be overstated, Dylan Griffiths casting doubt upon it by noting the similarities between government policy in Wales and England in a number of areas and the limited political salience of Welsh distinctiveness.[50] He argues that the interventionist policies pursued by Walker and Hunt reflected Thatcherism's attempts to facilitate enterprise through cooperation with the private rather than public sector. Within the framework of administrative devolution, key economic and social policies were applied Britain-wide with only limited account taken of the Welsh dimension. Walker and Hunt enjoyed some personal influence over policy and, during their period in office, the government took more account of Welsh than Scottish distinctiveness, thereby helping to limit dissent in the Principality. But this did not provide a secure foundation for Welsh exceptionalism – their successors, John Redwood and William Hague favoured more Thatcherite methods, stressing enterprise and a rolling back of the state.[51] Devolution had been resoundingly rejected in Wales in 1979 and Labour's proposals for a Welsh Assembly with only limited powers reflected that devolution has less salience in Wales than Scotland. Territorial management in Wales began to mirror the approach by Forsyth in Scotland, mixing limited changes to the apparatus of administrative devolution with a criticism of Labour's devolution proposals and an emphasis on enterprise. The role of the Welsh Grand Committee was enhanced, though the move to unitary local authorities and the growth in the number of quangos were criticized for by-passing Welsh opinion.[52] The Conservative case for the Union focused on its economic benefits and the protection of Welsh identity, noting that the Welsh language was given equal status with English in the conduct of public business under the 1993 Welsh Language Act. Ministers claimed that Labour's plans for a Welsh Assembly would produce constitutional instability and add an unwelcome bureaucratic tier.[53] But in the 1997 election, already low levels of Conservative support fell further and the party failed to win any seats in Wales.

NORTHERN IRELAND

Since 1972 Conservative and Labour governments have sought, without any great success, to broker agreement between the Northern Ireland constitutional parties on arrangements for power-sharing devolution (rather than a return to majoritarianism).[54] Conservative Shadow Northern Ireland Secretary Airey Neave had expressed doubts about the power-sharing option in 1976, suggesting improvements to the apparatus of direct rule which might open the door to majority rule in Northern Ireland.[55] The 1979 Conservative manifesto contained a commitment to introduce elected regional councils, but after Neave's murder, Secretary of State Humphrey Atkins and his successor Jim Prior reverted to the power-sharing formula.[56] Thatcher's instinctive unionism appeared hostile to the 'Irish dimension', the Prime Minister stating that Northern Ireland's status was a matter for domestic politics and rejecting the options put forward in the 1984 New Ireland Forum Report.[57] However, the failure of Prior's Assembly plan and external pressure moved the government towards enhanced Anglo-Irish intergovernmental co-operation.[58]

The Anglo-Irish Agreement

In Article One of the 1985 Anglo-Irish Agreement (AIA) the British and Irish governments affirmed that 'any change in the status of Northern Ireland would only come about with the consent of a majority of people', recognized that 'the present wish of a majority of the people of Northern Ireland is for no change in the status of Northern Ireland' and declared that, if a majority formally consented to a united Ireland, they would legislate accordingly. The Agreement also explicitly recognized the 'Irish dimension', institutionalizing inter-state cooperation in the form of an Intergovernmental Conference meeting at ministerial and official level to discuss Northern Ireland affairs, in which the Irish government would represent the interests of the nationalist community in the North.

The AIA restated the conditional status of Northern Ireland in the UK. Though it did not create joint authority, the Intergovernmental Conference and the Irish government's entitlement to be consulted on a range of Northern Ireland matters marked a further modification of British sovereignty. The Irish government was unwilling to make unilateral concessions on Articles 2 and 3 of the Irish Constitution which claimed sovereignty over the whole of the island of Ireland.[59] Despite the Republic's recognition that no change in the status of Northern Ireland would come about without the consent of the people of Northern Ireland, Unionists were angered by the enhanced 'Irish dimension', their lack of influence over arrangements for governing Northern Ireland within the UK and the failure of the British government to consult them. Senior British civil servants played a key role in the negotiations, Cabinet Secretary Sir Robert Armstrong persuading Thatcher that the Agreement would improve security and was good for the Union. Foreign Secretary Howe and Northern Ireland Secretary Douglas Hurd were also involved, neither sharing the Prime Minister's maximalist views on sovereignty. Howe did not regard sovereignty as a measurable commodity, preferring to 'provide for the interpenetration of influence between the several communities'.[60] Thatcher was concerned to improve cross-border security cooperation, marginalize Sinn Fein (whose electoral performance had improved considerably since the Maze hunger strikes, weakening the constitutional nationalist SDLP) and avoid any formal ceding of British sovereignty, rejecting joint authority and hoping that Article One plus her known support for the Union would reassure unionists.[61]

Although signalling a strategic shift towards intergovernmentalism, the AIA did not mark an abandonment of the government's search for power-sharing devolution. Indeed the AIA was designed to provide an incentive for Unionists to accept a power-sharing Assembly, the establishment of which would bring about a downgrading (but not dissolution) of the Intergovernmental Conference, thereby reducing Dublin's role and giving the Unionist parties a greater say in Northern Ireland affairs.[62] But the prospects of the AIA bearing fruit soon receded given the intensity of Unionist opposition plus disputes between the two governments over security and extradition policy, and Thatcher lost faith in the Agreement.[63]

The Downing Street Declaration and Framework Documents

Momentum was restored in 1990 by Major's desire to find a peaceful settlement and by Secretary of State Peter Brooke's efforts to bring about 'three strand' talks – firstly, talks between the constitutional parties on devolved government in Northern Ireland, secondly all-Ireland discussions and, thirdly, talks between the two governments.[64] Brooke also signalled changing perspectives when he stated that Britain had 'no selfish strategic or economic interest in Northern Ireland'. The talks process stalled and violence escalated, but subterranean movement was taking place through secret British contacts with the IRA and dialogue between SDLP leader John Hume and Sinn Fein leader Gerry Adams.The Irish government's interest in the latter and Major's activist approach encouraged a further inter-state initiative which ultimately produced the December 1993 Downing Street Declaration (DSD).[65]

Paragraph 4 of the DSD confirmed that the British government 'will uphold the democratic wish of a greater number of people of Northern Ireland' on its constitutional status and reiterated that it had no 'selfish strategic or economic interest in Northern Ireland. Their primary interest is to see peace, stability and reconciliation established by agreement among all the people who inhabit the island.' The government presented itself as neutral, an honest broker for a political settlement rather than a principled persuader for the Union, its role being 'to encourage, facilitate and enable' dialogue and a peaceful settlement which accorded 'parity of esteem', respecting the 'rights and identities of both traditions in Ireland'. British official language had a greener tinge, accepting the validity of the nationalist community's cultural identity and aspirations, but refused to accept the Hume-Adams formulation that the British government should be a 'persuader for an agreed Ireland'. A crucial (and complex) section of Paragraph 4 stated that

> The British government agree that it is for the people of the island of Ireland alone, by agreement between the two parts respectively, to exercise their right of self-determination on the basis of consent, freely and concurrently given, North and South to bring about a united Ireland, if that is their wish.

In another sign of movement, the government recognized that the development of the EU required new approaches to the Northern Ireland problem. The DSD aimed to kick-start the search for a peaceful settlement, Paragraph 10 suggesting that an IRA ceasefire would in due course allow Sinn Fein to join talks aimed at creating new structures. Some Unionist parties and Sinn Fein were unsatisfied with the Declaration – particularly the formula on consent and self-determination – but an open-ended IRA ceasefire was called in August 1994, followed by a Loyalist ceasefire.

In February 1995, the British and Irish governments published the Frameworks for the Future document which comprised two parts: the joint Anglo-Irish 'A New Framework for Agreement' and 'A Framework for Accountable Government in Northern Ireland', produced by the British government alone. The latter contained proposals for power-sharing devolution, including an elected 90-member Northern Ireland Assembly with a range of legislative and executive powers and a system of Assembly Committees. It would be complemented by an elected 3-person Panel. Power-sharing would be entrenched in the new arrangements: proportional representation would be used in elections, there would be a system of checks and balances, appointments to the Assembly Committees would be through weighted voting and minority rights would be protected.[66] However, the proposals were not presented as a settled blueprint.

'A New Framework for Agreement' reaffirmed the DSD principles of self-determination and consent, but saw both governments seeking 'an agreed new approach to traditional constitutional doctrines' (Paragraph 14). Thus, the British government offered to change its constitutional legislation to incorporate a commitment to accept the will of a majority of the people of Northern Ireland and to include a commitment to impartiality in their jurisdiction of Northern Ireland. The Irish government offered to support proposals to remove its territorial claim from the constitution. The document proposed a North/South body comprising elected representatives from, and accountable to, the new Northern Ireland Assembly and the Irish Parliament. It would have 'consultative, harmonizing and executive functions', where consultative functions include exchange of information; harmonizing powers could cover economic policy, health, education and industrial development; and executive functions include EU all-Ireland programmes. Further inter-state cooperation between the UK and Ireland was envisaged, including a standing Intergovernmental Conference. British ministers spoke of a 'triple lock' of consent being required for a change in Northern Ireland's status – from the parties engaged in political talks, through a referendum in Northern Ireland and a vote at Westminster.

The issue of decommissioning weapons proved problematic, a commitment to this having been made a precondition for Sinn Fein entry into talks by the British government. An international commission examining the question, chaired by former United States Senator George Mitchell, recommended in January 1996 that some decommissioning proceed in parallel with all-party talks, also putting forward six democratic principles which parties should accept before joining talks. The government was uneasy with some of the Mitchell proposals but, picking up on its suggestions for an elected body, announced elections to a new Forum as a means of promoting dialogue between the parties. The IRA ceasefire ended a month later meaning that the multi-party talks which began in June 1996 did so without Sinn Fein.

Conservatives and the Union

Conservative policy on Northern Ireland adds further to the evidence presented in this book that the Thatcher and Major Governments did not develop a coherent national strategy which consistently upheld the territorial integrity and sovereignty of the British nation-state or promoted national identity. Important contradictions in Conservative attitudes and policy between and within Scotland, Wales and Northern Ireland were evident.[67] With regard to Northern Ireland, the inter-state initiatives of this period marked an activist government role which contrasted with previous attempts at keeping Northern Ireland affairs out of mainstream British politics. They also clarified the message that Northern Ireland's status in the UK was conditional and not one vigorously defended through principled commitment to the Union. The government claimed its position was neutral in regard to the eventual status of Northern Ireland, vowing to respect the consent of the people of Northern Ireland if they wanted a united Ireland, though the DSD and Framework Documents recognized that at present a majority want Northern Ireland to remain in the UK. It saw its role as facilitating a settlement rather than steering it in a predetermined direction. But with regard to the arrangements for governing Northern Ireland within the UK, the government was not neutral, ruling out integration and joint authority while continuing to support power-sharing devolution despite failing to make real progess towards this goal.

The confirmation of the conditional status of Northern Ireland within the UK, plus the government's declared neutrality and support for power-sharing devolution, contrasted with its principled support for the Union between Scotland and England and opposition to legislative devolution in Scotland and Wales. These differences between Conservative unionism in relation to Scotland and Northern Ireland again reflected that the latter is treated as a 'place apart' requiring different solutions. Major explained the differences between his support for a devolved Assembly in Northern Ireland and his opposition to Labour's proposals for a tax-raising Scottish Parliament as follows:

> In Northern Ireland, the Assembly will not be tax-raising. The Assembly proposed for Scotland would be. In Northern Ireland, there has been a sectarian divide of remarkable proportions for years. That does not exist elsewhere. In Northern Ireland, none

of the parties can form part of the UK Government and lead that Government. That does not apply in any other part of the UK. In Northern Ireland, because of its history, there has been an Assembly in the past. That does not apply elsewhere. In Northern Ireland, a part of the population may wish to form part of a foreign country. That does not apply elsewhere.[68]

But these inconsistencies in territorial management were significant given that Conservatives criticized both the principle and details of Labour's proposals for legislative devolution.[69] The Major Government's emphasis on the necessity of the consent of the people of Northern Ireland for any moves towards a united Ireland, with a referendum the means of ascertaining consent, implied a principle of popular sovereignty (although in the 'triple lock', a vote by the Westminter Parliament is also required). Yet in Scotland, which has a tradition of popular sovereignty, the Major Government stressed the sovereignty of Parliament, although the language of the 1993 White Paper recognized that Scotland was part of the Union voluntarily and could not be held within it against its will. Constitutional conundrums such as the West Lothian Question, a key theme in Conservative opposition to Scottish devolution, were not regarded as particularly problematic during the lifetime of the Stormont Parliament.

The modification of Northern Ireland's status occurred at a time when the Conservative Party was taking a maximalist view of the Union between England and Scotland, acting as though the UK were a unitary state and restating that the Conservatives were the party of the Union. Thatcher and Major presented themselves as instinctive supporters of the Union, yet the former signed the AIA and the latter accepted that the government should not be a persuader for the Union. Nonetheless, ministerial statements showed that the government wanted Northern Ireland to remain within the Union. Thus, on the day the Framework Documents were released, Major told the Commons, 'I am a Unionist who wants peace for all the people of the Union. I cherish Northern Ireland's role in the Union', and at the 1996 Conservative Party conference stated 'I do not expect Northern Ireland to leave the United Kingdom, nor do I wish it to'.[70] But some Unionists felt that the failure to make a case for the Union reflected the views of some leading Conservatives that a united Ireland was inevitable or even desirable.[71]

The Ulster Unionist Party historically had organizational links with the Conservative Party, its MPs taking the Conservative whip at Westminster until 1974. The Unionists withdrew their representatives from the Conservative Party's National Union Executive Committee in 1985 in protest at the AIA and from its Central Council in 1990 following the creation of Conservative associations in Northern Ireland. Relations between the Unionist parties and the Conservative government were strained for much of the post-AIA period. Many commentators asserted that the Major Government's small (and decreasing) parliamentary majority after the 1992 election gave the Unionists greater influence over government policy.[72] Yet this appears to be only a partial truth. Although the government's room for manoeuvre was constrained by unfavourable parliamentary arithmetic during the peace process, it is unlikely that it would anyway have significantly altered its position on decommissioning. The creation of a Northern Ireland Select Committee had been accepted by the Commons Procedure Committee in 1990 – although it was not confirmed by the government until the day after the DSD was published. The parliamentary 'understanding' (rather than formal alliance) between the Conservatives and the Ulster Unionists, put in place for the final votes on the Maastricht Bill, was a fickle one: significant differences between the parties remained and Unionists were divided on its wisdom but were unlikely to want a Labour government. Overall the Unionist parties remained on the defensive, reacting in hostile fashion rather than significantly shaping the government's territorial strategy.

The movement to create Conservative associations in Northern Ireland illustrated and added to the strained relations between the Conservatives and Ulster Unionists. This grew out of the Campaign for Equal Citizenship which argued that the people of Northern Ireland were denied equal citizenship as they were unable to vote for parties which stood a chance of forming the UK government.[73] The campaign to organize in Northern Ireland won grassroots support from Conservative associations on the mainland, winning a 1989 party conference vote despite the initial opposition of the leadership.[74] The early performances of Northern Ireland Conservatives were respectable: Conservative candidates won 5.7 per cent of the vote in Northern Ireland in the 1992 general election, Laurence Kennedy scoring 32 per cent of the vote in North Down where the first association had been created. However, relations with the national party were often acrimonious given the Northern Ireland Conservatives' enthusiasm for integration and criticism of government policy, plus the Westminster 'understanding' with the Ulster Unionists. Following this, the electoral performance of Conservative candidates fell dramatically, failing to figure in the top ten parties in the 1996 Forum elections then winning just 1.3 per cent of the vote in the 1997 general election.

The uneasy relationship between the Conservatives and Ulster Unionism was not just a reaction to developments in government policy. More deep-rooted differences in the values and outlook of British Conservatives and Ulster Unionists are evident in the politics of nationhood. These were illustrated by Thatcher's confession that though her 'instincts are profoundly Unionist', she felt 'their [Unionists] patriotism was real and fervent, even if too narrow' and believed that 'even the most passionate English supporters of Ulster' do not 'fully understand' Northern Ireland.[75] The values, discourse and self-image of some parts of the heterogeneous Unionist family do not sit easily with the conservative nation. Ulster Unionism's symbols and language often differ markedly from the state patriotism of the conservative nation and the Thatcherite view of the nation. Jennifer Todd's ideal-type distinction between 'Ulster loyalist' and 'Ulster British' traditions in Unionist politics is useful in this context.[76] The 'imagined community' of the Ulster loyalist tradition is Northern Protestants and its loyalty to Britain is conditional, focusing on the Protestant Crown and becoming hostile to the British state if it is perceived as failing to defend Protestant Ulster from Irish republicanism. In contrast, the 'imagined community' of Ulster British ideology is Great Britain, supporting the Union for its economic benefits and the rights which accrue from British citizenship. Ulster British identity is multi-layered, drawing upon a more liberal reading of Northern Ireland's history than that found in the Ulster loyalist tradition plus a pluralist sense of Britishness.

In a speech in 1994, Mayhew stated that he saw in Unionism 'a historic political tradition that is authentically Irish' but claimed that some of its political beliefs 'form an important part of the British Conservative tradition'.[77] A number of Unionists have explored these links between Conservative politics and Unionism. Arthur Aughey, a member of the Conservative Political Centre's National Policy Group on the Constitution, has sought to bridge the Ulster British and Conservative integrationist perspectives, expressing the Unionist case in terms of conservative principles and conservative state patriotism. Aughey detaches Unionism from nationalist theory claiming that 'the identity of unionism has little to do with the idea of the nation and everything to do with the idea of the state'.[78] For him, 'intelligent unionists' owe allegiance to the 'idea of the Union', that is to the UK as a multiethnic state grounded in ideals of citizenship, state patriotism and the rule of law.

However, Aughey's assumptions are problematic.[79] Dual identities are a feature of the pluralist UK state but in Northern Ireland questions of identity are more politicized and disputed than elsewhere in the Union. The nature of 'Britishness' is disputed in Unionist thought and many Catholics do not identify with the British state. Rather than exhibiting the liberal individualist and pluralist values which Aughey places at the heart of Unionism, Ulster loyalism bears the hallmarks of an ethno-religious identity, being an activist form of patriotic politics rather than a limited state patriotism. Unionists aspiring to a civic identity have also had different historical experiences (in both the Stormont and direct rule periods) from mainland British Conservatives, and have been notably hostile to liberal values and minority citizenship rights. Finally, while Aughey constructs a pluralistic account of the Union based on state patriotism, the basis of the Thatcherite politics of nationhood became less integrative and more hostile to 'alien' political cultures. Aughey claimed that Major restored 'the idea of a constitutional people' and a 'reasonably clear-sighted conception of the integrity of the United Kingdom, based on constitutional patriotism'. But Major's strategy was pragmatic rather than principled, continuing the conditional loyalty to the Union shown by British governments which Aughey himself has criticized.[80]

Opinion on Northern Ireland in the parliamentary Conservative Party is malleable, usually following the leadership line, as many MPs do not have a direct interest in Northern Ireland affairs nor strong attachments to its place within the UK.[81] Public attitudes towards Northern Ireland also show limited emotional attachment to the Union and limited sympathy for the Unionists.[82] Since the late 1980s, Conservative activists have taken a greater interest in Northern Ireland issues and integrationist perspectives, sparked by the campaign for Conservative associations.[83] Supporters of the Ulster Unionist cause (more accurately, the Ulster British perspective) in the parliamentary party were critical of the government inter-state initiatives and faith in power-sharing devolution, advocating an integrationist alternative, influenced by Powell and T. E. Utley.[84] Twenty-two Conservative MPs voted against the Second Reading of Prior's Bill to establish a Northern Ireland Assembly, with Nicholas Budgen, Peter Lloyd and Viscount Cranborne resigning from the government in protest. Twenty-one Conservatives opposed the AIA, Thatcher's confidant Ian Gow resigning from the government.[85] The main integrationist ginger group has been the Friends of the Union, established by John Biggs-Davison in 1986, numbering Gow, Powell and Lamont among its authors.[86]

Integrationist perspectives vary, but all reject legislative devolution arguing that it perpetuates sectarian divisions and claim that treating Northern Ireland as a conditional part of the UK has encouraged violent republicanism. Conservative integrationists' anger that Northern Ireland was not treated as an integral part of the Union, that the government of the Republic of Ireland has a role in its affairs and at British neutrality was illustrated when Budgen asked the Prime Minister whether the government had 'no selfish strategic or economic interest in Wolverhampton' (Budgen's constituency).[87] Lamont's view that the British government should act as a persuader for the Union, especially as the Irish government represented the interests of the nationalist community in the Anglo-Irish Intergovernmental Conference, is typical of Conservative supporters of the Unionist cause: 'no government can be indifferent as to whether a component part of its country switches its allegiance elsewhere'.[88]

Integrationists are critical of the democratic deficit in the government of Northern Ireland which exists under direct rule, and suggested changes including Northern Ireland legislation following normal parliamentary routes rather than the Orders in Council procedure, stronger local government and a re-ordering of the Northern Ireland Office along the lines of the Scottish and Welsh Offices. Electoral integrationists backed the campaign to stand Conservative candidates in Northern Ireland.

Despite moves towards a more pro-integration stance whilst in Opposition, the Thatcher and Major Governments rejected the key tenets of the integrationist case, Prior arguing that integration would 'make a bad situation worse' by further alienating the Catholic minority.[89] However, in 1991, the Conservative Campaign Guide stated that, while power-sharing devolution remained the central objective, 'the government does not necessarily rule out some of the measures which form part of an integration policy, but the vital test of any structures of government is that they command widespread support'.[90] A number of changes to the apparatus of direct rule were introduced by the Major Government, including the creation of a Northern Ireland Select Committee in 1994 and a growing practice of including provisions for Northern Ireland within general UK legislation, despite its continued commitment to establishing a devolved assembly in Northern Ireland.[91] But the party leadership was at best half hearted in its backing for electoral integration. In the early days of the Blair Government, the new Conservative leadership gave tacit support to the softening of the British position on the decommissioning of IRA weapons, but should the IRA's second ceasefire breakdown or the 'Irish dimension' be further institutionalized, Conservative supporters of the Unionist and integrationist cause are likely to become more vocal.

THE EUROPEAN DIMENSION

The devolution campaign in Scotland, the SNP campaign for 'independence in Europe' and references to the European dimension in the Framework Documents reflected the growth of regionalism in Europe and the impact of the EU upon subnational government. The centre sought to oversee links between Scotland and the EU, creating Scotland Europa in 1992, but adopted a more innovative approach to relations between Northern Ireland and the EU. Thus, 'A New Framework for Agreement' recognized that European integration opened up new possibilities for cross-border cooperation, the two governments seeking a harmonized approach on a range of EU matters and proposing that a new North/South body be responsible for implementing and managing island-wide EC programmes. But whereas there was a trend towards decentralization and a greater role for subnational government in many Member States, the Conservative government sought to strengthen the central state, limiting the autonomy of local government and opposing legislative devolution. Regional aid was cut and some of the core functions of local government transferred to quangos. In 1994, ten integrated regional offices were created, taking over the regional responsibilities of a number of government departments. The Conservatives opposed Labour proposals for new, indirectly elected regional assemblies in England with a strategic role in economic development.[92] Differences between British and continental perspectives were also apparent on subsidiarity, Article 3b of the Maastricht Treaty stating that the Community should act only when objectives cannot be better achieved at a lower level. For most Member States, the concept of subsidiarity reaffirmed their support for autonomous regional government, but for the Major Governments it confirmed the leading role of the nation-state and central government.[93]

The centralizing measures introduced by the Conservatives prompted local authorities to seek new avenues of influence, local policy makers looking to local public–private sector cooperation and cross-regional partnerships to promote economic development. Developments in the EU also encouraged regionalism and subnational mobilization. The Maastricht Treaty established the Committee of the Regions, the government being defeated in the Commons when it proposed including non-elected members in the UK representation rather than just elected local councillors. Reforms of the Structural Funds doubled the EU aid available to poorer regions while the Commission stressed partnership, actively involving subnational government in EU regional policy and encouraging cross-regional collaboration. Subnational government has been 'Europeanized': regional lobbying and information offices have been set up in Brussels and local authorities are involved in policy networks in areas of EU competence which directly affect them. This has been characterized as 'multi-level governance' whereby the Commission, subnational government and central government are all involved in decision-making and policy implementation in EU regional policy.[94] The European dimension has opened up new avenues of influence for regional actors in the UK, but central government remains predominant: the resources available to subnational authorities are shaped by decisions made at the centre, regional elites often rely on central government to pursue their interests in the EU, and the absence of a coherent UK regional tier of government weakens their voice in Europe.[95]

CONCLUSIONS

Conservative approaches to territorial politics in the 1980s and 1990s offer further confirmation that the Thatcher and Major Governments did not achieve hegemony in the politics of nationhood nor develop a coherent national strategy built around the defence of the territorial integrity of the nation-state, national sovereignty and an integrative state patriotism. Important contradictions and inconsistencies in Conservative attitudes towards the component parts of the Union, and in government policy on Scotland and Northern Ireland, have been identified. Territorial politics posed a number of statecraft problems – electoral decline in Scotland, disputes within the party about Conservative unionism and a failure to win issue hegemony on devolution – and deeper questions about the self-image and strategy of the Conservative Party.

Under Thatcherism, a more assertive English cultural identity was apparent in Conservative politics, the defence of English interests and values informing the party's rejection of consensus politics and further European integration and the reworking of Conservative unionism. Whereas One Nation statecraft had sought to hold the union state together through administrative devolution and an integrative British state patriotism, Thatcherism was less conciliatory and conflated English and British identity. It departed from a One Nation statecraft in which British and imperial identities had been essential supports of the multinational UK state. In its place Thatcherism offered a post-imperial, authoritarian individualist understanding of the nation in which individualism and parliamentary sovereignty were central themes, viewing British state patriotism from an English cultural standpoint.[96] But despite becoming a more English party in terms of disposition and geographical representation, claims that the Conservatives had become an English nationalist party by the mid-1990s are overstated. The Conservatives remained a unionist party, though a more pronounced Englishness undermined Conservative unionism. A defence of British state patriotism, drawing upon Whig history but with Englishness afforded primary status, existed in tandem with authoritarian individualist themes in Thatcherite discourse. Despite their perceived English bias, the Thatcher and Major Governments did not radically alter some of the centre's key mechanisms for managing the union state, including preferential public spending arrangements and Scottish over-representation at Westminster. The Major Governments opposed Labour proposals to establish indirectly or directly elected assemblies in the English regions. Indeed the government determined to base its territorial strategy around a positive case for the Union which stressed the economic and political advantages it offered Scotland and Wales, rejecting an alternative English nationalist territorial strategy in which UK legislative devolution might allow the Conservatives to jettison the problematic Celtic nations and prosper as the dominant party in England, more explicitly defending English interests in a quasi-federal UK.

The anti-Establishment ethos of Thatcherism meant that traditional institutions central to conservative state patriotism, such as the monarchy, Parliament, the Church of England and the Union, were undermined. Maximalist interpretations of parliamentary sovereignty and the unitary state undermined Conservative statecraft in Scotland, but Northern Ireland remained a 'place apart' in which pragmatic modifications of British sovereignty occurred, including a limited acceptance that developments in the EU had important repercussions for UK territorial politics. The Major Governments paid greater attention to Scottish and Welsh distinctiveness, but limited reforms to the arrangements for administrative devolution, and a continuation of key Thatcherite policies did not sufficiently revive Conservative unionism.

As its electoral performance in Scotland, Wales and northern England worsened, the Conservative Party became more identified with southern England. Following the 1997 election, they look still more like an English national party, bereft of MPs in the other nations of the Union. As the concluding chapter of this book notes, legislative devolution will reshape British politics, Conservative statecraft and the politics of nationhood. The creation of a Scottish Parliament and Welsh Assembly may see the Conservatives once again seeking to portray themselves as a party which represents national distinctiveness but values the state patriotism of the multinational UK state. Alternatively, devolution may lead the Conservatives towards a more explicit defence of English interests, criticizing the perceived advantages enjoyed by Scotland and Wales within the British state, thereby marking a further weakening of Conservative unionism.

6 'Race' and Immigration

The changing context of Conservative ideology and policy in the politics of nationhood since the mid-1970s was also apparent in the politics of 'race' and immigration. The party leadership had rejected Powell's nationalist strategy with its demand for repatriation and warnings about the limits of integration. Under Thatcher and Major the Conservatives were committed to 'firm but fair' immigration controls, recognizing the potential electoral benefits of a populist anti-immigration stance, but also to managing the plural society and ensuring harmonious race relations.

The development of a plural, multicultural society in Britain presented a number of dilemmas for the Conservative politics of nationhood. The party's liberal wing sought to adapt the Conservative nation along inclusivist lines by accepting diversity and promoting shared vales, while Powellism proffered an exclusivist national strategy which sought to promote a homogenous British identity. The Conservative emphasis upon tradition, common culture and patriotic allegiance to the nation-state though precludes the easy integration of ethnic minority groups with distinct identities into the Conservative nation.[1]

The Thatcher era was significant for the politics of 'race' and immigration, marking a breakdown of the bipartisan consensus on the desirability of keeping 'race' issues off the political agenda. It also saw the Conservatives adopt a populist line, using popular fears of mass immigration for political advantage. Within Thatcherite thought are two distinct outlooks, a strong state emphasis on culture and nationhood plus a neo-liberal emphasis on individuals and markets. The language of the former informed a populist approach which politicized 'race' issues and potentially excludes some ethnic minorities from full membership of the national community. Neo-liberals reject this emphasis on culture and nationhood, focusing on individual actions and market solutions and rejecting positive state action aimed at addressing problems of racial inequality.

CONSERVATISM, 'RACE' AND NATIONHOOD

The expulsion of Powell from the Shadow Cabinet after his 'rivers of blood' speech showed that the mainstream of the party had no taste for his exclusivist national strategy, though the Tory Right continued to press for a more rigorous state-sponsored repatriation programme. But Powell did have a significant influence on Conservative discourse on 'race' and nationhood in the Thatcher period, influencing a limited reworking of the Conservative politics of nationhood which fused concepts of 'race', nation and culture in a new populist discourse.

The neo-liberal branch of New Right thought focuses on individual liberty rather than group-based politics, looking to 'colour-blind' market forces to promote integration and redress inequality. The state should play only a limited role in race relations, providing a legal framework of formal equality but not positive action which distorts the market, fosters dependency and creates new bureaucratic interests. The most significant developments in Conservative discourse on 'race' came though from the cultural conservative or social authoritarian wing of the New Right. Echoing Powell, cultural conservatives in the Salisbury Group sought to reassert British nationhood, claiming that immigration and multiculturalism had contributed to a crisis of national identity.[2] The nation is defined not in explicitly racist terms, but in terms of a homogeneous common culture, shared history and traditions, patriotic allegiance and a sense of kinship or belonging.[3] Defence of this common culture from external and internal threats, and a reawakening of Britishness were presented as an essential moral and political task. Immigration is seen as a threat to the British way of life as certain ethnic minorities cannot be successfully integrated into British society. They would remain 'alien wedges' with their own distinctive identities and cultures, often antithetical to British values, undermining social cohesion and order. Cultural conservatives denied that their defence of British culture was racist, presenting prejudice and the desire to live with people of one's own kind as natural or 'common sense'.[4]

The 'New Right, New Racism' thesis recognizes that the growth of theorising about 'race', culture and nation had a significant influence on Conservative discourse. However, it tends to exaggerate the coherence of Thatcherite ideology and the impact of the social authoritarian New Right on government policy. The national community envisaged by Thatcherism was one in which immigration is restricted and groups slow to adapt to British society are distrusted or regarded as undesirable. It was not, strictly speaking, an ethnically defined or ethnically exclusive nation.[5] Thatcherism's attitude towards ethnic minority groups was not uniform: groups such as the Indian community and 'black bourgeoisie' which had relatively successfully integrated into British society and adopted the 'vigorous virtues' of enterprise and individualism were praised and courted, but minorities who appeared unwilling to adopt Thatcherite values were ostracized. Krieger thus portrayed Thatcherism as a 'de-integrative strategy' dividing society into favoured groups which prospered and 'out-groups' (the 'enemy within') which were alienated and marginalized.[6]

Thatcherism tended towards a cultural or ethnic-ideological account of the nation in which ethnic minorities are accepted into the national community provided that they accept the primacy of British values and adapt accordingly. It thus bridged liberal and assimilationist language, accepting diversity and equality of opportunity, but stressing the primacy of British values and viewing excessive immigration as a threat. The costs of integration for minority groups are raised: diversity of cultures is acceptable but the British way of life is paramount and should be protected by the state. Thatcherism's terms for good race relations were tough: immigration is reduced and the onus is on ethnic minorities to 'learn to be British', abandoning or adapting those cultural facets which clash with the Thatcherite understanding of British values.[7] Although this does not go as far as the Powellite belief that ethnic minorities would remain an unassimilated 'alien wedge', Thatcherism's attachment to British nationhood and an 'authoritarian individualist' culture inevitably favoured the majority and discriminated against ethnic groups with different cultural values. Furthermore, it denied the existence of institutional racism and regarded popular concerns about excessive immigration as legitimate, which should be acted upon by politicians.

The direct impact of cultural conservatism on government policy on immigration and race relations was, however, limited. Thatcherism pushed immigration towards the top of the political agenda, at least in the early 1980s, but this did not constitute a coherent nationalist strategy setting out to redefine national identity along ethnically exclusivist lines. Legislation on immigration and asylum was punitive and racially discriminatory, but the government backed away from some of its 1979 manifesto commitments, did not adopt a policy of non-voluntary repatriation, reacted pragmatically over Hong Kong and did not use the 1981 British Nationality Act to link citizenship with allegiance. Government policies and outlook were a mix of liberal and authoritarian responses, but contributed to a climate in which some prejudices about immigration and ethnic pluralism were legitimized.

Conservative Policy on 'Race' and Immigration

Until 1976 the Conservative leadership stuck with the bipartisan consensus on depoliticizing 'race' issues and insulating the centre from demands for repatriation or that it play a key coordinating role in tackling racial inequality. Both parties accepted that limits on immigration were necessary and viewed equality of opportunity as the optimal means of encouraging peaceful integration. Responsibility for fostering harmonious race relations was delegated to local authorities, voluntary bodies and specialist agencies, which until the 1980s tended to play a relatively passive role.[8]

The centre's concentration on immigration control became more pronounced after 1979 as the Conservatives adopted a populist hardline tone, driven by expectations of electoral reward, intra-party pressure and Thatcher's unease with the bipartisan consensus.[9] Thatcher did not share the prevailing elite liberal attitude and in 1968 had 'strongly sympathized with the gravamen of [Powell's] argument about the scale of New Commonwealth immigration'.[10] In 1978 she urged stricter immigration controls, placing 'race' issues firmly in the arena of party competition. Thus, in a Granada Television interview Thatcher spoke of the fears the 'indigenous population' had about 'swamping' by alien cultures, echoing Powell's belief that such prejudices were legitimate and had to be addressed.

> People are really rather afraid that this country might be swamped by people with a different culture, and you know, the British character has done so much for democracy, for law and done so much throughout the world that if there is any fear that it might be swamped, people are going to react and be rather hostile to them coming in. So, if you want good race relations, you have got to allay people's fears about immigration.[11]

Thatcher felt that by adopting an attitude of 'civilized high mindedness' party leaders had chosen to ignore popular concerns about immigration.[12] By holding out the prospect of a halt to immigration, the Conservatives would allay people's fears and win back votes lost to the National Front. Opinion polls subsequently showed support for proposals to restrict immigration, but this was one among a number of factors contributing to the electoral decline of the National Front.[13] After its 1979 election victory, the first Thatcher Government set out to tighten immigration laws, introduce a new Nationality Bill, and manage the *status quo* in race relations.

CITIZENSHIP, IMMIGRATION AND ASYLUM

By the late 1970s widespread agreement existed on the need for reform of Britain's nationality laws. The 1948 British Nationality Act had created the category of Citizenship of the United Kingdom and Colonies (CUKC) under which British subjects and Commonwealth citizens had unrestricted right of entry and abode in the UK.[14] Subsequent immigration legislation, however, divorced citizenship of the UK and colonies from the right of abode, denying legal access to many CUKCs without 'close connection' to the UK through birth or residence. The 1971 Immigration Act established the status of 'patrial' to distinguish those CUKCs with right of abode in the UK from those subject to immigration controls. Patrials had a 'close connection' with the UK through birth, adoption, naturalization or registration in the UK, if either parent had acquired CUKC citizenship by one of these routes or if they had resided in the UK for a period of five years.[15] Non-patrials could still have the title of UK and Colonies Citizen, but were denied key citizenship rights, namely right of access to and abode in the territory of which they were legally a citizen. Patriality was a short-term solution dictated by concerns about immigration: the Home Office and the two main parties recognized that a new Nationality Act was needed to reunite British citizenship and right of abode. Conservatives wanted to formalize the link between citizenship and 'close connection', under which only those with close family connections to the UK would have right of abode, thus disproportionately favouring white citizens of Old Commonwealth states.[16] Some on the Tory Right highlighted allegiance and wanted the new nationality law to provide a clear statement of national identity.[17]

The British Nationality Act 1981

The 1981 British Nationality Act (BNA) aimed to provide a 'more meaningful citizenship for those who have close links with the United Kingdom' by creating a 'British citizenship based on the principle that citizenship should carry with it the right of abode in this country'.[18] The government also wanted to end the system under which anyone born within the UK automatically became a British citizen able to transfer this citizenship to their offspring, claiming that this was open to abuse by temporary residents and paved the way for future immigration. The BNA created three main categories of citizenship from the old CUKC category: British Citizen, British Dependent Territories Citizen and British Overseas Citizen.[19] It modified the traditional *ius soli* principle which had its roots in notions of allegiance to the sovereign on whose territory one was born. British citizenship was now to be transferred primarily through descent (the *ius sanguinis* principle) and was related to 'close association' with the UK. British citizens were those CUKCs who had close personal connection to the UK through one of their parents or grandparents, or through permanent settlement in the UK. Citizenship by descent was no longer to be transmissible as of right beyond the first generation for children born abroad; children born in the UK to non-British citizens would not automatically be entitled to citizenship. The Act also removed the right of a foreign woman married to a British citizen to register as British, requiring her to apply for naturalization.

Only the category of British Citizen entailed the right of abode in the UK, effectively codifying the status of patrial. The status of British Overseas Citizen followed existing immigration rules as it brought with it no right of access or abode. It was a largely meaningless category giving no substantial rights to its holders, except for the status of British national for the purpose of international law, and would fade out over time as it could not be transmitted to descendants. The status of 'British subject' was, though, phased out. With future immigration from Hong Kong in mind, the BNA also introduced a single category of British Dependent Territories Citizen (BDTC) which again did not bring with it right of abode in the UK. A number of Conservative backbenchers pressed for special treatment for various dependent territories, arguing that the new category weakened links with the colonies and adversely affected the citizenship rights of their residents. The government eventually agreed to special treatment for Gibraltar, the Falkland Islands (in 1983, after the Argentinian invasion) and, later, Hong Kong. Critics of the BNA claimed that it was primarily dictated by the Conservative's drive to strengthen immigration controls, accusing the government of racial discrimination for basing citizenship on close connection and affording special treatment to (predominantly white) residents of Gibraltar and the Falkland Islands. The requirements for close association through parents or grandparents born in the UK meant that very few residents of New Commonwealth states would have right of abode in Britain. The Act aimed to reunite citizenship and right of abode but the method for doing this was the category of patrial introduced in 1971. The new Nationality Act was inevitably racially discriminatory in character as the category of British Citizen marked a codification of existing immigration legislation, the purpose of which had been to halt primary immigration from the New Commonwealth. Ethnic minority communities in the UK feared that their status and rights would be weakened by changes to the *ius soli* principle, the need to register or naturalize and limits on citizenship for family members seeking to enter the UK.

The BNA provided a legal status of British citizenship, but it was not intended to provide a clear statement of nationhood or national identity. Dixon exaggerates the scope and clarity of the BNA when he claims that it meant the 'formalized expression of a reconstructed national identity based on imperial sentiments of racial superiority'.[20] The Act defined who is or is not British in legal terms, often in racially discriminatory ways, but it did not explicitly link citizenship with nationhood. Membership of the national community (in the subjective sense of Britishness) is not the same as legal citizenship which affords membership of the state as a political community. Many on the Tory Right were thus critical of the new nationality law, arguing that citizenship should be explicitly linked to allegiance to the Crown and claiming that the BNA did not address the weakening of national identity which a multicultural society entailed.[21] Legally resident, ethnic minority populations were citizens of the British state, but cultural conservatives continued to assert that ethnic minority communities could not easily become British.

Immigration Policy

The Conservative manifesto in 1979 and subsequent manifestos proclaimed a 'firm but fair' strategy of tighter immigration controls and equal opportunities for ethnic minorities in the UK.[22] The two were explicitly linked: integration and harmonious race relations would only be possible if the numbers of future immigrants entering the UK were minimized. Policy built upon a number of stated or unstated beliefs: high levels of immigration undermined social cohesion and stricter immigration laws were supported by the electorate; the integration of existing ethnic minority communities into British society had proved politically thorny; and responsibility for ensuring good race relations was best delegated to other agencies. Good race relations meant allaying the fears of the majority about immigration.

It would not be in the interests of the ethnic minorities themselves if there was a prospect of further mass inward movement. That prospect would increase social tensions, particularly in our cities. That is why we say firm immigration control is essential if we are to have good community relations.[23]

The 1979 manifesto made eight specific proposals to reduce immigration, including an end to the practice of allowing permanent settlement for those who came here for a temporary stay and a reduction in the secondary immigration of parents, grandparents and children over 18. However, several of the manifesto proposals quickly ran into difficulties. Two of the key proposals, a quota system placing a finite level on the number of immigrants to be allowed entry and a register of dependents, were dropped in the face of Home Office opposition.[24] The promised end to the 1974 concession to husbands and male fiancés was also modified. Changes to the immigration rules in 1980 restricted the entry of husbands of women with close connection with Britain, and aimed to prevent entry if its primary purpose was deemed to be settlement. This set the tone for future immigration policy by preventing the entry of persons without close personal connection to the UK and restricting the entry of those who would have to be supported by the state.

Further changes were introduced in 1982 in the light of the BNA. All British citizens were to be allowed to have their spouses and fiancés join them if they met the conditions of registration, but women who were not citizens did not enjoy this right. This was criticized by key figures on the Tory Right as a reversal of manifesto commitments and inconsistent with the stated goal of reducing immigration.[25] The decision to allow 10 000 Vietnamese refugees living in Hong Kong to come to Britain also revealed a pragmatism not in keeping with Thatcher's populist determination to reduce immigration to a minimum.

Immigration issues were not as high on the political agenda in the second Thatcher Government, as the BNA and tougher rules had greatly reduced the prospect of high levels of immigration. However, it remained determined to close loopholes in existing immigration law, even though the number of cases involved was small. The 1988 Immigration Act ended the automatic right for men settled in Britain to bring their dependants into the country and made right of entry for dependants conditional on them receiving accommodation and financial support from their families. Overstaying became a criminal offence, rights of appeal were restricted and the entry of second wives from polygamous marriages was outlawed.

The prospect of the transfer of sovereignty over Hong Kong to China in 1997 prompted the 1990 British Nationality (Hong Kong) Act. The BNA had made it clear that the government would not grant British citizenship to all Hong Kong British Dependent Territories Citizens (BDTCs), but the 1990 Act offered leading members of Hong Kong society the safeguard of right of abode in the UK. The Governor of Hong Kong would choose 50 000 'selected key people' resident in the colony who, with their spouses and families, would be assured of a British passport with right of abode in the UK. A points system and range of categories would be used to determine those eligible.[26] Subsequently, the Major Government announced that BDTCs, three million British Nationals (Overseas) passport holders and a post-1997 category of some two million Hong Kong Special Administrative Region passport holders would be allowed visa-free entry into the UK for visits of up to six months, but without right of residence. The government also guaranteed that if up to 8000 non-Chinese ethnic minorities without any other nationality were forced out of Hong Kong after the transfer of sovereignty they would be able to settle in the UK.[27]

Asylum Policy

In 1985 and 1986 the government acted to counter increases in asylum applications by imposing visa requirements on visitors from many New Commonwealth states, including Sri Lanka, India, Pakistan, Ghana and Nigeria. The 1987 Immigration (Carriers Liability) Act made it an offence for airlines to bring people into the UK without proper documentation, thus extending responsibility for the administration of immigration controls to airlines who could be fined £2000 each time they carried a passenger with inadequate or forged documents.

In the 1990s, the Major Governments continued this trend of restricting entry into the UK, legislating to deter asylum seekers and extending the number of countries from which nationals required visas to enter the UK. The government reacted to a rise in the number of asylum applications from 5000 a year in 1988 to 57 000 in 1991, claiming that only a small proportion of those coming to the UK had a well-founded fear of persecution as envisaged under the United Nations Convention on Refugees which forbade countries sending back genuine refugees. The majority of claimants were deemed to be economic migrants seeking a better standard of living in Britain and looking to by-pass her strict immigration rules.[28] An Asylum Bill was introduced in the 1991–2 Parliament but dropped prior to the general election. However, the 1992 manifesto included a commitment to reintroduce an Asylum Bill and, in the election campaign, Home Secretary Kenneth Baker claimed that Labour would allow a flood of refugees to enter the country.

The Asylum and Immigration Appeals Act 1993 introduced a faster appeals process to deal with 'bogus' asylum claims, which would be certified as 'without foundation' and made subject to an accelerated appeals system. The Act also included powers to rapidly deport asylum seekers whose claim had been rejected. Applicants whose asylum claim had been rejected had the right to an oral hearing in front of an independent adjudicator, while an additional appeal on points of law could be made by the Immigration Tribunal to the Court of Appeal. Asylum applicants and their dependants were to be fingerprinted to prevent multiple applications. Finally, the Act altered the duty of housing authorities to provide temporary accommodation for asylum applicants while their claims were being considered.[29]

After a fall in asylum applications in 1993–4, the number of claims rose again in 1995, prompting the Asylum and Immigration Act 1996, key elements of which were opposed by the Labour Party, defeated in the Lords and challenged in the courts. The Act extended the 'without foundation' criteria to include claims which do not fall within a strict reading of the 1951 Geneva Convention: where the grounds on which asylum is claimed are manifestly untrue or fraudulent; where the grounds cited no longer apply; where asylum is claimed only after leave to enter has been refused or action to deport has been initiated; and when the asylum seeker arrives with forged documents or without documents (unless there is a convincing explanation for this). The Home Secretary was empowered to draw up a 'white list' of countries designated as not giving rise to a 'serious risk of persecution'. Countries on the list generated significant numbers of asylum applications, a very high proportion of which prove unfounded, including Bulgaria, Poland, Romania, Cyprus, Ghana, India and Pakistan.[30] Asylum seekers from these states would not automatically be refused entry and would have the right of appeal to an independent adjudicator but not beyond it, though the presumption would be that there was no serious risk of persecution. Additionally, applications for asylum from people who travelled to Britain via a 'safe' third country were categorized as 'without foundation' under the 1993 and 1996 legislation. Appeals against refused asylum claims in such cases could only be made once the applicant had been returned to the third country. Following the Act, the number of people seeking asylum in Britain fell and the rate of refusal rose dramatically.

As well as tightening rules on entry and removal, the 1996 Act sought to prevent entry by making Britain an unattractive destination for economic migrants. It became a criminal offence to employ someone who was not entitled to work in the UK, forcing employers to check that prospective employees had a National Insurance number or valid work permit, measures criticized for shifting responsibility to employers and making them less willing to take on workers from ethnic minorities. A June 1996 Court of Appeal ruling overturned government regulations introduced through secondary legislation which denied welfare benefits to 8000 asylum seekers, but ministers evaded the ruling by pushing the measures through Parliament as primary legislation in the form of amendments to the Asylum and Immigration Bill.[31] These restricted welfare benefits to people making an asylum claim on arrival in the UK (at the point of entry rather than after entering the country) and removing entitlement to benefits once an application had been rejected by the Home Office. The government also overturned a House of Lords amendment extending the period in which migrants could claim refugee status to three days. The High Court and Court of Appeal subsequently ruled that local authorities had a legal obligation to provide warmth, food and shelter to asylum seekers.[32] Controversy also arose over the detention of asylum seekers while their claims were being heard and the deportation of claimants whose cases had been rejected.[33]

The European Context

The rise in applications for asylum was a cause of concern for most EC states in the late 1980s, the British government supporting intergovernmental cooperation but vigorously resisting supranational authority and the removal of UK border controls. It insisted that a General Declaration appended to the SEA allowed states to maintain border controls for security reasons, despite Article 8a defining the single market as 'an area without internal frontiers' ensuring 'the free movement of persons'. The Thatcher and Major Governments were resolute in their determination to retain border controls, even when seven of the Schengen Group states belatedly removed their internal frontiers in 1995. Ministers argued that Britain's island status made controls at frontiers the most effective means of regulating entry and were wary of identity cards.[34] A dispute over the status of Gibraltar held up the ratification of the External Frontiers Convention, and the government opposed a 1995 directive on the elimination of border controls and resisted proposals to bring matters concerning the crossing of external frontiers into Community competence.

Whilst accepting that increased migration required coordinated responses to asylum, illegal immigration, terrorism and organized crime, the government insisted that this must be on an intergovernmental basis which reflected the sensitivity of the issues and their centrality to national sovereignty.[35] In the late 1980s such matters were dealt with by a plethora of bodies, including the Trevi Group and the Ad Hoc Group on Immigration, and through agreements like the 1990 Dublin Convention. Britain welcomed the Justice and Home Affairs provisions of Title VI of the Maastricht Treaty which provided for enhanced cooperation on a primarily intergovernmental basis.[36] Article K.1 of the Treaty identified a number of areas as matters of common concern, including asylum and immigration policy plus the movement, entry and residence in the EU of nationals of third countries. Legal instruments took the form of joint positions, joint actions and conventions, on which unanimity was required.

Progress proved slow and the procedures complex and heterogeneous: the Commission had a limited role, QMV could be used in some areas and Member States could decide by unanimity to apply Article 100c to a number of areas of 'common interest'. Article 100c gave the Community competence on visa policy: in 1995, the Council adopted regulations on a uniform format for visas and agreed a common list of countries whose nationals would require a visa to enter the EU, though Member States could maintain their own visa requirement lists including additional countries. At the 1996–7 IGC, the Major Government proposed only limited reforms of the Title VI procedures to improve cooperation on justice and home affairs issues, defending its intergovernmental basis.[37]

The Major Government was unenthusiastic about the creation of a 'Citizenship of the European Union' in the Maastricht Treaty. Article 8 stated that 'every person holding the nationality of a Member State shall be a citizen of the Union'. A number of rights were conferred on Citizens of the Union: the right to free movement and residence within the EU, to vote and stand as a candidate at municipal and European Parliament elections, to diplomatic protection in a third country by the diplomatic authorities of any Member State, and to petition the European Parliament and Ombudsman. These largely confirmed existing rights and had a limited impact on the UK. The status of Citizenship of the Union is, however, a dynamic one, though Britain opposed proposals to extend the rights it entails. Citizenship of the Union would not replace national citizenship, but was built upon it as only nationals of Member States could become Citizens of the Union and nationality laws remained the prerogative of Member States.[38] However, like the Title VI arrangements, Citizenship of the Union made some inroads into national sovereignty, citizenship and the traditional role of the nation-state.[39]

EU action in the field of immigration and asylum remained primarily intergovernmental in this period, but those measures adopted had significant implications for national sovereignty and identity. Opposition to the removal of border controls and to Community competence in asylum and immigration policy confirmed that Britain's 'awkward partner' status owed something to the centrality of the politics of nationhood to Conservative politics, although the Blair Government was also determined to retain border controls.

RACE RELATIONS AND PUBLIC POLICY

The Conservative commitment to a 'firm but fair' immigration policy was coupled with a desire for harmonious race relations through equal opportunities for the ethnic minorities in a meritocratic society and their continued integration into British society. Whereas immigration and asylum were prioritized by the Thatcher and Major Governments, there was no coherent state-directed strategy for dealing with racial disadvantage and discrimination, the Home Office playing a regulatory rather than effective coordinating role.[40] Policy on race relations was often reactive, responding to events such as the 1981 inner city riots, or concerned with the hands-off management of a plural society rather than actively fostering a longer term strategy on integration. Policy responsibility continued to be delegated to agencies such as the Commission for Racial Equality (CRE) and local authorities.

The Conservatives claimed that their free market economic policies could tackle many of the problems of racial disadvantage, encouraging the growth of a black middle class stratum of professionals and businessmen who would provide an example of successful integration into British society which others would emulate.

> We want to see members of the ethnic minorities assuming positions of leadership alongside their fellow citizens and accepting their full share of responsibility. Racial discrimination is an injustice and can have no place in a tolerant and civilized society. Progress towards better community relations must be on a basis of equality. Reverse discrimination is itself an injustice and if it were to be introduced it would undermine the achievement and example of those who had risen on their merits.[41]

Improvements to the socio-economic position of ethnic minorities were to be achieved through enterprise and self-improvement in a meritocratic society. State action to redress racial inequality was regarded as costly and inefficient, undermining achievement and producing a culture of dependency. Although there is some evidence of ethnic minority upward mobility, racial disadvantage and discrimination remain deep rooted. Members of ethnic minority groups, particularly Bangladeshi, Pakistani and Black-African, are more likely to be unemployed and are disproportionately employed in the lowest positions in the labour market.[42] Government policy did little to ease the plight of inner city blacks suffering unemployment, poor housing, eroded welfare rights, educational disadvantage and racial discrimination. Thatcherite opposition to active state involvement and its emphasis on individual self-improvement and integration into British society rather than special treatment or group rights for ethnic minorities precluded a strengthening of state action countering racial inequality. A colour-blind market-based approach to the social integration of ethnic minorities was coupled with an emphasis on equality of opportunity as a means of eliminating racial discrimination. Legislation could check blatant discrimination, but 'ultimately racial harmony depends on the people of Britain as a whole, in all communities, being prepared to live and work together and to respect each other's way of life'.[43] Thatcherite discourse rejected the concept of institutionalized racism, claiming that British society is not racist, though some individuals may be. Major's personal commitment to good race relations was illustrated in a 1997 speech to the Commonwealth Institute when he spoke of the positive contributions to British society made by ethnic minorities, the importance of tolerance and his loathing of racism. His vision of a diverse but inclusive society drew upon familiar themes of enterprise and meritocracy, racial harmony engendered by the evolution of tolerance, colour-blind legislation rather than reverse discrimination and patriotism.[44]

The key elements of a liberal approach based on legal equality, equality of opportunity and the CRE's role in promoting good race relations remained in place, though the Thatcher Governments did not react positively to proposals to strengthen the CRE and Race Relations Act.[45] Legislation aimed at tackling racism was strengthened in some respects. The 1986 Public Order Act addressed incitement to racial hatred; the 1994 Criminal Justice and Public Order Act made the publication of racially inflammatory material an arrestable offence and created a new offence of intentional harassment as racially motivated attacks increased. Home Office funded community-level partnerships between police, local authorities and community groups remained the favoured way of tackling racism.[46] While supporting the EU's goal of tackling racism, the Major Government opposed parts of a plan to create a European Monitoring Centre on Racism and Xenophobia and IGC proposals to strengthen Treaty commitments on tackling racism, arguing that action at the national level was preferable and that existing legislation was adequate.[47] This, plus the tightening of immigration and asylum laws, reductions in benefits for asylum seekers and measures to tackle illegal employment had negative effects on race relations. Government attitudes to and policy on race relations were framed within the existing model of formal equality and administrative delegation, but were also shaped by concerns about social cohesion, an erosion of British values and the impact of local authority 'anti-racist' initiatives. Cultural conservatives questioned assumptions that ethnic minorities could be harmoniously integrated into British society, saw multiculturalism as a threat to nationhood, sought to uphold 'legitimate' concerns about integration and criticized mechanisms for dealing with racial discrimination. The competing demands of, on the one hand, a liberal emphasis on market forces and the delegation of responsibility for race relations, and, on the other, a social authoritarian critique of multiculturalism and management of a plural society are evident in the examples sketched below. Various instances of urban disorder prompted some limited attempts to tackle racial inequality but also an emphasis on law and order; centre–local relations were strained as 'race' policy issues were politicized; and the Rushdie affair pushed questions about the management of ethnic diversity in a liberal society more firmly into the political arena.

Law and Order

Since the mid-1970s, the popular Tory press, the police and sections of Conservative opinion had linked rising crime with black youth. Relations between police and young blacks in the inner cities had worsened and many blacks felt uneasy about the criminal justice system.[48] These issues exploded onto the political agenda in 1981 following a series of civil disturbances in the inner cities. The Scarman Report on these disturbances identified social and racial disadvantage plus poor relations between the police and black communities as important factors, urging positive action to tackle racial inequality. The Thatcher Government recognized the specific problems faced by ethnic minorities in the inner cities, but rejected claims that its economic and social policies contributed to this. It offered limited additional funding, but continued to look to local community projects as the optimal means of tackling racial inequality.[49] The Tory Right claimed that young blacks lacked respect for authority, Ivor Stanbrook complaining that the Scarman proposals meant 'going easy on the blacks'.[50] Following further disturbances in 1985, the government reverted to a law-and-order strategy identifying criminality rather than disadvantage as the prime cause of the riots.

Local Politics

The Conservative governments continued the trend of delegating responsibility for race relations matters to special agencies and local authorities.[51] Under section 11 of the 1966 Local Government Act, the Home Office gives grants to local authorities to be spent on strengthening opportunities for the ethnic minorities, while the Single Regeneration Budget finances business-related projects. Expectations that administrative delegation would depoliticize race relations issues by removing them from the national arena proved misplaced. Instead, disputes between the centre and some local authorities over appropriate policy measures emerged as a number of authorities introduced 'anti-racist' strategies stressing positive action to promote equal treatment and promote awareness of racism. This marked a politicization of local 'race' politics which spilled over into centre–local relations.

Multicultural and 'anti-racist' education policies were criticized by government ministers and heightened tensions between central and local government.[52] Claims made by Bradford headmaster Ray Honeyford that multi-ethnic education lowered standards, placed minority white pupils at a disadvantage and eroded the teaching of British values echoed those of cultural conservatives.[53] The 1985 Swann Report recommended that schools prepare all pupils for life in a multicultural society. However, the national curriculum introduced by the 1988 Education Reform Act squeezed multicultural teaching from many school timetables and instructed most schools to provide daily 'collective worship, wholly or mainly of a broadly Christian character'. Ministers also supported the teaching of British national history, Sir Keith Joseph claiming this was 'indispensable to understanding the society we live in, to an awareness by pupils of ... the developing story of the nation'.[54] Allowing schools to opt-out of local education control also prompted cases in which white parents sought to withdraw their children from schools where a majority of pupils were from ethnic minorities.

The Rushdie Affair

The Conservative desire to keep problems concerning the management of a plural society off the centre's political agenda was undermined by the controversy surrounding local 'anti-racist' strategies. However, the Rushdie affair brought the problems inherent in the management of a plural society to the fore.[55] This centred on the publication of Salmon Rushdie's novel *The Satanic Verses* which was deemed offensive by many Muslims, its author being condemned to death by Iranian leader Ayatollah Khomeini's fatwa in 1989. The case revealed tensions between Islamic fundamentalist values, which had gained support in sections of the British Muslim community, and liberal traditions of individual rights and colour-blind public policy. It also illustrated that treating 'blacks' as a uniform category ignored important differences between, as well divisions within, ethnic minority communities in Britain.[56]

Two open letters from John Patten, Home Office Minister with responsibility for race relations, outlined the government's position on the Rushdie affair and the management of a plural society. In the first letter, Patten stated that the government wanted a diverse society without separation in which ethnic minorities played a full participating role. Though applauding diversity, the onus was on ethnic minorities to adjust to the British way of life, its language, political culture and traditions.

> Of course, British Muslims should be brought up faithful in the religion of Islam and well-versed in the Holy Koran. But if they are also to make the most of their lives and opportunities as British citizens, then they must also have a clear understanding of British democratic processes, of its laws, the system of government and the history that lies behind them, and indeed of their own rights and responsibilities.[57]

Shared values and British national identity were the cement holding the plural society together. Patten stressed that this would not mean ethnic communities having to forfeit their faith or roots, but these would have to exist within a framework of British traditions, with respect for the rule of law and the obligations of living in Britain of paramount importance.

In the second letter, Patten argued that 'one cannot be British on one's own exclusive terms or to a selective basis, nor is there room for dual loyalties where those loyalties openly contradict one another'. Civil disobedience and support for the fatwa were incompatible with the duty to respect the rule of law which went with British citizenship. He wanted 'integration and active involvement in the mainstream', whereby Muslims would ensure that their children were fluent in the English language and had a good understanding of British history and culture. Though arguing that this did not mean assimilation and was compatible with toleration of diversity, conflicts of loyalties could only be managed if Muslims' overriding loyalty was to the British state and liberal values.

THE POLITICS OF 'RACE' AND THE CONSERVATIVE PARTY

Conservative leaders in this period insisted that racism was unwelcome and rare in the party, Major in particular stressing his abhorrence of racism and disassociating himself from racist comments made by party members. A Powellite rump remained in the parliamentary party but few of its members held government posts or had direct influence over policy. Indeed, the Tory Right was critical of government policy on immigration and race relations, its adherents voting against the government or abstaining on a number of occasions. They criticized the government for not doing more to halt immigration, supported repatriation, demanded the abolition of the CRE and claimed that social cohesion and British nationhood were being undermined.[58] A Young Conservative Report in 1984 claimed that 'extremist and racialist forces are at work in the Conservative party' with the Monday Club an important channel for racist sentiments. It also accused MPs on the Right of the party of using race 'in an emotive manner, whipping up bigotry and prejudice' and berated Mrs Thatcher for not doing enough to combat racism in the party.[59] Tebbit emerged as a key figure on the Tory Right, claiming in 1990 that many members of ethnic minority communities refused to adapt to the British way of life, failing his 'cricket test' of patriotic loyalty, and leading a rebellion on the British Nationality (Hong Kong) Act.[60]

One Nation Conservatives rejected the Tory Right's brand of cultural conservatism calling instead for tolerance, diversity and equal opportunity. A 1982 Tory Reform Group pamphlet argued that racial inequality and discrimination were unacceptable, making a number of proposals for positive action on multicultural education, community policing and employment.[61]

Ethnic Minority Electoral Support

Conservative Central Office has recognized the potential electoral significance of ethnic minority voters in a number of marginal seats. At the 1992 election there were 51 constituencies (16 marginal) in which ethnic minorities made up at least 15 per cent of the population, 17 of them held by the Conservatives.[62] To promote the party's appeal to potential ethnic minority supporters, particularly Indian professionals and businessmen, Central Office established an Ethnic Monitoring Unit in the late 1970s. Anglo-Asian and Anglo-West Indian Conservative Societies were also created, the former being the most significant. But these were abolished in 1987 amid internal conflict and replaced by the 'One Nation Forum', an advisory body based at Central Office made up of ethnic minority members which advises MPs and constituencies on building up their ethnic minority membership.[63]

Participation by members of the ethnic minorities in the Conservative Party in the mid-1990s remained low. At the 1992 general election the party fielded eight ethnic minority candidates, but only three in winnable seats. Ultimately, only the Sri Lankan-born Nirj Deva in Brentford and Isleworth was successful; Cheltenham, scene of much controversy over the selection of John Taylor, was lost to the Liberal Democrats. Eleven ethnic minority candidates stood for the Conservatives in 1997, few in winnable seats and all, including sitting MP Nirj Deva, were defeated, though the average swing against the Tories in seats contested by ethnic minority candidates (8.9 per cent) was less than the national swing (10.5 per cent). In two seats where the party fielded Asian candidates, Bradford West and Bethnal Green and Bow, the swing was 5 per cent from Labour to the Conservatives.[64]

Since 1976 the Conservatives have adopted a twin-track approach to the electoral politics of 'race', on the one hand adopting a populist, hardline message on immigration, but on the other stressing a commitment to good race relations and believing that the votes of ethnic minority groups in certain marginal seats could be electorally significant and might be won by the Conservatives if the party were able to target these voters effectively.[65] Balancing the two elements inevitably proved tricky: immigration laws which might be perceived as racially discriminatory by ethnic minority voters and negative publicity produced by racist remarks by some Conservatives undermined attempts to woo black voters. The 1983 Conservative election poster 'Labour Says He's Black, We Say He's British' was intended to illustrate the party's message of equal opportunity and meritocracy, but confirmed that it was the 'black bourgeoisie' who came closest to meeting the Conservative ideal of Britishness. In successive elections, the party courted the votes of the Indian community in Britain. In a keynote speech ahead of the 1997 election, Major restated claims that the Conservatives were their natural home given the shared commitment to enterprise, self-reliance and discipline.[66] Party strategists hoped that as Indians in the UK benefited from Conservative economic policies and became more integrated into British society, their voting record would mirror that of the British Jewish community by showing a significant swing from Labour to the Tories. Thatcher had good relations with leading members of the Jewish community nationally and in her own Finchley constituency.[67]

There is no substantial evidence to suggest that the Conservative attempt to make inroads into the Asian vote proved successful. A 1991 opinion poll indicated that only 14 per cent of Asian voters supported the Conservatives, declining from 23 per cent at the 1987 general election, although an NOP poll taken closer to the election put support at 19 per cent. A MORI opinion poll in early 1997 showed 25 per cent of Asians favouring the Conservatives, indicating a growth in support compared with the national swing to Labour. Only 15 per cent of Asians, however, viewed the Conservatives as the party most likely to look after Asian interests, despite Tory strategists making this a central plank of their drive to win ethnic minority support, indicating that Asian voters were primarily concerned with broader issues. According to these opinion polls, a majority of Asian voters supported Labour (67 per cent in 1987, 64 per cent in 1992, 70 per cent in 1997) while in 1997 86 per cent of Afro-Caribbeans backed Labour and just 8 per cent the Conservatives.[68] Labour continued to attract a substantial majority of ethnic minority votes, variously accounted for in terms of class location, residual loyalty to Labour and negative perceptions of the Conservatives. An opinion poll in 1997, however, found that 60 per cent of Asian voters felt that current immigration laws were 'about right' or 'not strict enough'.[69]

Black electoral participation is complex and far from uniform: the belief, shared by Conservative strategists, that ethnic minority voters in marginal constituencies can be successfully targeted by the two main parties has also been challenged.[70] By 1983 the electoral saliency of immigration had declined, being rarely cited in polls of key issues. The party appeared less inclined to play the 'race card' as the Thatcher and Major era progressed, immigration and asylum issues reappearing only sporadically in Conservative election campaigns, such as in 1992 when ministers warned of a flood of asylum seekers under a Labour government. Individual candidates, notably Nicholas Fairbairn in 1992 and Nicholas Budgen in 1997, attacked immigration and multiculturalism but were chastized by the leadership and did not appear to gain any electoral dividend.[71] The controversy over John Taylor's selection in Cheltenham confirmed that racism still existed in the party, while a survey in 1992 reported 70 per cent of party members agreeing that the government should encourage the repatriation of immigrants and 91 per cent supporting a further tightening of immigration rules.[72]

CONCLUSIONS

Thatcherism abandoned the bipartisan consensus on 'race' politics, adopting a hardline stance on immigration and asylum and a populist discourse in which good race relations were predicated upon the acceptance of British values by ethnic minorities. Despite a populist approach on immigration and assertions that good race relations would require the acceptance of British values by ethnic minorities, the Thatcher and Major Governments did not pursue a coherent or consistent approach to the politics of nationhood in the field of 'race' and immigration. Although cultural conservative themes found their way into Thatcherite rhetoric, there was not the level of theorizing on 'race', culture and nation associated with the social authoritarian New Right. Equally Powell's influence on Conservative politics on 'race' issues was apparent in the departure from the bipartisan consensus on immigration, but the leadership rejected his repatriation strategy and warnings about 'rivers of blood'.

The politics of 'race' and immigration will continue to raise important dilemmas for Conservative leaders in the 1990s. The conservative nation is constructed around ideas of authority, patriotic allegiance, national character and the organic evolution of institutions, which sit uneasily with a plural society. The dividing line between integration and assimilation became more blurred in the Thatcher and Major era as harmonious race relations were predicated upon ethnic minorities accepting cultural values associated with Britishness. Though not strictly an ethnic account of national identity, the emphasis on cultural homogeneity meant that becoming British required some cultural assimilation. Conservative leaders sought to manage race relations in a hands-off manner with the centre playing only a limited role, but fostered an atmosphere in which concerns that immigration and multiculturalism were problematic and detrimental to national identity were more freely aired. The balance between a liberal individualist approach to race relations, stressing meritocracy and equal opportunity, and a cultural conservative approach urging a reassertion of a homogenous British national identity will continue to exercise Conservatives in the 1990s.

The commitment to 'firm but fair' immigration policies is likely to survive the Conservative's election defeat, but the Labour Government is likely to accept much existing legislation. Immigration does not have the electoral potency it had in the 1970s and a tougher Conservative line would further reduce the Conservatives' chances of increasing their support among ethnic minority voters. Europe is also a key part of the equation in the politics of 'race'. Labour is determined to maintain British border controls and the intergovernmental character of EU decision-making on justice and home affairs, lessening the chances of Europe and immigration combining as a potent weapon in the Conservative armoury. But increased cooperation between EU Member States is required to deal effectively with international migration, and the limited progress made to date has nonetheless already impinged upon the role of the nation-state.

7 Conclusions

The politics of nationhood has historically and ideologically had a central position in modern British Conservative politics, in conservative thought from the late eighteenth century and in the statecraft of the Conservative Party from the late nineteenth century. By this time the Conservative Party was the dominant actor in the politics of nationhood, having constructed a One Nation political strategy in which the Conservatives positioned themselves as the patriotic party defending national institutions, upholding the Union, extending Empire, promoting social cohesion and making effective use of patriotic discourse. This national strategy was an important means of realizing the core goals of Conservative statecraft, namely upholding the relative autonomy of its leaders in office in matters of high politics, fostering an image of governing competence, achieving issue hegemony in these areas and extending the party's electoral appeal.[1] However, even in this relatively successful period, the Conservative politics of nationhood did not always prove easily manageable as disputes over Ireland and tariff reform illustrated.

In the post-war consensus period, the Conservative Party's predominance in the politics of nationhood began to ebb away as the foundations of its national strategy crumbled and its near-monopoly over populist patriotic discourse waned. Economic decline, decolonization, moves towards EC membership, immigration and multiculturalism, plus problems of territorial management undermined the One Nation or Conservative collectivist national strategy. The Heath Government, albeit briefly and with limited conviction, and Powellism offered contrasting prescriptions for reworking the Conservative politics of nationhood in the light of changed circumstances. Heath viewed British membership of the EC as the prerequisite for economic (and to a lesser extent, political) modernization, sought to depoliticize 'race' issues and promote harmonious integration and supported legislative devolution in Scotland. However, the Heath Government's attempts to revise the politics of nationhood were beset by problems – EC membership was achieved but with only a limited Europeanization of the British political system, immigration rules were tightened in the face of popular pressure, proposals for a Scottish Parliament were not

Conclusion 155

enacted and direct rule over Northern Ireland was introduced following escalating conflict. Powell rejected Heath's approach, constructing an alternative nationalist strategy based around the defence of parliamentary sovereignty and a homogeneous national community. He opposed EC membership, warned about the failure of integration, demanded a halt to immigration and a state-sponsored repatriation programme and supported the further integration of Northern Ireland into the British political system.

Thatcherism departed from key elements of One Nation statecraft, reacting to the failings of Heath and Powell's attempts to rework the Conservative politics of nationhood. Though drawing upon New Right thinking, this was not translated into a blueprint for government policy. Tensions between the neo-liberal and cultural conservative views of the nation and nation-state worked against the development of a coherent Thatcherite idea of the nation, while concepts of sovereignty and identity remained problematic. Policy on European integration, territorial politics and the politics of 'race' was often shaped by statecraft considerations such as governing competence and electoral success, plus the longer-term goals of maintaining the Conservatives' role as the patriotic party and defending the relative autonomy of its leaders in office. Thatcherism sought to defend the nation-state – in terms of executive autonomy, national sovereignty and the Union – and revitalize national identity through economic renewal, to be achieved by an emphasis on free market individualism and enterprise, English cultural nationalism and populist patriotic discourse.

The Thatcher Governments enjoyed some success in the politics of nationhood, placing free market individualism at the heart of its vision of a revitalized national identity and developing a populist patriotic discourse. But they did not develop or pursue a coherent and consistent national or nationalist strategy, often acting pragmatically, facing constraints on their actions and contradictions within the Thatcherite political project. The latter included: a defence of national sovereignty but support for the Single European Market project; staunch unionism in Scotland but support for devolution and intergovernmentalism in Northern Ireland; the imperialist echoes in Conservative discourse during the Falklands conflict but the general post-imperial orientation of the Thatcherite politics of nationhood; and its mix of liberal individualist and cultural conservative approaches to race relations. Thatcherism thus did not achieve hegemony over the politics of nationhood. Instead, Britain's role in the

European Union, territorial politics and the management of a multicultural society posed awkward problems for Conservative statecraft. These difficulties became acutely apparent under the Major Governments, with statecraft failings in the politics of nationhood – particularly divisions over Europe, sterling's withdrawal from the ERM and the government's opposition to legislative devolution in Scotland – contributing to the Conservative's heavy election defeat in 1997.

The detailed studies of Conservative government policy on European integration, territorial management and immigration and race relations provided in Chapters 4 to 6 noted the relative importance of statecraft over ideological considerations, examined the opportunities and problems which the politics of nationhood raised for Conservative statecraft in the Thatcher and Major period and assessed the constraints on government action in these policy areas. As noted in Chapter 4, the difficulties encountered by Conservative leaders on European policy in this period in part resulted from deep-seated difficulties concerning the adaptation of British policy and the British political system to EU membership. European integration proved problematic for foreign economic policy, Conservative Party statecraft and the conservative concept of the nation. The defence of the nation-state and national identity were central to Conservative politics but were increasingly challenged by developments in the EC. An attachment to the nation-state and a state patriotism built around the Union were also evident in territorial politics. But Thatcherism undermined Conservative unionism in Scotland, being perceived as promoting English values but failing to take account of Scottish distinctiveness, while the Major Governments' defence of administrative devolution failed to restore the party's fortunes. In Northern Ireland, modifications to British sovereignty reflected Northern Ireland's status as a 'place apart', government support for devolution here contrasting with its opposition to a Scottish Parliament. The Conservatives employed the 'race card' in the late 1970s, but immigration dropped down the political agenda by the mid-1980s, though an increase in asylum applications prompted further government action in the 1990s. The government adopted a managerial approach to race relations, though tensions concerning the appropriate balance between a liberal emphasis on equality of opportunity and a cultural conservative concern with upholding British values were evident in the Conservative Party.

THE CONSERVATIVE POLITICS OF NATIONHOOD AFTER 1997

The politics of nationhood will continue to have a central place in Conservative politics following the 1997 election defeat, but will continue to raise important and divisive questions about the aims, values and policies of the Conservative Party. These questions about the future direction of Conservatism – whether to move towards the centre ground and accept elements of Labour's agenda or seek 'clear blue water' between Conservative and Labour policy on devolution, European integration and the politics of 'race' – have been made more acute by the erosion of the foundations of the Conservative politics of nationhood.[2] Thatcherism sought to reconstruct a Conservative national strategy and restore Conservative predominance in the politics of nationhood at a time when the party's One Nation strategy had been undermined by British decline, decolonization, moves towards EC membership, challenges to territorial management and the development of a plural society. In the late 1990s, external developments and the failings of the Thatcherite project necessitate a further reworking of the Conservative politics of nationhood. Should the party regain power at the next or next-but-one general election, it is likely to be faced with an environment at odds with the key tenets of Conservative policy on Europe and the constitution under the Thatcher and Major Governments.

The electoral decline of the Conservatives in Scotland, Wales and northern England was dramatically confirmed in the 1997 election which left the party without any MPs in three of the four component nations of the United Kingdom. Geographically, the Conservatives look still more like an English national party. The 'Yes' votes in the Scottish and Welsh devolution referendums necessitated rethinking on the appropriate Conservative response to devolution, William Hague having maintained the party's opposition to the principle and details of legislative devolution during the referendum campaigns. But the scale of the election and referendum defeats in Scotland were a stark confirmation of the failings of Major's attempt to forge a constructive Conservative unionism built around administrative devolution. Change in Conservative policy became inevitable – the leadership thus indicated that it would not seek to abolish the Scottish Parliament and will contest elections to the new body in 1999. This will provide a chance for the Conservatives to rebuild their support in Scotland, but they will first have to clarify the policy on devolution and this review process will highlight differences between Scottish Conservatives and tensions between the Scottish party and the leadership. Following the close Welsh referendum vote, Constitutional Affairs spokesman Michael Ancram continued to voice concerns about the Assembly proposals, but recognized that policy would have to be adapted if devolution went ahead.[3]

The prospect of substantial changes in the territorial management of the UK following legislative devolution has led some Conservatives to suggest that the party become more explicitly one defending English interests, condemning the perceived special treatment afforded to Scotland and Wales. At the 1997 party conference, Ancram indicated that the party would address the 'English dimension' of devolution, suggesting that in the House of Commons two days per week could be set aside for English matters, and that Scottish and Welsh MPs be prevented from speaking or voting on English primary legislation. The leadership is critical of Labour's (now postponed) proposals for English regional assemblies, but some envisage an English parliament as the long-term consequence of Scottish and Welsh devolution.[4] Alternatively, the Conservatives may again try to portray themselves as a party upholding national distinctiveness but one which values the state patriotism of the multinational UK state, a scenario made more likely if Scottish and Welsh Conservatives gain greater autonomy within the party organization. Developments in Northern Ireland will also raise questions for a Conservative leadership supportive of the peace process but wary of concessions to republicans. A sizeable number of Conservative MPs remain close to the Ulster Unionist cause, are sceptical of government policy and may try to raise the profile of the integrationist option should the peace process run aground or be perceived as offering too many concessions. Labour's wider constitutional reform agenda (the incorporation of the European Convention on Human Rights into UK law, reform of the House of Lords and possible electoral reform) also impacts upon Conservative statecraft and the politics of nationhood. Defence of the constitution has been a central theme of the conservative nation, with national institutions viewed as part of an organic whole which reflects the national character and shared history and which are a defining feature of British state patriotism.

A concerted revival of Labour patriotism also seems likely as senior Labour politicians seek a modernized British national identity, with devolution, constitutional reform and a pro-European outlook, including preparation for membership of the single currency, key aspects of this vision. Gordon Brown's 1997 Spectator/ Allied Dunbar lecture was one such example of Labour's attempt to re-establish Labour patriotism, mixing a recognition of the legitimacy of the nation-state and national identity with the desire for a modernized British identity.[5] Brown noted that Thatcher had recognized 'the need for Britain to reinvent itself and rediscover a new self-confidence', drawing on a common past and shared bonds to build a better future. But the Conservative project failed in this task, offering only a narrow and damaging vision, 'rebuilding the concept of Britishness from individual self-interest and mistrust of foreigners' and clinging to outdated institutions as an expression of national identity. Brown restated familiar themes in Labour patriotism – democracy, freedom from arbitrary power, internationalism and a recognition of the diversity of British society – but in the context of a pooling of sovereignty in the EU and constitutional reform.

Conservative policy on the politics of 'race' appears more settled following the immigration and asylum legislation of the 1980s and 1990s and the leadership's reluctance to exploit 'race' issues. Labour has accepted much of the immigration legislation it inherited, though its decision to abolish the primary purpose rule drew a critical reaction from the Conservative frontbench. Conservative efforts to win support from ethnic minorities are likely to continue, Hague also seeking increased ethnic minority representation in the party. The leadership has declined to overtly play the 'race card', given the fall in immigration and its declining political salience, and wishes for harmonious race relations and greater ethnic minority electoral support. But the Rushdie affair confirmed that the plural society has the potential to raise problems for Conservative statecraft and conservative concepts of the nation, the Tory Right remaining critical of multiculturalism. Thus at the 1997 party conference, Tebbit claimed that multiculturalism was divisive as ethnic minorities were not fully integrated into British society, remaining 'foreigners holding British passports' with their own identities, and warning of Yugoslavia-style ethnic conflict in the UK.[6] This ethnic-ideological account of the nation argues that 'one cannot ... be loyal to two nations ... it perpetuates ethnic divisions because nationality is in the long term more about culture than ethnics'. These sub-Powellite views remain marginalized in the Conservative Party and were firmly rebuffed by the leadership, Hague seeking a 'patriotism without bigotry'.

The new Conservative leadership faces continued problems regarding Britain's role in the European Union and the optimal response to further European integration, more acute given the party's limited influence over EU (and now UK) policy developments and the difficulties of forging a policy behind which the majority of the parliamentary party can unite. Given the continued dynamism of the EU agenda, especially the launch of the third stage of EMU in 1999 involving all but a handful of Member States, and the intensity of intra-party disputes, Conservative divisions on Europe are unlikely to be healed or contained in the medium term. Hague quickly moved the party further along a moderate Euro-sceptic path, his new policy on EMU proclaiming that Britain should not join the single currency for the lifetimes of the current and next Parliament, a period of some ten years. The Conservative Party will thus officially oppose entry at the next general election and campaign for a 'No' vote in a referendum held in this period, though backbenchers would be allowed a free vote on the parliamentary legislation and be free to campaign for a referendum 'Yes' vote. The moderate Euro-sceptic line is evident in other policy areas, Hague stating in his first conference speech as leader that 'there is a limit to European integration and... in my opinion, we are near that limit now'.[7] Euro-sceptic voices are strongly represented in the Shadow Cabinet: John Redwood and Michael Howard have claimed that the EU is a threat to the nation-state, are hostile to the single currency in principle and are keen to repatriate policy competences.

The leadership's new stance on EMU is still in part a pragmatic one designed, like its 'wait and see' predecessor, to contain Conservative divisions. It is broadly acceptable to much of the parliamentary party and the voluntary party, though hardline Euro-sceptics are opposed to entry at any time as a matter of principle, while pro-European concern was soon made apparent by the resignation of two Conservative frontbenchers and criticism from Clarke and Heseltine. Within months of the election defeat, Major and Clarke stated that Britain should not be in the first wave of single currency entrants.[8] For Major, the lack of sufficient lasting convergence between European currencies and concerns about political pressure on the European Central Bank made EMU entry 'a risk too far' for the foreseeable future, noting that, even if there were an overwhelming economic case for entry some day, the political implications are 'unpalatable'. Clarke also cited the lack of long-term convergence as cause for opposing first wave entry, but is broadly supportive of the single currency and will support entry in a second wave should EMU prove successful. Major's support helped Hague's cause but angered Euro-sceptics who felt, albeit without compelling evidence, that a similar statement before the election would have strengthened the Conservative case.

The parliamentary Conservative Party remains divided on European issues. Euro-scepticism has pushed the Conservative politics of nationhood towards a more doctrinaire manifestation, alienating Europhile Tories. Pro-European MPs Emma Nicholson and Hugh Dykes left the party to join the Liberal Democrats, while remaining pro-Europeans had few inhibitions about disobeying the leadership line, putting principle before party loyalty as Euro-sceptics had done under Major. Philip Norton's analysis of the post-election parliamentary party revealed that the balance between the Euro-sceptic Right (30 per cent of Conservative MPs), the pro-European Left (21 per cent) and the party faithful (50 per cent) had not been greatly altered, the scale of the election defeat nullifying the relative strength of Euro-sceptics among new Conservative candidates.[9] Crucially though, the centre of gravity lies with a moderate Euro-sceptic position as, in addition to the Right, a majority of the party faithful (some 29 per cent of the party) are Euro-sceptic leaning. Norton's analysis also indicated that support for Hague in the leadership contest, as with Major in 1990, came disproportionately from the party faithful, Hague picking up the majority of Euro-sceptic votes only on the third ballot and then by a margin of less than two to one. Hague was not the preferred choice of the Euro-sceptics; this, plus the new leader's unwillingness to oppose EMU entry in principle, means he cannot rely on their support as a matter of course.

The moderate Euro-sceptic elements in Major's vision of a flexible, deregulated Europe of nation-states are likely to be further embellished by opposition to early involvement in EMU and demands for a limited repatriation of policies. But further integration and a more positive British role in the EU under Labour would make it more difficult to win domestic and European allies for such a package and present the Conservative vision of the EU as realistic, achievable and beneficial to British interests. Euro-sceptics believe that a vigorous 'No' campaign in an EMU referendum would revive

Conservative fortunes and weaken the Labour Government, but a concerted anti-single currency stance also threatens to split the party while some moderate Euro-sceptics recognize that excessive anti-European rhetoric can be counter-productive. Conservative opposition to EMU entry also threatens to undermine further relations with the City and British industry. Since the 1997 election, the CBI has indicated its support for entry into a successful single currency while the government is actively preparing business for eventual entry. Should the Conservatives oppose EMU entry despite warnings from the financial and business communities that exclusion would be damaging to British interests, a divorce between the interests of the Conservative Party and the national interest, which Major talked of in the 1997 campaign, might become more apparent.

RETHINKING THE CONSERVATIVE NATION

Alongside these statecraft challenges, long-term changes to the nation-state and national identity pose important questions of the conservative concept of the nation. British conservative thought has been slow to react to a revived interest in concepts of nationality, patriotism, community and citizenship by political theorists uneasy with liberal individualism. Much communitarian thought is hostile to conservative and New Right thinking, but a number of the themes it addresses and promotes are of relevance to contemporary conservatism.[10] Communitarian claims that the free market, individualist ethos of Thatcherism damaged the traditional institutions and practices of civil society have been prominent in British political discourse in the 1990s. Thus John Gray claims that the hegemony of neo-liberal thought on the British Right means 'the conditions under which conservatism as a coherent form of political thought and practice no longer exist', Thatcherism having undermined a core element of conservatism, namely the belief that neither markets nor political institutions can be treated as autonomous from the culture in which they are found.[11]

Nonetheless, Conservatives have undertaken a re-evaluation of the relationship between markets and communities, one of the most significant being David Willetts' attempt to marry the two in a 'civic conservatism'. Willetts recognizes that 'the communitarians are on to something and to retreat into simple-minded individualism is not true to the Conservative condition', but criticizes communitarian thought for looking to state action to foster solidarity and for its abstract view of community.[12] He thus places free markets in the particular context of the institutions and traditions of British political culture and civil society, claiming that the market, enterprise and private property are deeply embedded in Britain's history as a nation of 'traders and developers, entrepreneurs and speculators, free-booters and buccaneers'.[13] Civic conservatism believes that Britain is 'not a lumpy enough country' but its notion of citizenship and intermediate institutions are limited in character.

As noted in Chapter 3, contemporary conservative thinking on the concept of the nation has coalesced around two approaches, a political account of the nation which looks to a limited politics of state patriotism and a cultural account stressing the pre-political basis of nationhood and a common culture. Willetts offers a political account, a 'micro-conservatism' in which the nation-state is one among a series of communities: 'a shared cultural tradition, limited government, the free market and loyalty to the central institutions of the nation-state, are the integrating forces in which a conservative trusts'.[14] The state's role in upholding the shared political culture and an integrative, state patriotism is a limited one; the diverse communities within civil society have significant autonomy. 'The nation-state can command our loyalty as the protector of these communities but we certainly cannot look to it as one organic whole embodying detailed moral purposes which we all share.'[15]

Scruton's cultural conservatism rejects contractual membership as a basis for national unity, focusing instead on the cultural basis of national identity, that is a shared language, shared associations, shared history and a common culture.

> Nations have an identity through time which is distinct from that of the state, and independent of institutions, even those dearest to its people ... the identity of a nation through time has a clear moral aspect, and the reaffirmation of this identity, through acts of pride and contrition, is a part of belonging and of living under immovable obligations.[16]

Allegiance to authority is a central feature of British nationhood, but is undermined by multiculturalism as competing loyalties within the nation-state undermine obligation, shared loyalties and state authority.

David Miller has claimed that 'nationality is not a conservative idea' as it 'invokes the activist idea of a people collectively determining its destiny' whereas conservatism is concerned with 'politics as a limited activity'.[17] But activist politics are best viewed as associated with ideological nationalism, which conservatives are often uneasy about, rather than with patriotism or the concept of the nation *per se*. Indeed, rather than treating conservative politics and nationhood as uneasy bedfellows, it has been argued in this book that British Conservatism has developed a coherent concept of the nation built around the limited politics of conservative state patriotism. The conservative nation is an amalgam of civic and cultural elements, linking a concern for limited government and 'little platoons' with a defence of the nation-state and shared political culture. State patriotism based on a shared civic culture, allegiance to common institutions and membership of a historic community offers a sense of national identity and commonality. Here citizens share a sense of belonging and a common idea of a society with a long-lived but evolving constitutional framework characterized by limited politics and shared traditions. The nation has both civic and cultural elements, with peoples linked by citizenship and political culture looking to build a common future for the national community. Thus, the authors of the 1996 Conservative Political Centre report, *Strengthening the United Kingdom*, depicted Britishness as a form of constitutional patriotism denoting allegiance to the constitution and its underlying principles, while allowing for diverse identities within this framework.[18]

But neither the civic nor cultural conservative accounts of the nation is fully equipped to deal with the current challenges to British identity and conservative politics. The myth of national and cultural homogeneity espoused by cultural conservatives misrepresents the basis of British nationhood and is unwilling to accept or adapt to the inevitable, but gradual, changes in national identity which occur over time.[19] The political account of the nation offers a more attractive vision of Britishness in which diverse identities coexist within a framework of common adherence to existing institutions and values such as the rule of law. A revitalised conservative idea of nationhood requires that the state both fosters a common identity and respects devolved power and dual identities so that loyalty to the whole is not undermined by allegiance to the particular, but gains vitality from it. But when linking state patriotism with the defence of a shared political culture, recent manifestations of the conservative nation have tended to embrace English cultural values and downplay the importance of elected local institutions. The constitutional settlement which the Conservative Party and conservative idea of the nation celebrates has also been bedevilled by legimitacy problems in recent years, public opinion favouring significant reforms of parliament, the constitution and the monarchy rather than viewing them as valued elements of British identity in their current form.

Both the cultural and political accounts oppose further European integration, often maintaining a strong attachment to the nation-state and an uncritical view of sovereignty. Yet the problems which Conservatism and the Conservative Party face in respect of the politics of nationhood reflect broader questions about the continued efficacy of the nation-state and national sovereignty. The globalization thesis claims that in an increasingly interdependent world of global markets and communications, nation-states have less autonomy, their capacity to achieve core policy goals and exercise sovereignty within their borders diminished.[20] Although useful in recognizing important changes in the world economy and the erosion of state autonomy, exponents of the globalization thesis underestimate the continued significant role of the nation-state, plus the legitimacy and resilience of both it and national identity.[21]

Sovereignty is a key theme in the Conservative politics of nationhood, but treating it in an absolutist or zero-sum manner precludes effective analysis of the impact of European integration on the British state and society. A pluralistic approach, treating sovereignty as a multi-dimensional concept, is more fruitful but it also needs to be assessed in conjunction with concepts of power, legitimacy and autonomy.[22] *De jure* sovereignty has clearly been eroded by EU membership given, for example, the supremacy of Community law and the extension of QMV and Community competence. European integration has also had repercussions for the location of sovereign authority within the nation-state. In some respects, executive autonomy has been enhanced by the dominant role national governments play in shaping major EU decisions. But developments in the Single Market, regional policy and EMU constrain executive autonomy, giving supranational institutions and domestic actors an enhanced role in the EU's multi-level policy-making process.[23]

In the context of the shrinking capacity for effective state action, transferring or 'pooling' formal sovereignty in the EU can enhance its *de facto* sovereignty or policy capacity. Through EU membership, governments may gain greater executive autonomy in the domestic arena, more effectively manage interdependence and achieve socio-economic policy outcomes which may otherwise prove beyond their reach. However, as noted in Chapter 4, Britain's 'awkward partner' status within the EU and the problematic adaptation of its political system to membership have limited the extent to which the capacity of the British state and government might be enhanced.

In a number of Member States, EU membership is bound up with state identity, resistance to further integration being more evident in states such as Britain and Denmark where sovereignty is central to nationhood.[24] The erosion of national sovereignty has not been matched by an equivalent erosion of national identity: the nation-state remains the focal point of identity and legitimacy. Neither has the development of the EU been matched by that of a European identity, although multiculturalism, regionalism and the EU's Citizenship of the Union signal the emergence of more pluralistic forms of citizenship and identity politics.[25]

The political and conceptual difficulties identified in this and previous chapters show that instead of achieving a comfortable hegemony, British Conservatism has found the politics of nationhood problematic territory in recent years. European integration and the erosion of state autonomy will continue to pose significant challenges for a Conservative politics of nationhood – both Conservative statecraft and the conservative concept of the nation – which is still largely premised upon the defence of the nation-state and national sovereignty. Domestically, a multicultural society, legislative devolution and attempts by the Labour Government to modernize British identity will also require a reworking of the Conservative politics of nationhood. Pragmatic moves towards a reforming, pro-European centre ground would have political benefits and mark a development of themes evident in an earlier Conservative national strategy: but it would erode the distinctiveness of the Conservative politics of nationhood. Alternatively, further moves in the direction of a nationalist strategy built around Euroscepticism and English nationalism would establish a clear Conservative vision of the nation-state and national identity, but would consign the party to a reactive and outdated view of the nation-state and might allow Labour to establish predominance in the politics of nationhood. A modernization of British national identity shaped from top-down by a Labour Government but reflecting wider changes in a plural British society, particularly the popular support for institutional and cultural change evident after the death of Diana, Princess of Wales, would have significant repercussions for the

Conservative Party and the politics of nationhood. The Conservative Party has benefited from being seen as a responsible national party in tune with the instincts and values of the British people. But in the late 1990s Conservatives risk finding that this key weapon in their armoury has lost its potency in a changing environment, is prone to inflict more damage on the Conservative Party than on its former targets, or has been seized by a Labour Government intent on using the politics of nationhood to its own advantage.

Notes and References

INTRODUCTION

1. M. Thatcher, *The Keith Joseph Memorial Lecture: Liberty and Limited Government*. (London: Centre for Policy Studies, 1996) pp. 9–10; T. Garel-Jones, 'Patriots Must be Europeans', *The Independent*, 6 June 1996; J. E. Powell, *Enoch Powell on 1992*. Edited by Richard Ritchie. (London: Anaya Publishers, 1989) p. 126; J. Major, speech to a Conservative election press conference, *The Guardian*, 17 April 1997.

1 CONSERVATISM AND THE POLITICS OF NATIONHOOD

1. H. Cunningham, 'The Conservative Party and Patriotism', in R. Colls and P. Dodd (eds), *Englishness: Politics and Culture, 1880–1930*. (London: Croom Helm, 1986) pp. 283–307.
2. See H. Kearney, *The British Isles: A History of Four Nations*. (Cambridge: Cambridge University Press, 1994); A. Grant and K. Stringer (eds), *Uniting the Kingdom? The Making of British History*. (London: Routledge, 1995); B. Crick, 'The Sense of Identity of the Indigenous British', *New Community*, 21 (1995) pp. 167–82.
3. See C. Tilly (ed.), *The Formation of National States in Western Europe*. (Princeton: Princeton University Press, 1975).
4. E. Hobsbawm and T. Ranger (eds), *The Invention of Tradition*. (Cambridge: Cambridge University Press, 1983).
5. See A. Fletcher, 'The First Century of English Protestantism and the Growth of National Identity', in S. Mews (ed.), *Religion and National Identity*. Studies in Church History, Vol. 18. (Oxford: Basil Blackwell, 1982) pp. 309–17. See also, Grant and Stringer, *Uniting the Kingdom?*, Part II of which explores medieval foundations of English identity and Part III, the Tudor and Stuart period.
6. H. Kohn, 'The Genesis and Character of English Nationalism', *Journal of the History of Ideas*, 1 (1940) pp. 69–94.
7. G. Newman, *The Rise of English Nationalism: A Cultural History, 1740–1830*. (London: Weidenfeld and Nicolson, 1987); B. Crick, 'The English and the British', in B. Crick (ed.), *National Identities: The Constitution of the United Kingdom*. (London: Blackwell, 1991) pp. 90–104; S. Haseler, *The English Tribe: Identity, Nation and Europe*. (London: Macmillan, 1996) Chs 1 and 2.
8. On radical patriotism, see H. Cunningham, 'The Language of Patriotism', in R. Samuel, *Patriotism: The Making and Unmaking of British National Identity*. Vol. 1. (London: Routledge, 1989) pp. 57–89. New Right interpretations include A. Macfarlane, *The Origins of English Individualism: The Family, Property and Social Transition*. (Oxford:

Blackwell, 1978) and J .C. D. Clark, 'The History of Britain: A Composite State in a Europe des Patries', in J. C. D. Clark (ed.), *Ideas and Politics in Modern Britain*. (London: Macmillan, 1990) pp. 32–49.
9. L. Colley, *Britons: Forging the Nation, 1707–1837*. (London: Yale University Press, 1992). See also, Grant and Stringer, *Uniting the Kingdom?*, Part IV.
10. D. Marquand, 'The Twilight of the British State? Henry Dubb versus Sceptred Awe', *Political Quarterly*, 64 (1993) pp. 210–21; D. Marquand, 'After Whig Imperialism? Can There be a New British Identity', *New Community*, 21 (1995) pp. 183–94; Crick, 'The Sense of Identity of the Indigenous British'.
11. Colley, *Britons*, pp. 195–236; H. T. Dickinson, 'Popular Conservatism and the French Wars, 1789–1815', in H. T. Dickinson (ed.), *Britain and the French Revolution, 1789–1815*. (London: Macmillan, 1989) pp. 103–25; F. O'Gorman, 'Pitt and the "Tory" Reaction to the French Revolution, 1789–1815', in Dickinson, *Britain and the French Revolution*, pp. 21–37.
12. L. Colley, 'Whose Nation? Class and National Consciousness in Britain, 1750–1830', *Past and Present*, 113 (1986) p. 109.
13. D. Miller, *Philosophy and Ideology in Hume's Political Thought*. (Oxford: Clarendon Press, 1981). Hume rejected myths of a continuous English national history and claimed that the diversity of English society meant it had no clear national character. Rather than being an organic community, 'a nation is nothing but a collection of inidvidual s'; D. Hume, 'Of National Characters', in *The Philosophical Works*. Vol. 3. Edited by T. Green & T. Grose. (Germany: Scintia Verlay Allen, 1964) p. 244. See also H. Bolingbroke, *The Works of Lord Bolingbroke*. (London: Frank Cass, 1967).
14. F. O'Gorman, *Edmund Burke: His Political Philosophy*. (London: George Allen and Unwin, 1973), and M. Freeman, *Edmund Burke and the Critique of Political Radicalism*. (Oxford: Basil Blackwell, 1980). Burke's 'theory of nationality' is discussed in A. Cobban, *Edmund Burke and the Revolt against the Eighteenth Century*. (London: George Allen and Unwin, 1962) Ch. 4.
15. On conservatism and conservative values see A. Aughey, G. Jones and W. Riches, *The Conservative Political Tradition in Britain and the United States*. (London: Pinter, 1992); R. Eatwell and N. O'Sullivan (eds), *The Nature of the Right*. (London: Pinter, 1989); T. Honderich, *Conservatism*. (London: Hamish Hamilton, 1990); A. Vincent, 'British Conservatism and the Problem of Ideology', *Political Studies*, 42 (1994) pp. 204–27.
16. Quoted in J. Casey, 'One Nation: The Politics of Race', *The Salisbury Review*, 1 (1982) p. 23.
17. F. Dreyer, *Burke's History: A Study in Whig Orthodoxy*. (Ontario: Laevier University Press, 1979) pp. 54–67.
18. E. Burke, 'Speech on Reform of Representation in the House of Commons, 1784', in *The Speeches of the Right Hon. Edmund Burke*. (Dublin: James Duffy, 1867) p. 408.
19. E. Burke, *Reflections on the Revolution in France*. (London: Penguin, 1986 edition) p. 100.

20. On limited politics, see N. O'Sullivan, *Conservatism*. (London: J. M. Dent, 1976). On philosophical scepticism see L. Allison, *Right Principles: A Conservative Philosophy of Politics*. (Oxford: Basil Blackwell, 1984).
21. E. Burke, 'Appeal from the New to the Old Whigs', quoted in F. O'Gorman, *British Conservatism: Conservative Thought from Burke to Thatcher*. (London: Longman, 1986) p. 96.
22. Burke, *Reflections*, p. 181.
23. On America, see 'Speech on Conciliation with the Colonies' and on India, 'From a Speech in Opening the Impeachment of Warren Hastings', in B. Hill (ed.), *Edmund Burke: On Government, Politics and Society*. (Brighton: Fontana, 1975) pp. 159–87 and 263–76. On Ireland, see C. C. O'Brien, 'Introduction' to Burke, *Reflections*. (London: Penguin, 1986) pp. 30–41.
24. M. Thompson, 'Ideas of Europe during the French Revolution and Napoleonic Wars', *Journal of the History of Ideas*, 55 (1994) pp. 40–7.
25. P. Arter, *Nationalism*. (London: Edward Arnold, 1989) pp. 14–18.
26. W. H. Greenleaf, *The British Political Tradition*. Vol. 2. *The Ideological Heritage*. (London: Methuen, 1983); P. Norton and A. Aughey, *Conservatives and Conservatism*. (London: Temple Smith, 1981) pp. 53–89.
27. On conservatism and political practice, see Norton and Aughey, *Conservatives and Conservatism*; J. Fair and J. Hutcheson, 'British Conservatism in the Twentieth Century: An Emerging Ideological Tradition', *Albion*, 19 (1987) pp. 549–78.
28. R. Blake, *The Conservative Party from Peel to Thatcher*. (London: Fontana, 1986) p. 130. P. Smith, *Disraelian Conservatism and Social Reform*. (London: Routledge and Kegan Paul, 1967) p. 323, depicts populist patriotism as more important than social reform to the Disraelian legacy.
29. B. Disraeli, *A Vindication of the English Constitution*. (London, 1835); J. Vincent, *Disraeli*. (Oxford: Oxford University Press, 1990).
30. Reprinted in T. E. Kebbel, *Speeches of the Earl of Beaconsfield*. Vol. 2. (London, 1882).
31. B. Coleman, *Conservatism and the Conservative Party in Nineteenth Century Britain*. (London: Edward Arnold, 1988).
32. P. Marsh, *The Discipline of Popular Government: Lord Salisbury's Domestic Statecraft, 1881–1902*. (Brighton: Harvester Press, 1978).
33. R. E. Quinault, 'Lord Randolph Churchill and Tory Democracy, 1880–1885', *The Historical Journal*, 22 (1979) pp. 141–65.
34. Smith, *Disraelian Conservatism and Social Reform*, p. 3.
35. M. Pugh, 'Popular Conservatism in Britain: Continuity and Change, 1880–1987', *Journal of British Studies*, 27 (1988) pp. 254–82; J. Cornford, 'The Transformation of Conservatism in the Late Nineteenth Century', *Victorian Studies*, 7 (1963) pp. 35–66; and R. McKenzie and A. Silver, *Angels in Marble: Working Class Conservatives in Urban England*. (London: Heinemann, 1968).
36. M. Pugh, *The Tories and the People, 1880–1935*. (Oxford: Basil Blackwell, 1985).
37. McKenzie and Silver, *Angels in Marble*, pp. 72–3.
38. D. Cannadine, 'The Context, Performance and Meaning of Ritual: The

British Monarchy and the "Invention of Tradition", c1820–1977', in Hobsbawm and Ranger, *The Invention of Tradition*, pp. 101–64; Pugh, *The Tories and the People*, pp. 72–8.
39. T. Nairn, *The Enchanted Glass: Britain and its Monarchy*. (London: Radius, 1988) Ch. 2.
40. Cunningham, 'The Conservative Party and Patriotism', p. 302.
41. G. Bennett (ed.), *The Concept of Empire: Burke to Attlee, 1774–1947*. 2nd edn (London: Adam and Charles Black, 1962) Parts 12–13; R. Koerner and H. dan Schmidt, *Imperialism: The Story and Significance of a Political Word, 1840–1960*. (Cambridge: Cambridge University Press, 1964) Chs 4–7; and P. Cain and A. Hopkins, *British Imperialism: Innovation and Expansion, 1688–1914*. (London: Longman, 1993).
42. R. Price, 'Society, Status and Jingoism: The Social Roots of Lower Middle Class Patriotism, 1870–1900', in G. Crossick (ed.), *The Lower Middle Class in Britain, 1870–1914*. (London: Croom Helm, 1977) pp. 89–112; J. M. MacKenzie, *Propaganda and Empire: The Manipulation of British Public Opinion, 1880–1960*. (Manchester: Manchester University Press, 1985).
43. P. Rich, *Race and Empire in British Politics*. (Cambridge: Cambridge University Press, 1986); C. Bolt, 'Race and the Victorians', in C. C. Eldridge (ed.), *British Imperialism in the Nineteenth Century*. (London: Macmillan, 1984) pp. 126–47.
44. See C. A. Bodelsen, *Studies in Mid-Victorian Imperialism*. (London, Heinemann, 1960) Ch. 3; A. Thompson, 'The Language of Imperialism and the Meanings of Empire: Imperial Discourse in British Politics, 1895–1914', *Journal of British Studies*, 36 (1997) pp. 147–77.
45. Marquand, 'After Whig Imperialism?', p. 188.
46. E. H. H. Green, *The Crisis of Conservatism: The Politics, Economics and Ideology of the British Conservative Party, 1880–1914*. (London: Routledge, 1995) pp. 1–23.
47. N. Blewett, 'Free Fooders, Balfourites, Whole Hoggers: Factionalism within the Unionist Party, 1906–10', *The Historical Journal*, 11 (1968) pp. 95–124.
48. J. Bulpitt, *Territory and Power in the United Kingdom: An Interpretation*. (Manchester: Manchester University Press, 1983) pp. 104–33.
49. Quoted in J. Mitchell, *Conservatives and the Union: A Study of Conservative Party Attitudes to Scotland*. (Edinburgh: Edinburgh University Press, 1990) p. 19.
50. S. Kendrick and D. McCrone, 'Politics in a Cold Climate: The Conservative Decline in Scotland', *Political Studies*, 37 (1989) pp. 589–603.
51. D. G. Boyce, 'The Marginal Britons: The Irish', in Colls and Dodd (eds), *Englishness*, pp. 230–53.
52. D. G. Boyce, *The Irish Question and British Politics, 1868–1986*. (London: Macmillan, 1986) pp. 23 and 28–33.
53. Boyce, 'The Marginal Britons', p. 235; Boyce, *The Irish Question*, p. 31.
54. A. V. Dicey, *England's Case Against Home Rule*. (Surrey: Richmond Publishing, 1973 edition). J. H. Grainger, *Patriotisms: Britain, 1900–1939*. (London: Routledge and Kegan Paul, 1986) p. 245, states that

'if there was a prototypical, United Kingdom, Anglo-Britannic nationalist, it was surely Dicey'.
55. Marsh, *The Discipline of Popular Government*, p. 68.
56. L. P. Curtis, *Coercion and Conciliation in Ireland, 1880–1892: A Study in Conservative Unionism*. (Princeton: Princeton University Press, 1963). On Chamberlain, see J. Loughlin, 'Joseph Chamberlain, English Nationalism and the Ulster Question', *History*, 77 (1992) pp. 202–19.
57. J. Fair, 'From Liberal to Conservative: The Flight of the Unionists after 1886', *Victorian Studies*, 29 (1986) pp. 291–314; J. France, 'Salisbury and the Liberal Unionists', in R. Blake and H. Cecil (eds), *Salisbury: The Man and his Policies*. (London: Macmillan, 1987) pp. 219–51.
58. C. Shannon, *Arthur J. Balfour and Ireland, 1874–1922*. (Washington DC: Catholic University of America Press, 1988) pp. 82–135; D. Dutton, *His Majesty's Loyal Opposition: The Unionist Party in Opposition, 1905–1915*. (Liverpool: Liverpool University Press, 1992) Ch. 9.
59. F. Coetzee, *For Party or Country: Nationalism and the Dilemmas of Popular Conservatism in Edwardian England*. (Oxford: Oxford University Press, 1989); G. Searle, 'The "Revolt from the Right" in Edwardian Britain', in P. Kennedy and A. Nicholls (eds), *Nationalist and Racialist Movements in Britain and Germany before 1914*. (London: Macmillan, 1981) pp. 21–39; A. Sykes, 'The Radical Right and the Crisis of Conservatism before the First World War', *The Historical Journal*, 26 (1983) pp. 661–76.
60. P. Jalland, 'United Kingdom Devolution, 1910–14: Political Panacea or Tactical Diversion?', *English Historical Review*, 94 (1979) pp. 757–85.
61. A. Bonar Law, 'Preface', in A. Balfour, *Against Home Rule: The Case for the Union*. (London: Frederick Warne, 1912) p. 13.
62. R. Murphy, 'Faction in the Conservative Party and the Home Rule Crisis, 1912–14', *History*, 71 (1986) pp. 222–34.
63. Boyce, 'The Marginal Britons', p. 242. See also T. Hennessey, 'Ulster Unionist Territorial and National Identities 1886–1893: Province, Ireland, Kingdom and Empire', *Irish Political Studies*, 3 (1993) pp. 21–36.
64. J. Turner, 'Letting Go: The Conservative Party and the End of Union with Ireland', in Grant and Stringer, *Uniting the Kingdom?*, pp. 255–74; Bulpitt, *Territory and Power in the United Kingdom*, pp. 129–30.
65. Notions of 'national character' gained popularity in this period. See P. Rich, 'A Question of Life and Death to England: Patriotism and the British Intellectuals, c1886–1945', *New Community*, 15 (1989) p. 499.
66. P. Williamson, 'The Doctrinal Politics of Stanely Baldwin', in M. Bentley (ed.), *Public and Private Doctrine: Essays in British History Presented to Maurice Cowling*. (Cambridge: Cambridge University Press, 1993) p. 191. See also, B. Schwarz, 'The Language of Constitutionalism: Baldwinite Conservatism', in *Formations of Nation and People*. (London: Routledge and Kegan Paul, 1984) pp. 1–18.
67. See S. Howe, 'Labour Patriotism 1939–83', in Samuel, *Patriotism*. Vol. 1, pp. 127–39; and M. Taylor, 'Patriotism, History and the Left in Twentieth Century Britain', *The Historical Journal*, 33 (1990) pp. 971–87. George Orwell provided the most significant socialist thinking on English identity. See G. Orwell, *England Your England and Other Essays*.

(London: Secker and Warburg, 1954), and 'The Lion and the Unicorn', in S. Orwell and I. Angus (eds), *The Collected Essays, Journalism and Letters of George Orwell*. Vol. 2. (London: Secker and Warburg, 1968) pp. 56–109. Here Orwell argued that 'patriotism has nothing to do with Conservatism. It is actually the opposite of Conservatism since it is a devotion to something that is always changing and yet is felt to be mystically the same.' (p. 103).

2 HEATH AND POWELL – TWO NATIONAL STRATEGIES

1. P. Rich, 'British Imperial Decline and the Forging of English Patriotic Memory, c1918–1968', *History of European Ideas*, 9 (1988) pp. 669–77.
2. The term 'authoritarian individualism' is used by Clark, 'The History of Britain', pp. 44–5.
3. D. Goldsworthy, *Colonial Issues in British Politics, 1945–61*. (Oxford: Clarendon Press, 1971) pp. 182–8 and 193–202.
4. Goldsworthy, *Colonial Issues in British Politics*, pp. 169–73 and 289–95.
5. Goldsworthy, *Colonial Issues in British Politics*, pp. 295–300; H. Berrington, 'The Conservative Party: Revolts and Pressures, 1955–61', *Political Quarterly*, 32 (1961) pp. 363–73; M. Beloff, 'The Crisis and its Consequences for the Conservative Party', in R. Louis and R. Owen (eds), *Suez 1956: The Crisis and its Consequences*. (Oxford: Clarendon Press, 1989) pp. 319–34.
6. P. Norton, *Dissension in the House of Commons, 1945–74*. (London: Macmillan, 1975) pp. 255–6; P. Seyd, 'Factionalism Within the Conservative Party: The Monday Club', *Government and Opposition*, 17 (1972) pp. 464–87.
7. A. Horne, *Macmillan, 1957–1986*. (London: Papermac, 1991) pp. 173–211 and 388–425.
8. D. Sanders, *Losing an Empire, Finding a Role: British Foreign Policy Since 1945*. (London: Macmillan, 1990) pp. 101–12.
9. See J. Young, *Britain and European Unity*. (London: Macmillan, 1993) pp. 43–66; W. Kaiser, *Using Europe, Abusing the Europeans: Britain and European Integration, 1945–63*. (London: Macmillan, 1996) Chs 2–4.
10. Kaiser, *Using Europe, Abusing the Europeans*, Ch. 5; J. Tratt, *The Macmillan Government and Europe*. (London: Macmillan, 1997).
11. H. Macmillan, *At the End of the Day*. (London: Macmillan, 1973) p. 5.
12. D. Dutton, 'Anticipating Maastricht: The Conservative Party and Britain's First Application to Join the European Community', *Contemporary Record*, 7 (1993) pp. 522–40; R. Butt, 'The Common Market and Conservative Party Politics, 1961–2', *Government and Opposition*, 2 (1967) pp. 372–86; and N. Ashford, 'The European Economic Community', in Z. Layton-Henry (ed.), *Conservative Party Politics*. (London: Macmillan, 1980) pp. 97–102.
13. Dutton, 'Anticipating Maastricht', p. 527; Butt, 'The Common Market and Conservative Party Politics', p. 386.
14. H. Macmillan, *Britain, the Commonwealth and Europe*. (London: Conservative Central Office, 1961) pp. 6–7.

15. Ashford, 'The European Economic Community', p. 102; Kaiser, *Using Europe, Abusing the Europeans*, pp. 146–51.
16. Horne, *Macmillan*, p. 447; Kaiser, *Using Europe, Abusing the Europeans*, pp. 200–3.
17. Z. Layton-Henry, 'The State and New Commonwealth Immigration: 1951–56', *New Community*, 14 (1987) pp. 64–75; J. Ramsden, *The Winds of Change: Macmillan to Heath, 1957–1975*. (London: Macmillan, 1996) pp. 41–6.
18. J. Bulpitt, 'Continuity, Autonomy and Peripheralisation: The Anatomy of the Centre's Race Statecraft in England', in Z. Layton-Henry and P. Rich (eds), *Race, Government and Politics in Britain*. (London: Macmillan, 1986) pp. 17–44.
19. C. Waters, '"Dark Strangers" in Our Midst: Discourses on Race and Nation in Britain, 1947–63', *Journal of British Studies*, 36 (1997), pp. 207–38.
20. P. Foot, *Immigration and Race in British Politics*. (Harmondsworth: Penguin, 1965), pp. 124–60; Ramsden, *The Winds of Change*, pp. 151–2; Macmillan, *At the End of the Day*, pp. 73–83.
21. Z. Layton-Henry, *The Politics of Immigration*. (Oxford: Blackwell, 1992), pp. 75–6; Foot, *Immigration and Race in British Politics*, pp. 138–42.
22. Foot, *Immigration and Race in British Politics*, Chs 1–4.
23. Z. Layton-Henry, 'Immigration and the Heath Government', in S. Ball and A. Seldon (eds), *The Heath Government 1970–74: A Reappraisal*. (London: Longman, 1996) p. 216.
24. See A. Gamble, *The Conservative Nation*. (London: Routledge and Kegan Paul, 1974); Ball and Seldon, *The Heath Government*.
25. C. Lord, *British Entry to the European Community under the Heath Government of 1970–4*. (Aldershot: Dartmouth, 1993) p. 9.
26. E. Heath, 'Realism in British Foreign Policy', *Foreign Affairs*, 48 (1969) p. 40.
27. E. Heath, 'European Unity over the Next Ten Years: From Community to Union', *International Affairs*, 64 (1988) p. 199.
28. See W. Wallace, 'What Price Independence? Sovereignty and Interdependence in British Politics', *International Affairs*, 62 (1986), pp. 367–89; C. Lord, 'Sovereign or Confused? The "Great Debate" About British Entry to the European Community 20 Years On', *Journal of Common Market Studies*, 30 (1992) pp. 419–36; W. Kaiser, 'Using Europe and Abusing the Europeans: The Conservatives and the European Community', *Contemporary Record*, 8 (1994), pp. 387–8.
29. *Hansard*, Vol. 889, cols 1274–86, 9 April 1975.
30. Lord, *British Entry to the European Community*, pp. 36–44; *The United Kingdom and the European Communities*. (London: HMSO, 1971), Cm 8715.
31. See J. Young, 'The Heath Government and British Entry into the European Community', in Ball and Seldon, *The Heath Government*, p. 283, footnote 93.
32. Lord, *British Entry to the European Community*, p. 28; Heath, 'Realism in British Foreign Policy', pp. 43–50.
33. Kaiser, *Using Europe, Abusing the Europeans*, pp. 383–4.

34. Young, 'The Heath Government and British Entry', pp. 266–7.
35. Young, 'The Heath Government and British Entry', pp. 278–82.
36. Ashford, 'The European Economic Community', pp. 103–8 and 110–12; J. Critchley, 'Stresses and Strains in the Conservative Party', *Political Quarterly*, 44 (1973) pp. 401–10.
37. P. Norton, *Conservative Dissidents: Dissent Within the Parliamentary Conservative Party, 1970–74*. (London: Temple Smith, 1978) pp. 61–82.
38. S. Saggar, *Race and Politics in Britain*. (Hemel Hempstead: Harvester Wheatsheaf, 1992) pp. 77–92.
39. Z. Layton-Henry, 'Race, Electoral Strategy and the Major Parties', *Parliamentary Affairs*, 31 (1978) pp. 268–81.
40. Saggar, *Race and Politics in Britain*, pp. 82–93; Layton-Henry, *The Politics of Immigration*, pp. 46–56.
41. Norton, *Dissension in the House of Commons*, p. 280; Ramsden, *The Winds of Change*, pp. 290–3.
42. J. Edmonds and R. Behrens, 'Kippers, Kittens and Kipper-Boxes: Conservative Populists and Race Relations', *Political Quarterly*, 52 (1981) pp. 342–8.
43. A. Dummett and A. Nicol, *Subjects, Citizens, Aliens and Others: Nationality and Immigration Law*. (London: Weidenfeld and Nicolson, 1990) Ch. 11.
44. Ramsden, *The Winds of Change*, pp. 294–5.
45. Z. Layton-Henry, 'Immigration', in Layton-Henry, *Conservative Party Politics*, pp. 62–3.
46. D. Studlar, 'Policy Voting in Britain: The Coloured Immigration Issue in the 1964, 1966 and 1970 General Elections', *American Political Science Review*, 72 (1978) pp. 46–72. A more sceptical verdict is given in N. Deakin and J. Bourne, 'Powell, the Minorities and the 1970 Election', *Political Quarterly*, 41 (1970) pp. 399–415. D. Studlar, 'Elite Responsiveness or Elite Autonomy: British Immigration Policy Reconsidered', *Ethnic and Racial Studies*, 3 (1980) pp. 207–23, argues that 'members of the British political elite are responsive on the immigration issue because they think they have to be in order to survive politically'. (p. 217).
47. Dummett and Nicol, *Subjects, Citizens, Aliens and Others*, Ch. 12.
48. P. Norton, 'Intra-Party Dissent in the House of Commons: A Case Study of the Immigration Rules 1972', *Parliamentary Affairs*, 29 (1972) p. 404.
49. Layton-Henry, 'Immigration and the Heath Government', p. 234.
50. J. Mitchell, *Conservatives and the Union: A Study of Conservative Party Attitudes to Scotland*. (Edinburgh: Edinburgh University Press, 1990) pp. 8–14.
51. R. Crossman, *Diaries of a Cabinet Minister*. Vol. 2. (London: Hamish Hamilton, 1976) pp. 550–1.
52. D. W. Urwin, 'Scottish Conservatism: A Party Organisation in Transition', *Political Studies*, 14 (1966) pp. 145–62.
53. Mitchell, *Conservatives and the Union*, pp. 53–7; V. Bogdanor, 'Devolution', in Layton-Henry, *Conservative Party Politics*, pp. 79–82.
54. *Scotland's Government: The Report of the Scottish Constitutional*

Committee. (Edinburgh: Scottish Constitutional Committee, 1970), quote from p. 62. See also, Bogdanor, 'Devolution', pp. 82–5.
55. G. Smith, 'Devolution and Not Saying What You Mean', *The Spectator*, 26 February 1977; Mitchell, *Conservatives and the Union*, pp. 61–8.
56. Mitchell, *Conservatives and the Union*, pp. 69–74.
57. P. Arthur, 'The Heath Government and Northern Ireland', in Ball and Seldon, *The Heath Government*, pp. 235–58; B. O'Leary and J. McGarry, *The Politics of Antagonism: Understanding Northern Ireland.* (London: Athlone Press, 1993) pp. 183–5.
58. Arthur, 'The Heath Government and Northern Ireland', pp. 239–44; John Campbell, *Edward Heath: A Biography.* (London: Jonathan Cape, 1993), pp. 430–4.
59. B. Hadfield, 'The Constitution of Northern Ireland', in B. Hadfield (ed.), *Northern Ireland: Politics and the Constitution.* (Buckingham: Open University Press, 1992) pp. 1–12; Arthur, 'The Heath Government and Northern Ireland', pp. 244–8.
60. Arthur, 'The Heath Government and Northern Ireland', pp. 248–56; O'Leary and McGarry, *The Politics of Antagonism*, pp. 185–202; Campbell, *Edward Heath*, pp. 549–53.
61. P. Norton, 'Conservative Politics and the Abolition of Stormont', in P. Catterall and S. McDougall (eds), *The Northern Ireland Question in British Politics.* (London: Macmillan, 1996) pp. 129–42; Ramsden, *The Winds of Change*, pp. 341–4, reports that a working group rejected the option of standing Conservative candidates in Ulster.
62. J. E. Powell, *Enoch Powell on 1992.* Edited by R. Ritchie. (London: Anaya Publishers, 1989) p. 126.
63. J. E. Powell, *A Nation Not Afraid: The Thinking of Enoch Powell.* Edited by J. Wood. (London: B. T. Batsford, 1965) p. 24.
64. D. Schoen, *Enoch Powell and the Powellite*s. (London: Macmillan, 1977).
65. J. E. Powell, *Freedom and Reality.* Edited by J. Wood. (Surrey: Elliot Right Wing Books, 1969) pp. 242–57.
66. Quoted in P. Cosgrave, *The Lives of Enoch Powell.* (London: Bodley Head, 1989) p. 300.
67. Powell, *A Nation Not Afraid*, p. 136.
68. Powell, *A Nation Not Afraid*, p. 137.
69. Powell, *A Nation Not Afraid*, p. 139.
70. J .E. Powell, *Reflections of a Statesman: The Writings and Speeches of Enoch Powell*. Edited by R. Collings. (London: Bellew Publishing, 1991) p. 502.
71. Powell, *Reflections of a Statesman*, pp. 34–5.
72. J. E. Powell, *The Common Market: Renegotiate or Come Out.* (Surrey: Elliot Right Wing Books, 1973) pp. 41–2.
73. *Hansard*, Vol. 809, cols 1372–3, 21 January 1971.
74. *Hansard*, Vol. 831, cols 699–703, 17 February 1972; Powell, *Enoch Powell on 1992*, Chs 2 and 5.
75. Powell, *Reflections of a Statesman*, p. 476.
76. Powell, *Reflections of a Statesman*, p. 257.
77. *Hansard*, Vol. 809, cols 1376–7, 21 January 1971.
78. Powell, *Freedom and Reality*, pp. 246–57.

Notes and References

79. J. E. Powell, *Still to Decide*. Edited by J. Wood. (Surrey: Elliot Right Wing Books, 1972) p. 177.
80. Cosgrave, *The Lives of Enoch Powell*, pp. 373–82; R. Lewis, *Enoch Powell: Principle in Politics*. (London: Cassell, 1979) pp. 204–19.
81. Powell, *Reflections of a Statesman*, pp. 507–10.
82. *Hansard*, Vol. 922, cols 1809–20, 16 February 1976; Lewis, *Enoch Powell*, pp. 241–5.
83. The speech is reprinted in Powell, *Freedom and Reality*, pp. 213–19. See also, Schoen, *Enoch Powell and the Powellites*, pp. 25–44; P. Foot, *The Rise of Enoch Powell*. (London: Penguin, 1969).
84. Lewis, *Enoch Powell*, pp. 122–7.
85. Quoted in Foot, *The Rise of Enoch Powell*, p. 119.
86. Powell, *Reflections of a Statesman*, p. 35.
87. B. Parekh, 'The "New Right" and the Politics of Nationhood', in G. Cohen et al., *The New Right: Image and Reality*. (London: Runnymede Trust, 1986) pp. 33–43.
88. Cosgrave, *The Lives of Enoch Powell*, p. 248.
89. J. E. Powell, 'The United Kingdom and Immigration', *The Salisbury Review*, 7 (1988) pp. 40–5.
90. *Hansard*, Vol. 997, col. 967, 21 January 1981.
91. Cosgrave, *The Lives of Enoch Powell*, p. 476.

3 THATCHERISM AND THE POLITICS OF NATIONHOOD

1. A. King, 'Margaret Thatcher: The Style of a Prime Minister', in A. King (ed.), *The British Prime Minister*. 2nd edn (London: Macmillan, 1985) pp. 96–140.
2. See G. Ionescu, *Leadership in an Interdependent World*. (Harlow: Longman, 1991) Ch. 3, and P. Sharp, *Thatcher's Diplomacy: The Revival of British Foreign Policy*. (London: Macmillan, 1997), both of whom emphasize the foreign policy significance of Thatcher's patriotism and defence of national sovereignty.
3. H. Thompson, 'Joining the ERM: Analysing a Core Executive Policy Disaster', in R. Rhodes and P. Dunleavy (eds), *Prime Minister, Cabinet and Core Executive*. (London: Macmillan, 1995) pp. 248–74.
4. P. Riddell, *The Thatcher Government*. (Oxford: Martin Robertson, 1983) p. 7.
5. Quoted in V. Bevan, *The Development of British Immigration Law*. (London: Croom Helm, 1986) p. 85.
6. I. Gilmour, *Dancing with Dogma: Britain under Thatcherism*. (London: Pocket Books, 1992).
7. Greenleaf, *The British Political Tradition*, Vol. 2.
8. F. A. Hayek, 'Why I am Not a Conservative', in *The Constitution of Liberty*. (London: Routledge and Kegan Paul, 1960) pp. 397–411. See also B. Rowland, *Ordered Liberty and the Constitutional Framework: The Political Thought of F. A. Hayek* (New York: Greenwood Press, 1987).
9. F. A. Hayek, *Law, Legislation and Liberty*. Vol. 2. (London: Routledge, 1982) p. 58.

10. Hayek, *Law, Legislation and Liberty*. Vol. 3, p. 56.
11. M. Oakeshott, *On Human Conduct*. (Oxford: Clarendon Press, 1975) and M. Oakeshott, *Rationalism in Politics and Other Essays*. (London: Methuen, 1962). See also P. Franco, *The Political Philosophy of Michael Oakeshott*. (London: Yale University Press, 1990).
12. R. Scruton, *The Meaning of Conservatism*. 2nd edn (London: Macmillan, 1984). See also C. Covell, *The Redefinition of Conservatism*. (London: Macmillan, 1986).
13. R. Scruton, 'In Defence of the Nation', in Clark, *Ideas and Politics in Modern Britain*, pp. 53–86.
14. G. Dawson, 'Freedom, State and Tradition', *Salisbury Review*, 2 (1984), pp. 47–8.
15. Casey, 'One Nation: The Politics of Race'.
16. S. Hall, *The Hard Road to Renewal: Thatcherism and the Crisis of the Left*. (London: Lawrence and Wishart, 1988) pp. 150–60.
17. See A. M. Smith, *New Right Discourse on Race and Sexuality: Britain 1968–90*. (Cambridge: Cambridge University Press, 1994).
18. A. O'Shea, 'Trusting the People: How Does Thatcherism Work?', in *Formations of Nation and People*, pp. 19–41 (p. 20).
19. O'Shea, 'Trusting the People', p. 25.
20. Quoted in A. Barnett, *Iron Britannia*. (London: Allison and Busby, 1982) p. 30.
21. Sharp, *Thatcher's Diplomacy*, Chs 4 and 5.
22. Quoted in Barnett, *Iron Britannia*, p. 150.
23. Quoted in Barnett, *Iron Britannia*, pp. 151–2.
24. R. Gray, 'The Falklands Factor', in S. Hall and M. Jacques (eds), *The Politics of Thatcherism*. (London: Lawrence and Wishart, 1983) pp. 271–80; E. Hobsbawm, 'Falklands Fallout', in Hall and Jacques, *The Politics of Thatcherism*, pp. 257–70.
25. S. Letwin, *The Anatomy of Thatcherism*. (London: Fontana, 1992).
26. Letwin, *The Anatomy of Thatcherism*, pp. 304 and 306. See also R. W. Johnson, 'Pomp and Circumstance', in his *The Politics of Recession*. (London: Macmillan, 1985) pp. 224–55.
27. M. Thatcher, *The Downing Street Years*. (London: Harper Collins, 1993), pp. 753 and 595–6.
28. J. Bulpitt, 'The Discipline of the New Democracy: Mrs Thatcher's Domestic Statecraft', *Political Studies*, 34 (1986) pp. 19–39 (pp. 21 and 28).
29. J. Bulpitt, 'The European Question', in D. Marquand and A. Seldon (eds), *The Ideas that Shaped Post-War Britain*. (London: Fontana, 1996) pp. 214–56.
30. Bulpitt, *Territory and Power in the United Kingdom*.
31. Bulpitt, 'Continuity, Autonomy and Peripheralisation'.
32. A. Gamble, *The Free Economy and the Strong State: The Politics of Thatcherism*. 2nd edn (London, Macmillan, 1994) p. 4.
33. Gamble, *The Free Economy and the Strong State*, pp. 172 and 199.
34. A. Gamble, 'The Entrails of Thatcherism', *New Left Review*, 198 (1993) pp. 117–28.
35. D. Marquand, 'The Twilight of the British State?'

36. B. Jessop, K. Bonnett, S. Bromley and T. Ling, *Thatcherism: A Tale of Two Nations*. (Cambridge: Polity, 1988).
37. C. Hay, *Re-Stating Social and Political Change*. (Buckingham: Open University Press, 1996) pp. 127–57.
38. D. Marsh, 'Explaining "Thatcherite" Policies: Beyond Unidimensional Explanation', *Political Studies*, 43 (1995) pp. 595–613.
39. D. Marsh and R. Rhodes (eds), *Implementing Thatcherite Policies: Audit of an Era*. (Buckingham: Open University Press, 1992).
40. I. Crewe, 'The Thatcher Legacy', in A. King (ed.), *Britain at the Polls 1992*. (Chatham, NJ: Chatham House, 1992) pp. 1–28; P. Norton, 'The Lady's Not for Turning, But What About the Rest? Margaret Thatcher and the Conservative Party 1979–89', *Parliamentary Affairs*, 43 (1990) pp. 249–59.
41. J. Moon, 'Evaluating Thatcher: Sceptical Versus Synthetic Approaches', *Politics*, 14 (1994) pp. 43–9; Hay, *Re-Stating Social and Political Change*, pp. 151–3.
42. S. Ludlam and M. Smith, 'The Character of Contemporary Conservatism', in S. Ludlam and M. Smith (eds), *Contemporary British Conservatism*. (London: Macmillan, 1996) pp. 264–81.
43. Hay, *Re-Stating Social and Political Change*, pp. 158–73.
44. A. Gamble, 'The Crisis of Conservatism', *New Left Review*, 214 (1995) pp. 3–25.
45. Quoted in Haseler, *The English Tribe*, p. 65.

4 EUROPEAN INTEGRATION

1. R. Putnam, 'Diplomacy and Domestic Politics', *International Organization*, 42 (1988) pp. 427–61; S. Bulmer, 'Domestic Politics and European Community Policy-Making', *Journal of Common Market Studies*, 21 (1983) pp. 349–63.
2. S. Bulmer, 'Britain and European Integration: Of Sovereignty, Slow Adaptation and Semi-Detachment', in S. George (ed.), *Britain and the European Community: The Politics of Semi-Detachment*. (Oxford: Clarendon Press, 1992) pp. 1–29; S. George, 'A Reply to Buller', *Politics*, 15 (1995) pp. 43–7.
3. Bulpitt, 'The Discipline of the New Democracy'; Gamble, *The Free Economy and the Strong State*.
4. Sharp, *Thatcher's Diplomacy*, Chs 4 and 5.
5. Thatcher, *The Downing Street Years*, p. 545.
6. 'Europe – The Future', *Journal of Common Market Studies*, 23 (1984) pp. 73–81.
7. Thatcher, *The Downing Street Years*, pp. 550–4.
8. See A. Moravcsik, 'Negotiating the Single European Act: National Interests and Conventional Statecraft', *International Organization*, 45 (1991) pp. 19–56.
9. Thatcher, *The Downing Street Years*, p. 536.
10. Compare Thatcher, *The Downing Street Years*, p. 555 and N. Lawson, *The View From Number Eleven* (London: Corgi, 1993), pp. 893–4.

180 Notes and References

11. W. Wallace and H. Wallace, 'Strong State or Weak State in Foreign Policy? The Contradictions of Conservative Liberalism', *Public Administration*, 68 (1990) pp. 83–100.
12. Thatcher, *The Downing Street Years*, p. 547.
13. Thatcher, *The Downing Street Years*, p. 728.
14. M. Thatcher, *Britain and Europe*. Text of the speech delivered by the Prime Minister on 20 September 1988. (London: Conservative Political Centre, 1988).
15. Thatcher, *The Downing Street Years*, pp. 688–705; H. Thompson, *The British Conservative Government and the European Exchange Rate Mechanism 1979–94*. (London: Pinter, 1996); P. Stephens, *Politics and the Pound: The Tories, The Economy and Europe*. (London: Papermac, 1997).
16. Thatcher, *The Downing Street Years*, pp. 689–91; Lawson, *The View From Number Eleven*, pp. 888–913.
17. Thatcher, *The Downing Street Years*, pp. 709–15; Lawson, *The View From Number Eleven*, pp. 927–35; G. Howe, *Conflict of Loyalty*. (London: Macmillan, 1994), pp. 566–80.
18. *An Evolutionary Approach to Economic and Monetary Union*. (London: HM Treasury, 1989); House of Lords Select Committee on the European Communities, Economic and Monetary Union and Political Union, *EMU: Beyond Stage I – The Hard Ecu*. HL88 (1988–9) Vol. 2.
19. Thatcher, *The Downing Street Years*, pp. 20–1 and 725; A. Seldon, *John Major: A Political Life*. (London: Weidenfeld and Nicolson, 1997) pp. 107–9.
20. Thatcher, *The Downing Street Years*, pp. 721–4; Stephens, *Politics and the Pound*, pp. 142–63; Thompson, *The British Conservative Government and the European Exchange Rate Mechanism*, pp. 163–77.
21. *Hansard*, Vol. 178, col. 873, 30 October 1990.
22. J. Major, *The Evolution of Europe*. (London: Conservative Political Centre, 1991) p. 12; Seldon, *John Major*, pp. 166–8; S. Hogg and J. Hill, *Too Close To Call: Power and Politics – John Major in No. 10*. (London: Little Brown, 1995) pp. 72–9. Major claimed in 1997 that he had meant that Britain should be at the heart of European debate.
23. P. Cradock, *In Pursuit of British Interests: Reflections on Foreign Policy under Margaret Thatcher and John Major*. (London: John Murray, 1997) p. 139; Hogg and Hill, *Too Close to Call*, pp. 138–62; Seldon, *John Major*, pp. 242–51. See also A. Blair, 'The United Kingdom and the Negotiation of the Maastricht Treaty'. Unpublished PhD thesis, University of Leicester, 1997.
24. Seldon, *John Major*, pp. 368–71 and 384–91; T. Gorman, *The Bastards*. (London: Pan, 1993).
25. S. Ludlam, 'The Spectre Haunting Conservatism: Europe and Backbench Rebellion', in S. Ludlam and M. Smith (eds), *Contemporary British Conservatism*. (London: Macmillan, 1996) pp. 110–17.
26. See D. Cameron, 'British Exit, German Voice, French Loyalty: Defection, Domination and Cooperation in the 1992–93 ERM Crisis'. Paper presented at the annual conference of the American Political

Science Association, Washington DC, 1993; Seldon, *John Major*, pp. 309–23; P. Stephens, *Politics and the Pound*, pp. 226–62.
27. Seldon, *John Major*, p. 465.
28. J. Major, 'Raise Your Eyes, There is a Land Beyond', *The Economist* (25 September 1993) pp. 23–7.
29. M. Rifkind, 'Britain's Modern Vision of Europe', speech to the French Chamber of Commerce, London, 23 January 1997.
30. M. Rifkind, 'Europe: Which Way Forward?', speech to the Konrad Adenauer Stiftung, Bonn, 19 February 1997.
31. Rifkind, 'Europe: Which Way Forward?'.
32. J. Major, 'A Competitive Europe: The Enterprise Approach', speech to the European Policy Forum, Brussels, 4 February 1997.
33. Seldon, *John Major*, pp. 648–52.
34. J. Major, speech at Ellesmere Port, 31 May 1994.
35. J. Major, 'Europe: A Future that Works', speech at Leiden, 7 September 1994.
36. *A Partnership of Nations: The British Approach to the Intergovernmental Conference*. (London: HMSO, 1996) Cm 3181. See also S. George, 'The Approach of the British Government to the 1996 Intergovernmental Conference of the European Union', *Journal of European Public Policy*, 3 (1996) pp. 45–62.
37. 'The European Court of Justice'. IGC Memorandum by the British Government, July 1996.
38. *Hansard*, Vol. 255, col. 1068, 1 March 1995; J. Major, 'We Must Not Allow EMU to be Fudged', *The Times*, 5 October 1996.
39. *Hansard*, Vol. 288, col. 1071, 23 January 1997.
40. *The Guardian*, 17 April 1997.
41. B. Laffan, 'The Politics of Identity and Political Order in Europe', *Journal of Common Market Studies*, 34 (1996) pp. 85–7.
42. W. Wallace, 'National Identity in the United Kingdom', *International Affairs*, 67 (1991) pp. 65–80.
43. Thatcher, *Britain and Europe*, pp. 1–2; Letwin, *The Anatomy of Thatcherism*, pp. 301–6.
44. Thatcher, *Britain and Europe*, p. 4.
45. *Hansard*, Vol. 199, col. 292, 20 November 1991.
46. Thatcher, *The Downing Street Years*, p. 791; *The Independent on Sunday*, 15 July 1990; N. Ridley, 'Saying the Unsayable about the Germans', *The Spectator* (14 July 1990) pp. 8–9; Kaiser, *Using Europe, Abusing the Europeans*, pp. 222–5.
47. Lawson, *The View From Number Eleven*, p. 900.
48. *Hansard*, Vol. 154, col. 1121, 15 June 1989; *Hansard*, Vol. 178, col. 875, 30 October 1990.
49. Seldon, *John Major*, p. 110.
50. *The Financial Times*, 4 April 1995.
51. J. Major, speech to Conservative Group for Europe, London, 22 April 1993.
52. Thompson, *The British Conservative Government and the European Exchange Rate Mechanism*, p. 62.
53. P. Lynch, 'Sovereignty and the European Union: Eroded, Enhanced,

Fragmented', in J. Hoffman and L. Brace (eds), *Reclaiming Sovereignty*. (London: Cassell, 1997) pp. 42–61.
54. A. Dicey, *Introduction to the Study of the Law of the Constitution*. (Indianapolis: Liberty Classics, 1982 edn) p. xviii.
55. N. Malcom, 'Sense on Sovereignty', in M. Holmes (ed.), *The Eurosceptical Reader*. (London: Macmillan, 1996) pp. 342–67.
56. D. Pollard and M. Ross, *European Community Law*. (London: Butterworths, 1994) pp. 397–406.
57. Pollard and Ross, *European Community Law*, pp. 404–5.
58. D. Held, *Political Theory and the Modern State*. (Cambridge: Polity, 1989) pp. 214–42; W. Wallace, 'What Price Independence? Sovereignty and Interdependence in British Politics', *International Affairs*, 62 (1986) pp. 367–89.
59. J. Camilleri and J. Falk, *The End of Sovereignty? The Politics of a Shrinking and Fragmented World*. (Aldershot: Edward Elgar, 1992).
60. G. Howe, 'Sovereignty and Interdependence: Britain's Place in the World', *International Affairs*, 66 (1990) pp. 675–95 (p. 676).
61. Howe, 'Sovereignty and Interdependence', p. 678.
62. D. Judge, 'Incomplete Sovereignty: The British House of Commons and the Completion of the Internal Market in the European Communities', *Parliamentary Affairs*, 41 (1988) pp. 441–55.
63. D. Willetts, *Modern Conservatism*. (London: Penguin, 1992) p. 171.
64. Willetts, *Modern Conservatism*, p. 177; N. Nugent, 'Sovereignty and Britain's Membership of the European Union', *Public Policy and Administration*, 11 (1996) pp. 10–11.
65. See A. Milward and V. Sørensen, 'Interdependence or Integration? A National Choice', in F. Lynch, A. Milward, F. Romero, R. Ranieri and V. Sørensen (eds), *The Frontier of National Sovereignty*. (London: Routledge, 1994) pp. 1–32.
66. A. Moravcsik, 'Preferences and Power in the European Community: A Liberal Intergovernmentalist Approach', *Journal of Common Market Studies*, 31 (1993) pp. 473–524; Moravcsik, 'Negotiating the Single European Act', pp. 25–7.
67. A. Moravcsik, *Why the European Community Strengthens the State: Domestic Politics and International Cooperation*. Centre for European Studies Working Paper Series, No. 52. (Cambridge, MA: Harvard University, 1994).
68. H. Wallace, 'Britain Out On a Limb?', *Political Quarterly*, 66 (1995) pp. 46–58.
69. Moravcsik, 'Negotiating the Single European Act', pp. 61–3.
70. P. Norton, 'The United Kingdom: Political Conflict, Parliamentary Scrutiny', *Journal of Legislative Studies*, 1 (1995) pp. 92–109.
71. See G. Edwards, 'Central Government', in George, *Britain and the European Community*, pp. 64–90; K. Armstrong and S. Bulmer, 'United Kingdom', in D. Rometsch and W. Wessels (eds), *The European Union and Member States: Towards Institutional Fusion?* (Manchester: Manchester University Press, 1996) pp. 267–74. On the 'core executive', see R. Rhodes and P. Dunleavy (eds), *Prime Minister, Cabinet and Core Executive*. (London: Macmillan, 1995).

72. J. Bulpitt, 'The European Question', in D. Marquand and A. Seldon (eds), *The Ideas That Shaped Post-War Britain*. (London: Fontana, 1996) pp. 244–6. See also A. Busch, 'Central Bank Independence and the Westminster Model', *West European Politics*, 17 (1994) pp. 53–72.
73. H. Thompson, 'Joining the ERM: Analysing a Core Executive Policy Disaster', in Rhodes and Dunleavy, *Prime Minister, Cabinet and Core Executive*, p. 273.
74. Armstrong and Bulmer, 'United Kingdom', pp. 259–65.
75. G. Marks, L. Hooghe and K. Blank, 'European Integration from the 1980s: State-Centric v Multi-Level Governance', *Journal of Common Market Studies*, 34 (1996) pp. 341–78. See also S. Bulmer, 'The Governance of the European Union: A New Institutionalist Approach', *Journal of Public Policy*, 13 (1994) pp. 351–80.
76. J. Peterson, 'Decision-Making in the European Union: Towards a Framework for Analysis', *Journal of European Public Policy*, 2 (1995) pp. 69–93.
77. See F. Scharpf, 'Community and Autonomy: Multi-Level Policy-Making in the European Union', *Journal of European Public Policy*, 1 (1994) pp. 219–42; G. Majone, 'The Rise of the Regulatory State in Europe', *West European Politics*, 17 (1994) pp. 77–101.
78. D. Butler and M. Westlake, *British Politics and European Elections 1994*. (London: Macmillan, 1995) pp. 100–6 and 112–13; *A Strong Britain in a Strong Europe*. (London: Conservative Central Office, 1994).
79. *The Guardian*, 17 April 1997.
80. N. Nugent, 'British Public Opinion and the European Community', in George, *Britain and the European Community*, pp. 172–201; J. Rasmussen, '"What Kind of Vision is That?" British Public Attitudes Towards the European Community During the Thatcher Era', *British Journal of Political Science*, 27 (1997) pp. 111–18.
81. D. Sanders, 'Voting and the Electorate', in P. Dunleavy et al., *Developments in British Politics 5*. (London: Macmillan, 1997) p. 50.
82. P. Kellner, 'Why the Tories were Trounced', *Parliamentary Affairs*, 50 (1997) pp. 627–8.
83. I. Crewe, '1979–1996', in A. Seldon (ed.), *How Tory Governments Fall*. (London: Fontana, 1996) pp. 419–35; P. Whiteley, 'The Conservative Campaign', *Parliamentary Affairs*, 50 (1997) pp. 542–54.
84. *The Campaign Guide 1997*. (London: Conservative Central Office, 1997) pp. 717–45.
85. P. Norris, 'Anatomy of a Labour Landslide', *Parliamentary Affairs*, 50 (1997) p. 526; Kellner, 'Why the Tories were Trounced', pp. 618–19; J. Curtice and M. Steed, 'The Results Analysed', in D. Butler and D. Kavanagh, *The 1997 General Election*. (London: Macmillan, 1997) pp. 301–8.
86. *The Times*, 1 May 1997; *The Financial Times*, 21 April 1997.
87. P. Whiteley, P. Seyd and J. Richardson, *True Blues: The Politics of Conservative Party Membership*. (Oxford: Clarendon Press, 1994) pp. 57–8.
88. The 1996 survey is reported in *The Financial Times* (28 March 1996).

On conference motions see M. Ball, *The Conservative Conference and Euro-Sceptical Motions 1992–95*. The Bruges Group Occasional Paper No. 23. (London, 1996).
89. *Shaping the Future: A Europe That Works*. (London: Confederation of British Industry, 1995).
90. *The Financial Times*, 11 November 1996.
91. *The Financial Times*, 10 March 1997.
92. D. Baker, A. Gamble and S. Ludlam, '1846 . . . 1906 . . . 1996? Conservative Splits and European Integration', *Political Quarterly*, 64 (1993) pp. 420–34.
93. See P. Cowley, 'Men (and Women) Behaving Badly? The Conservative Parliamentary Party since 1992', *Talking Politics*, 9 (1996) pp. 94–9.
94. Seldon, *John Major*, pp. 685–8.
95. M. Sowemimo, 'The Conservative Party and European Integration 1988–95', *Party Politics*, 2 (1996) pp. 77–97.
96. M. Spicer, *A Treaty Too Far: A New Policy For Europe*. (London: Fourth Estate, 1992) pp. 167–75. Some sceptics refer to themselves as 'Eurorealists'.
97. See D. Baker, A. Gamble and S. Ludlam, 'Mapping Conservative Fault-Lines: Problems of Typology', in P. Dunleavy and J. Stanyer (eds), *Contemporary Political Studies*. Vol. 1. (Belfast: Political Studies Association, 1994) pp. 278–98.
98. N. Tebbit, *Unfinished Business*. (London: Weidenfeld and Nicholson, 1991) Ch. 4.
99. See, for example, *A Europe of Nations*. (London: The European Research Group, 1995) pp. 8–9; N. Lamont, *Sovereign Britain*. (London: Duckworth, 1995) pp. 78–83; and the policy paper issued by the 'Whipless Eight', 19 January 1995.
100. M. Thatcher, *The Path to Power*. (London: Harper Collins, 1995) p. 483.
101. Thatcher, *The Path to Power*, p. 497.
102. Lamont, *Sovereign Britain*, p. 22.
103. J. Bulpitt, 'Conservative Leaders and the "Euro-Ratchet"', *Political Quarterly*, 63 (1992) pp. 272–4.
104. Lamont, *Sovereign Britain*, pp. 25–32. See also J. Redwood, *Our Currency, Our Country: The Dangers of European Monetary Union*. (London: Penguin, 1997) pp. 191–206.
105. Spicer, *A Treaty Too Far*, pp. 75–103; Holmes, *The Eurosceptical Reader*, Part III.
106. Lamont, *Sovereign Britain*, pp. 26–8.
107. Gorman, *The Bastards*, p. 190.
108. J. Major, speech to the Institute of Directors, London, 24 April 1996.
109. Quoted in I. Loveland, 'Parliamentary Sovereignty and the European Community: The Unfinished Revolution?', *Parliamentary Affairs*, 49 (1996) p. 527. Loveland also examines scenarios in which Parliament challenges Community law, pp. 531–5.
110. See G. Ress, 'The Constitution and the Maastricht Treaty: Between Co-operation and Conflict', *German Politics*, 3 (1994) pp. 47–74.

111. See for example, M. Portillo, 'Between the Phobes and the Philes', *The Spectator*, 25 October 1997.
112. Baker et al., 'Mapping Conservative Fault-Lines', pp. 278–98.
113. G. Howe, 'No Longer Part of the Convoy', *The Financial Times*, 11 March 1996.
114. Q. Davis, 'The Case for the Single Currency', *Reformer* (Autumn 1996) pp. 9–11.
115. M. Thatcher, *The Keith Joseph Memorial Lecture: Liberty and Limited Government*. (London: Centre for Policy Studies, 1996) p. 10.
116. T. Garel-Jones, 'Patriots Must be Europeans', *The Independent*, 6 June 1996.

5 TERRITORIAL POLITICS

1. Bulpitt, *Territory and Power in the United Kingdom*.
2. J. Kellas, *The Scottish Political System*. 4th edn (Cambridge: Cambridge University Press, 1989) pp. 1–19; A. Midwinter, M. Keating and J. Mitchell, *Politics and Public Policy in Scotland*. (London: Macmillan, 1991) pp. 195–202.
3. R. Rose, *Ministers and Ministries: A Functional Analysis*. (Oxford: Clarendon Press, 1987) Chs 5–7.
4. R. Rose, 'Is the United Kingdom a State? Northern Ireland as a Test Case', in P. Madgwick and R. Rose (eds), *The Territorial Dimension in United Kingdom Politics*. (London: Macmillan, 1982) pp. 100–36 (p. 125).
5. See B. Hadfield, 'The Constitution of Northern Ireland'.
6. Thatcher, *The Path to Power*, pp. 321–6.
7. Kendrick and McCrone, 'Politics in a Cold Climate', pp. 595–6.
8. Urwin, 'Scottish Conservatism', pp. 145–62.
9. T. Nairn, 'Tartan and Blue', *Marxism Today*, 32 (June 1988) pp. 30–3.
10. I. Holliday, 'Scottish Limits to Thatcherism', *Political Quarterly*, 63 (1992), 448–59; J. Mitchell, *Conservatives and the Union*, pp. 102–6.
11. Thatcher, *The Downing Street Years*, pp. 623 and 619. Lawson also dubbed Scotland a 'dependency culture', *The Scotsman*, 24 November 1987.
12. Holliday, 'Scottish Limits to Thatcherism', pp. 448–59.
13. R. Barker, 'Legitimacy in the United Kingdom: Scotland and the Poll Tax', *British Journal of Political Science*, 22 (1992) pp. 521–33.
14. N. Acheson, 'The Forsyth Saga', *The Independent on Sunday*, 16 September 1990.
15. Mitchell, *Conservatives and the Union*, pp. 119–23; M. Thatcher, *The Revival of Britain: Speeches on Home and European Affairs, 1975–88*. (London: Aurum Press, 1989) pp. 235–55.
16. A. Marr, *The Battle for Scotland*. (London: Penguin, 1995).
17. Thatcher, *The Downing Street Years*, p. 624.
18. J. Mitchell, 'Conservatives and the Changing Meaning of Union', *Regional and Federal Studies*, 6 (1996) pp. 30–44.
19. S. Rokkan and D. Urwin, 'Introduction: Centres and Peripheries in

Western Europe', in S. Rokkan and D. Urwin (eds), *The Politics of Territorial Identity: Studies in European Regionalism.* (London: Sage, 1982) p. 11.
20. A 1990 International Communications and Marketing opinion poll found that 79 per cent of Scots agreed that the Conservative Party was mainly an English party with little relevance to Scotland. See D. Seawright, 'Being Scottish, But Looking English', *Parliamentary Brief* (October 1994) p. 40. Thatcher, *The Downing Street Years*, p. 624, claims that the Conservatives appeared English 'because the Union is inevitably dominated by England by reason of its greater population'.
21. J. Cooper, 'The Scottish Problem: English Conservatives and the Union with Scotland in the Thatcher and Major Eras', in J. Lovenduski and J. Stanyer (eds), *Contemporary Political Studies 1995*, Vol. 3. (Belfast: Political Studies Association, 1995) pp. 1384–93.
22. Hogg and Hill, *Too Close To Call*, pp. 246–9.
23. *The Scotsman*, 6 April 1992.
24. Marr, *The Battle for Scotland*, pp. 230–2.
25. J. Curtice and D. Seawright, 'The Decline of the Scottish Conservative and Unionist Party 1950–92: Religion, Ideology or Economics?', *Contemporary Record*, 9 (1995) pp. 319–42.
26. *The Scotsman*, 11 March 1993.
27. M. Forsyth, *Fighting for Scotland.* (London: Conservative Political Centre, 1996) p. 38.
28. I. Lang, 'Local Government Reform: Change for the Better', *Scottish Affairs*, 6 (1994) pp. 14–24; R. Paddison, 'The Restructuring of Local Government in Scotland', in J. Bradbury and J. Mawson (eds), *British Regionalism and Devolution: The Challenges of State Reform and European Integration.* (London: Jessica Kingsley, 1997) pp. 99–117.
29. J. Major, *Scotland in the United Kingdom.* (London: Conservative Political Centre, 1992) pp. 7–8.
30. Forsyth, *Fighting for Scotland*, pp. 40–52.
31. *Scottish Conservative Manifesto 1992, 'The Best Future for Scotland'.* (Edinburgh: Scottish Conservative and Unionist Party, 1992) pp. 49–50.
32. 'Introduction by the Secretary of State for Scotland', *Scotland in the Union: A Partnership for Good.* (London: HMSO, 1993) Cm 2225, p. 8.
33. See M. Burch and I. Holliday, 'The Conservative Party and Constitutional Reform: The Case of Devolution', *Parliamentary Affairs*, 45 (1992) pp. 368–98.
34. CPC National Policy Group on the Constitution, *Strengthening the United Kingdom.* (London: Conservative Political Centre, 1996) pp. 8 and 16–18. Though not formal party policy, this drew upon discussions with the Secretaries of State for Scotland and Wales.
35. CPC, *Strengthening the United Kingdom*, p. 15.
36. *Scotland's Parliament, Scotland's Right.* (Edinburgh: Scottish Constitutional Convention, 1995); *Scotland's Parliament.* (Edinburgh: HMSO, 1997) Cm 3658.
37. See, for example, *The United Kingdom: Maintaining the Union of its Peoples.* (London: Conservative Political Centre, 1995) pp. 100–2;

J. Major, *Our Nation's Future*. (London: Conservative Political Centre, 1997) pp. 46–57.
38. See Midwinter et al., *Politics and Public Policy in Scotland*, pp. 98–114; N. Lyndon, 'Let the English Voice be Heard', *The Independent*, 23 July 1997.
39. The ICM opinion poll showed support for the *status quo* at 30 per cent, its highest for ten years. See J. Curtice, 'Sailing into Stormy Waters', *The Scotsman*, 22 April 1997.
40. A 1997 Gallup poll showed only 27 per cent of English voters feared for the future after devolution and 47 per cent of Tory voters had no objection to a Scottish Parliament. *The Scotsman*, 11 March 1997.
41. A. Brown, 'Scotland: Paving the Way for Devolution', *Parliamentary Affairs*, 50 (1997) pp. 658–71. Major's keynote speeches on the Union are reported in *The Daily Telegraph*, 5 April and 29 April 1997.
42. See Mitchell, 'Conservatives and the Changing Meaning of Union', pp. 40–3; J. Bradbury, 'Conservative Governments, Scotland and Wales: A Perspective on Territorial Management', in Bradbury and Mawson, *British Regionalism and Devolution*, pp. 80–6.
43. J. Kellas, 'The Scottish and Welsh Officers as Territorial Managers', *Regional Politics and Policy*, 1 (1991) pp. 87–100; R. Parry, 'Being Different, While Being the Same', *Parliamentary Brief* (February 1995) pp. 6–7.
44. J. Mitchell, 'Reviving the Union State? The Devolution Debate in Scotland', *Politics Review* (February 1996) p. 17.
45. Marr, *The Battle for Scotland*, p. 224; Hogg and Hill, *Too Close To Call*, p. 247.
46. See, for example, A. Gamble, 'Territorial Politics', in P. Dunleavy et al., *Developments in British Politics 4*. (London: Macmillan, 1993) pp. 83–4.
47. P. Walker, *Staying Power*. (London: Bloomsbury, 1991) pp. 202–3. Thatcher, *The Downing Street Years*, pp. 602–3, notes only Walker's plans for housing.
48. Walker, *Staying Power*, p. 212.
49. Quoted in D. Griffiths, 'The Welsh Office and Policy Exceptionalism During the 1980s – Some Reflections', in P. Dunleavy and J. Stanyer (eds), *Contemporary Political Studies 1994*, Vol. 2. (Belfast: Political Studies Association, 1992) p. 1028.
50. D. Griffiths, *Thatcherism and Territorial Politics: A Welsh Case Study*. (Aldershot: Avebury, 1996). See also, Bradbury, 'Conservative Governments, Scotland and Wales', pp. 87–91.
51. J. Redwood, 'The Challenge of the Future', in *Politics Today, Wales: The Challenge and the Record*. (London: Conservative Research Department, 1994) pp. 91–3; W. Hague, 'Foreword', in *Politics Today, A New Wales*. (London: Conservative Research Department, 1996) pp. 276–7; Bradbury, 'Conservative Governments, Scotland and Wales', pp. 91–4.
52. A. Thomas, 'The Hardliners Riding for a Fall', *Parliamentary Brief* (March 1995) pp. 59–60.
53. J. Redwood, *Views from Wales*. (Cardiff: Conservative Political Centre, 1994).

54. P. Maguire, 'Why Devolution?', in Hadfield (ed.), *Northern Ireland: Politics and the Constitution*, pp. 13–28; B. O'Leary, 'The Limits to Coercive Consociationalism in Northern Ireland', *Political Studies*, 37 (1989) pp. 562–88.
55. A. Aughey, 'Conservative Party Policy and Northern Ireland', in B. Barton and P. Roche (eds), *The Northern Ireland Question: Perspectives and Politics*. (Aldershot: Avebury, 1994) pp. 132–6.
56. J. Prior, *A Balance of Power*. (London: Hamish Hamilton, 1986) pp. 194–201.
57. In the early 1980s, Thatcher stated she was 'rock firm for the Union' and said that 'Northern Ireland is as British as Finchley'. See also, Prior, *A Balance of Power*, pp. 196–7.
58. C. O'Leary, S. Elliott and R. Wilford, *The Northern Ireland Assembly, 1982–86: A Constitutional Experiment*. (London: Hurst, 1988).
59. See S. Hopkins, 'The Search for Peace and a Political Settlement in Northern Ireland: Sovereignty, Self-Determination and Consent', in Hoffman and Brace, *Reclaiming Sovereignty*, pp. 62–79.
60. Howe, *Conflict of Loyalty*, pp. 426–7. Prior, *A Balance of Power*, pp. 241–2, also believed the government should 'pool sovereignty' on Northern Ireland.
61. Thatcher, *The Downing Street Years*, pp. 395–405.
62. B. O'Leary and J. McGarry, *The Politics of Antagonism: Understanding Northern Ireland*. (London: Athlone Press, 1993), pp. 229–39; Thatcher, *The Downing Street Years*, pp. 402–4.
63. Thatcher, *The Downing Street Years*, p. 415, claimed that given the disappointing results of the AIA, it was 'time to consider an alternative approach'.
64. Seldon, *John Major: A Political Life*, pp. 263–8.
65. E. Mallie and D. McKittrick, *The Fight for Peace: The Secret Story Behind the Irish Peace Process*. (London: Heinemann, 1996); Seldon, *John Major: A Political Life*, pp. 418–30.
66. A. Lijphart, 'The Framework Document on Northern Ireland and the Theory of Power-Sharing', *Government and Opposition*, 31 (1996) pp. 267–74.
67. B. O'Leary, 'The Conservative Stewardship of Northern Ireland, 1979–97: Sound-bottomed Contradictions or Slow Learning?', *Political Studies*, 45 (1997) pp. 663–76.
68. *Hansard*, Vol. 255, cols 480–1, 23 February 1995.
69. Peter Lynch, 'The Northern Ireland Peace Process and Scottish Constitutional Reform: Managing the Unions of 1800 and 1707', *Regional and Federal Studies*, 6 (1996) pp. 45–62.
70. *Hansard*, Vol. 255, col. 355, 22 February 1995; speech to the Conservative Party Conference, Bournemouth, 11 October 1996.
71. F. Cochrane, 'Any Takers? The Isolation of Northern Ireland', *Political Studies*, 42 (1994), p. 385. During secret contacts with Sinn Fein, a British government representative is reported to have stated that while stressing consent, the government wanted 'a North/South settlement that won't frighten Unionists. The final solution is union. It is going to happen anyway. The historical train – Europe – determines that'.

Quoted in P. Bew and G. Gillespie, *The Northern Ireland Peace Process 1993-1996: A Chronology*. (London: Serif, 1996) p. 31.
72. See P. Dixon, '"The Usual English Doubletalk": The British Political Parties and the Ulster Unionists 1974-94', *Irish Political Studies*, 9 (1994) pp. 34-9. But on the 'understanding' with the Unionists, see Seldon, *John Major: A Political Life*, pp. 386-7.
73. A. Aughey, *Under Siege: Ulster Unionism and the Anglo-Irish Agreement*. (London: Hurst & Co, 1989) pp. 146-65. In a 1990 survey, 19 per cent of Northern Ireland voters chose the Conservative Party when asked about party identification, the majority of these being Unionist voters. J. Curtice and T. Gallagher, 'The Northern Ireland Dimension', in R. Jowell et al., *British Social Attitudes: The 7th Report*. (Aldershot: Gower, 1990) p. 191.
74. M. Cunningham and R. Kelly, 'Standing for Ulster', *Politics Review*, 5 (November 1995) pp. 20-3.
75. Thatcher, *The Downing Street Years*, p. 385.
76. J. Todd, 'Two Traditions in Unionist Political Culture', *Irish Political Studies*, 2 (1987), pp. 1-26. See also, C. Coulter, 'The Character of Unionism', *Irish Political Studies*, 9 (1994) pp. 1-24, and N. Porter, *Rethinking Unionism: An Alternative Vision for Northern Ireland*. (Belfast: The Blackstaff Press, 1996).
77. Quoted in Bew and Gillespie, *The Northern Ireland Peace Process*, p. 52.
78. Aughey, *Under Siege*, pp. 1-30 (p. 18).
79. Coulter, 'The Character of Unionism', pp. 15-17; J. McGarry and B. O'Leary, *Explaining Northern Ireland: Broken Images*. (Oxford: Blackwell, 1995), pp. 128-36; Porter, *Rethinking Unionism*, Ch. 4.
80. A. Aughey, 'Batting Well on a Sticky Wicket', *Parliamentary Brief*, (December, 1994), pp. 27-8; Aughey, *Under Siege*, p. 25.
81. Aughey, 'Conservative Party Policy and Northern Ireland', p. 147.
82. Cochrane, 'Any Takers? The Isolation of Northern Ireland', pp. 386-9.
83. Cunningham and Kelly, 'Standing for Ulster', p. 22.
84. Cosgrave, *The Lives of Enoch Powell*, Ch. 8; T. E. Utley, *The Lessons of Ulster*. (London: Dent, 1975).
85. M. Cunningham, 'Conservative Dissidents and the Irish Question: The "Pro-Integrationist" Lobby 1973-94', *Irish Political Studies*, 10 (1995), pp. 26-42. Conservative dissidents on the two votes totalled 32, drawn mainly from the party's Euro-sceptic Right.
86. See *The Untried Solution: A Stronger Union*. (London: Friends of the Union, 1993). The *Daily Telegraph* and *The Times* have in recent years been sympathetic to the Unionist cause.
87. *Hansard*, Vol. 234, col. 1086, 15 December 1993.
88. Lamont, *Sovereign Britain*, p. 117.
89. Prior, *A Balance of Power*, pp. 192-4.
90. *The Conservative Campaign Guide 1991*. (London: Conservative Central Office, 1991) p. 571.
91. R. Wilford and S. Elliott, 'The Northern Ireland Affairs Select Committee', *Irish Political Studies*, 10 (1995), pp. 216-24.
92. B. Hogwood, 'Regional Administration in Britain since 1979: Trends

and Explanations', *Regional and Federal Studies*, 5 (1995), pp. 267–91; Bradbury and Mawson, *British Regionalism and Devolution*, Part II.
93. A. Scott, J. Peterson and D. Millar, 'Subsidiarity: A "Europe of the Regions" v the British Constitution?', *Journal of Common Market Studies*, 32 (1994), pp. 47–67.
94. Marks et al., 'European Integration from the 1980s'.
95. See Bradbury and Mawson, *British Regionalism and Devolution*, Part III; I. Bache, S. George and R. Rhodes, 'The European Union, Cohesion Policy and Subnational Authorities in the United Kingdom', in L. Hooghe (ed.), *Cohesion Policy and European Integration: Building Multi-Level Governance*. (Oxford: Clarendon Press, 1996) pp. 294–319.
96. Gamble, 'The Entrails of Thatcherism'; Marquand, 'The Twilight of the British State'?

6 'RACE' AND IMMIGRATION

1. See F. Reeves, *British Racial Discourse*. (Cambridge: Cambridge University Press, 1983) Ch. 5.
2. G. Seidel, 'Culture, Nation and "Race" in the British and French New Right', in R. Levitas (ed.), *The Ideology of the New Right*. (Cambridge, Polity Press, 1986) pp. 107–35.
3. Parekh, 'The "New Right" and the Politics of Nationhood'.
4. M. Barker, *The New Racism: Conservatives and the Ideology of the Tribe*. (Maryland: Aletheira Books, 1981) Chs 2 and 3.
5. Compare this with H. Goulbourne, *Ethnicity and Nationalism in Post-Imperial Britain*. (Cambridge: Cambridge University Press, 1991) who argues that Conservatives define the British nation in ethnic terms (pp. 111–25).
6. J. Krieger, *Reagan, Thatcher and the Politics of Decline*. (Cambridge: Polity Press, 1986).
7. J. Solomos and L. Back, *Race, Politics and Social Change*. (London: Routledge, 1995) pp. 119–20.
8. Bulpitt, 'Continuity, Autonomy and Peripheralisation'; S. Saggar, 'The Politics of "Race" Policy in Britain', *Critical Social Policy*, 37 (1993) pp. 39–45.
9. Compare A. Messina, 'Race and Party Competition in Britain', *Parliamentary Affairs*, 38 (1985) pp. 423–36 and D. Studlar, 'Elite Responsiveness or Elite Autonomy: British Immigration Policy Reconsidered', *Ethnic and Racial Studies*, 3 (1980) pp. 207–23.
10. M. Thatcher, *The Path to Power*, p. 146.
11. Quoted in V. Bevan, *The Development of British Immigration Law*. (London: Croom Helm, 1986) p. 85.
12. Thatcher, *The Path to Power*, pp. 405–8.
13. C. Husbands, 'Extreme Right Wing Politics in Great Britain: The Recent Marginalization of the National Front', *West European Politics*, 11 (1988) pp. 65–79.
14. I. Macdonald and N. Blake, *Immigration Law and Practice in the United Kingdom*. (London: Butterworths, 1995) pp. 118–27.

15. Macdonald and Blake, *Immigration Law and Practice*, pp. 127–9.
16. Committee of the Society of Conservative Lawyers, *Towards a New Citizenship*. (London: Conservative Political Centre, 1975).
17. See E. Gardner, *Who Do We Think We Are*. (London: Conservative Political Centre, 1980); R. Plender, *Defining the Nation: The Need for a New Nationality Law*. (London: The Bow Group, 1978).
18. W. Whitelaw, *Hansard*, Vol. 97, col. 935, 28 January 1981 and Vol. 5, col. 1155, 4 June 1981.
19. Macdonald and Blake, *Immigration Law and Practice*, pp. 130–44.
20. D. Dixon, 'Thatcher's People: The British Nationality Act 1981', *Journal of Law and Society*, 10 (1983) pp. 161–80.
21. See, for example, speeches by Ivor Stanbrook, John Stokes, Harvey Proctor and Nicholas Budgen in the debate on the Act's Second Reading, *Hansard*, Vol. 997, 28 January 1981.
22. *The Conservative Party Manifesto 1979*. (London: Conservative Central Office, 1979). The 1983 manifesto stated that 'to have good community relations, we have to maintain effective immigration control' (p. 35); the 1987 manifesto promised a further tightening of immigration laws as 'firm but fair immigration controls are essential for harmonious and improving community relations' (p. 59).
23. Douglas Hurd, *Hansard*, Vol. 122, col. 779, 16 November 1987.
24. Z. Layton-Henry, *The Politics of Immigration*. (Oxford: Blackwell, 1992) pp. 186–90.
25. See the debate on immigration, *Hansard*, Vol. 31, cols 692–761, 11 November 1982.
26. Macdonald and Blake, *Immigration Law and Practice*, pp. 149–50.
27. *The Guardian*, 5 March 1996.
28. On the definition of 'refugee' see Macdonald and Blake, *Immigration Law and Practice*, pp. 372–400.
29. On asylum practice after the 1993 Act, see Macdonald and Blake, *Immigration Law and Practice*, pp. 403–20.
30. *The Independent*, 14 November 1996 reported a dispute between Foreign Secretary Malcom Rifkind and Home Secretary Michael Howard over the latter's plans to include Pakistan as a 'safe' country.
31. *The Guardian*, 22 June and 25 June 1996.
32. *The Guardian*, 9 October 1996 and 18 February 1997.
33. R. Cohen, *Frontiers of Identity: The British and the Others*. (Harlow: Longman, 1994) pp. 99–129.
34. The British position is outlined in K. Baker, *The Turbulent Years*. (London: Faber and Faber, 1993) pp. 439–43. See also D. O'Keeffe, 'The Free Movement of Persons and the Single European Market', *European Law Review*, 17 (1992) pp. 3–20.
35. *A Partnership of Nations: The British Approach to the Intergovernmental Conference*. (London: HMSO, 1996) Cm 3181.
36. See D. Cullen, J. Monar and P. Myers, *Cooperation in Justice and Home Affairs*. (Brussels: European Interuniversity Press, 1996).
37. *The Reflection Group's Report*. (Brussels, 1995) pp. 15–18.
38. A. Evans, 'Nationality Law and European Integration', *European Law Review*, 16 (1991) pp. 190–215, and C. Closa, 'Citizenship of the Union

and Nationality of Member States', *Common Market Law Review*, 32 (1995) pp. 487–518.
39. H. Jessurun d'Oliveira, 'Union Citizenship: Pie in the Sky?', in A. Rosas and E. Antola (eds), *A Citizen's Europe: In Search of a New Order* (London: Sage, 1995) pp. 58–84.
40. J. Nixon, 'The Home Office and Race Relations Policy: Coordinator and Initiator', *Journal of Public Policy*, 2 (1982) pp. 365–78.
41. *1987 Conservative Manifesto*, p. 59.
42. See *Social Focus on Ethnic Minorities*. (HMSO: London, 1996) and Policy Studies Institute, *Ethnic Minorities in Britain: Diversity and Discrimination*. (London: Policy Studies Institute, 1997).
43. *Politics Today*, 11 (London: Conservative Central Office,1981), p. 200.
44. J. Major, *Britain: The Best Place in the World*. Text of a speech at the Commonwealth Institute, London, 18 January 1997. (London: One Nation Forum, 1997). See also, *The Campaign Guide 1997*. (London: Conservative Central Office, 1997) pp. 480–3; Seldon, *John Major: A Political Life*, pp. 28–30 and 696–7.
45. J. Solomos, 'Equal Opportunities Policies and Racial Inequality: The Role of Public Policy', *Public Administration*, 67 (1989) pp. 79–93.
46. See, for example, Home Office Press Releases on tackling racial harassment in East London, 16 November 1995, and projects involving Muslim communities, 29 March 1996.
47. *The Guardian*, 27 January 1997; Home Office Press Release, 27 January 1997.
48. J. Solomos, *Race and Racism in Britain*. 2nd edn (London: Macmillan, 1993) Chs 5–7.
49. T. Raison, 'The View from the Government', in J. Benyon (ed.), *Scarman and After*. (London: Pergamon, 1984) pp. 244–58.
50. *Hansard*, Vol. 14, col. 1045, 10 December 1981.
51. S. Saggar, 'The Politics of "Race Policy" in Britain', *Critical Social Policy*, 37 (1993) pp. 36–45.
52. P. Gordon, 'A Dirty War: The New Right and Local Authority Anti-Racism', in W. Ball and J. Solomos (eds), *Race and Local Politics*. (London: Macmillan, 1990) pp. 175–90.
53. R. Honeyford, 'Education and Race – an Alternative View', *The Salisbury Review*, 6 (1984) pp. 30–2. See also F. Palmer (ed.), *Anti-Racism: An Assault on Education and Value*. (London: Sherwood Press, 1986).
54. K. Joseph, 'Why Teach History in School?', *The Historian*, 2 (1984) p. 10. A critical perspective is presented in H. Kaye, 'The Use and Abuse of the Past: The New Right and the Crisis of History', *The Socialist Register 1987*, pp. 332–64.
55. B. Parekh, 'The Rushdie Affair: A Research Agenda for Political Philosophy', *Political Studies*, 38 (1990) pp. 695–709.
56. T. Modood, 'British Asian Muslims and the Rushdie Affair', *Political Quarterly*, 61 (1990) pp. 143–60; 'The Changing Context of "Race" in Britain: A Symposium', *Patterns of Prejudice*, 30 (1996) pp. 3–42.
57. J. Patten, 'Letter of 4 July 1989 from Mr John Pattern, Minister of State at the Home Office, to a Number of Leading British Muslims', in Commission for Racial Equality, *Law, Blasphemy and Religion in a*

Multi-Faith Society: Report of a Seminar. (London: CRE, 1990, pp. 84–7 (85).
58. H. Proctor and J. Pinniger, *Immigration, Repatriation and the Commission for Racial Equality*. (London: The Monday Club, 1981).
59. Layton-Henry, *The Politics of Immigration*, pp. 199–203. Messina, 'Race and Party Competition in Britain', estimated that there were 60 Conservative MPs with strong illiberal views on 'race' in the early 1980s (pp. 426–8).
60. See Tebbit's speech on the Second Reading of the British Nationality (Hong Kong) Act, *Hansard*, Vol. 170, cols 1596–1602, 19 April 1990.
61. *Young, British and Black*. (London: Tory Reform Group, 1982) p. 2.
62. K. Amin and R. Richardson, *Politics for All: Equality, Culture and the General Election 1992*. (London: Runnymede Trust, 1992).
63. Solomos and Back, *Race, Politics and Social Change*, pp. 159–60.
64. S. Saggar, 'Racial Politics', *Parliamentary Affairs*, 50 (1997) pp. 693–707.
65. Z. Layton-Henry, 'Race, Electoral Strategy and the Major Parties', *Parliamentary Affairs*, 31 (1978) pp. 268–81.
66. E. Cashmore, 'Songs of the New Blues', *New Statesman and Society*, 23 August 1991, pp. 21–3; 'The Race to Charm the Asian Voter', *The Independent*, 27 February 1997; Major, *Britain: The Best Place in the World*.
67. K. Alderman, 'The Jewish Dimension in British Politics since 1945', *New Community*, 20 (1993) pp. 9–25.
68. The 1987 figures are discussed in S. Saggar, 'Competing for the Black Vote', *Politics Review*, 2, 4 (1993) p. 28; the 1991 survey in K. Amin and R. Richardson, *Politics for All*; and the 1992 NOP poll in Z. Layton-Henry, 'Immigration and Contemporary Politics', *Politics Review*, 5, 3 (1996) p. 23. The 1997 opinion poll was reported in *The Financial Times*, 25 February 1997.
69. Mori-ZeeTV poll reported in *The Financial Times*, 25 February 1997.
70. See S. Saggar, 'Analysing Race and Voting', *Politics Review*, 2, 3 (1993) pp. 9–12 and Saggar, 'Racial Politics'.
71. S. Saggar, 'Can Political Parties Play the Race Card in General Elections? The 1992 Poll Revisited', *New Community*, 19 (1993) pp. 693–9; N. Budgen, 'How Long Shall We Avoid the Immigration Issue?' *The Independent*, 27 February 1997; 'Immigration and Race: United in Extreme Caution', *The Times*, 18 April 1997.
72. P. Whiteley, P. Seyd and J. Richardson, *True Blues: The Politics of Conservative Party Membership*. (Oxford: Clarendon Press, 1994) pp. 253 and 265.

7 CONCLUSIONS

1. Bulpitt, 'The Discipline of the New Democracy'.
2. Gamble, 'The Crisis of Conservatism'.
3. M. Ancram, speech to the Conservative Party Conference, 8 October 1997.

4. See E. Heathcoat Amory's critiques, 'The English Impatient', *The Spectator*, 4 October 1997, and 'Advertising the End of Britain', *The Spectator*, 1 November 1997.
5. G. Brown, 'Outward Bound', *The Spectator*, 8 November 1997. See also M. Leonard, *Britain: Renewing Our Identity*. (London: Demos, 1997).
6. *The Independent*, 8 October 1997.
7. W. Hague, speech to the Conservative Party Conference, 10 October 1997.
8. See J. Major, 'Why I Now Say No to Europe's Currency', *The Sunday Telegraph*, 5 October 1997.
9. P. Norton, 'Electing the Leader: The Conservative Leadership Contest 1997', *Politics Review*, 7 (1998).
10. On nationality and patriotism, see D. Miller, *On Nationality*. (Oxford: Clarendon Press, 1995); A. Macintyre, *Is Patriotism a Virtue?* (Lindley Lecture, University of Kansas, 1984), and S. Nathanson, 'In Defense of "Moderate Patriotism"', *Ethics*, 99 (1989) pp. 535–52. On community and citizenship, see M. Walzer, *Spheres of Justice*. (Oxford: Martin Robertson, 1983) and D. Heater, *Citizenship: The Civic Ideal in World History, Politics and Education*. (London: Longman, 1990).
11. J. Gray, *The Undoing of Conservatism*. (London: Social Market Foundation, 1994) p. 14. See also J. Gray, *Beyond the New Right: Markets, Government and the Common Environment*. (London: Routledge, 1994).
12. D. Willetts, 'The Free Market and Civic Conservatism', in K. Minogue (ed.), *Conservative Realism: New Essays in Conservatism*. (London: Harper Collins, 1996) pp. 80–97 (p. 85); D. Willetts, *Civic Conservatism*. (London: Social Market Foundation, 1994); Willetts, *Modern Conservatism*.
13. Willetts, 'The Free Market and Civic Conservatism', pp. 96–7.
14. Willetts, *Modern Conservatism*, p. 184.
15. Willetts, *Modern Conservatism*, p. 106.
16. Scruton, 'In Defence of the Nation'.
17. D. Miller, 'In Defence of Nationality', *Journal of Applied Philosophy*, 10 (1993) p. 9.
18. *Strengthening the United Kingdom*, pp. 15–16.
19. Parekh, 'The New Right and the Politics of Nationhood'.
20. Camilleri and Falk, *The End of Sovereignty?*; M. Horsman and A. Marshall, *After the Nation State*. (London: Harper Collins, 1994).
21. See A. Smith, *Nations and Nationalism in a Global Era*. (Cambridge: Polity, 1995); P. Hirst and G. Thompson, *Globalisation in Question*. (Cambridge: Polity Press, 1996).
22. Lynch, 'Sovereignty and the European Union'.
23. Marks et al., 'European Integration from the 1980s'.
24. See U. Hedetoft, 'The State of Sovereignty in Europe: Political Concept or Cultural Self-Image', in S. Zetterholm (ed.), *National Cultures and European Integration*. (Oxford: Berg, 1994) pp. 13–48; Laffan, 'The Politics of Identity and Political Order in Europe'.
25. See A. Smith, 'National Identity and the Idea of European Unity', *International Affairs*, 68 (1992) pp. 55–76; E. Meehan, *Citizenship and the European Community*. (London: Sage, 1993); A. Rosas and E. Antola (eds), *A Citizen's Europe: In Search of a New Order*. (London: Sage, 1995).

Select Bibliography

Aughey, A. 'Conservative Party Policy and Northern Ireland', in B. Barton and P. Roche (eds), *The Northern Ireland Question: Perspectives and Politics*. Aldershot: Avebury, 1994, pp. 121–50.
Baker, D., Gamble, A. and Ludlam, S. '1846 . . . 1906 . . . 1996? Conservative Splits and European Integration', *The Political Quarterly*, 64 (1993) pp. 420–34.
Ball, S. and Seldon, A. (eds) *The Heath Government, 1970–74: A Reappraisal*. London: Longman, 1996.
Barnett, A. *Iron Britannia*. London: Allison and Busby, 1982.
Bulpitt, J. *Territory and Power in the United Kingdom: An Interpretation*. Manchester: Manchester University Press, 1983.
Bulpitt, J. 'The Discipline of the New Democracy: Mrs Thatcher's Domestic Statecraft', *Political Studies*, 34 (1986) pp. 19–39.
Casey, J. 'One Nation: The Politics of Race', *The Salisbury Review*, 1 (1982) pp. 23–9.
Conservative Political Centre. *Strengthening the United Kingdom*. London: Conservative Political Centre, 1996.
Cosgrave, P. *The Lives of Enoch Powell*. London: Bodley Head, 1989.
Cunningham, H. 'The Conservative Party and Patriotism', in R. Colls and P. Dodd (eds), *Englishness: Politics and Culture, 1880–1930*. London: Croom Helm, 1986, pp. 283–307.
Gamble, A. *The Conservative Nation*. London: Routledge and Kegan Paul, 1974.
Gamble, A. 'The Entrails of Thatcherism', *New Left Review*, 198 (1993) pp. 117–28.
Gamble, A. *The Free Economy and the Strong State: The Politics of Thatcherism*. 2nd edn. London: Macmillan, 1993.
Gamble, A. 'The Crisis of Conservatism', *New Left Review*, 214 (1995) pp. 3–25.
George, S. (ed.) *Britain and the European Community: The Politics of Semi-Detachment*. Oxford: Clarendon Press, 1992.
Hall, S. *The Hard Road to Renewal: Thatcherism and the Crisis of the Left*. London: Laurence and Wishart, 1988.
Holmes, M. (ed.) *The Eurosceptical Reader*. London: Macmillan, 1996.
Howe, G. 'Sovereignty and Interdependence: Britain's Place in the World', *International Affairs*, 66 (1990) pp. 675–95.
Layton-Henry, Z. *The Politics of Immigration*. Oxford: Blackwell, 1992.
Layton-Henry, Z. and Rich, P. (eds) *Race, Government and Politics in Britain*. London: Macmillan, 1986.
Letwin, S. *The Anatomy of Thatcherism*. London: Fontana, 1992.
Levitas, R. (ed.) *The Ideology of the New Right*. Cambridge: Polity Press, 1986.
Ludlam, S. and Smith, M. J. (eds), *Contemporary British Conservatism*. London: Macmillan, 1996.

Marquand, D. 'The Twilight of the British State? Henry Dubb versus Sceptred Awe', *Political Quarterly*, 64 (1993) pp. 210–21.
Mitchell, J. *Conservatives and the Union: A Study of Conservative Party Attitudes to Scotland*. Edinburgh: Edinburgh University Press, 1990.
Mitchell, J. 'Conservatives and the Changing Meaning of Union', *Regional and Federal Studies*, 6 (1996) pp. 30–44.
New Community special issue, 'British National Identity in a European Context'. 21, 2 (1995).
Parekh, B. 'The "New Right" and the Politics of Nationhood', in G. Cohen et al., *The New Right: Image and Reality*. London: Runnymede Trust, 1986, pp. 33–43.
Powell, J. E. *Reflections of a Statesman: The Writings and Speeches of Enoch Powell*. Edited by Rex Collings. London: Bellew Publishing, 1991.
Scruton, R. 'In Defence of the Nation', in J. C. D. Clark (ed.), *Ideas and Politics in Modern Britain*. London: Macmillan, 1990, pp. 53–86.
Seldon, A. *John Major: A Political Life*. London: Weidenfeld and Nicolson, 1997.
Thatcher, M. *The Downing Street Years*. London: Harper Collins, 1993.
Wallace, W. 'What Price Independence? Sovereignty and Interdependence in British Politics', *International Affairs*, 62 (1986) pp. 367–89.
Wallace, W. 'National Identity in the United Kingdom', *International Affairs*, 67 (1991) pp. 65–80.

Index

Aughey, Arthur, 124–5

Blair, Tony, 91
 Blair Government, 113, 127, 143
British constitution, 36, 37
 Conservative Party's defence of, 10, 15, 19–20, 65, 111–13, 158, 164
 conservative views on, 2, 5–6, 8, 42, 111, 125, 164–5
British identity, 1–4, 14, 39, 78–9, 95, 162–3, 166–7
 in a multicultural society, 27–8, 42–5, 132–3, 137, 148–9, 153
 and Northern Ireland, 16–19, 124–5
 state patriotism, 2, 8, 35, 38–9, 61, 158–9
 see also conservative state patriotism; patriotism
British Nationality Act 1981, 136–7
Bruges speech (Thatcher), 51, 78–9, 94
Budgen, Nicholas, 126, 152
Bulpitt, Jim, 16, 59, 97, 103
Burke, Edmund, 4–8, 9, 20, 52, 54, 56

Casey, John, 55
Chamberlain, Joseph, 11, 13, 17
Churchill, Randolph, 11, 17
citizenship, 7, 8, 52, 54, 111, 123–5, 149, 162–4
 British legislation, 27, 34, 42, 44–5, 57, 134, 135–7, 139
 EU Citizenship of the Union, 143, 166
Clarke, Kenneth, 95, 96, 100–1, 160–1
Commonwealth, 24–8, 41, 135
conservatism, 4–8, 52–6, 110–12, 124–5, 157, 162–4
 cultural conservatism, 54–6, 132–3, 137, 146, 147, 163–4

 as ideology, 6, 9, 51–3, 58, 164
 One Nation Conservatism, 1, 9–11, 15, 49, 51, 57, 58, 60, 63, 106, 129, 149, 154–5, 157
 see also New Right; Thatcherism
conservative nation, 4–9, 14–15, 20, 38, 51–6, 124, 152, 158, 163–6
 and New Right, 8, 43–4, 51–6, 131–3
Conservative Party
 and Empire, 9–10, 12–15, 22–5, 49
 and European integration, 25–7, 32–3, 73, 89–96, 99–102, 160–2
 and immigration, 27–8, 33–5, 134–5, 138–9, 150–2, 159
 and Northern Ireland, 122–6, 158
 and patriotic discourse, 9–12, 19–21, 22, 51, 56–7, 64, 154
 and the politics of nationhood, 1, 9–21, 22–7, 45–7, 48–50, 60–5, 77–80, 93–4, 101–2, 128–30, 152–3, 154–7, 165–7
 and Scotland, 16, 35–6, 105–15, 157–8
 and the Union, 15–19, 35–6, 60–1, 103, 107–15, 122–6, 128–9, 158
 see also statecraft
conservative state patriotism, 7–9, 11–15, 19–21, 23–4, 63–4, 124–5
 see also British identity; patriotism
constitution *see* British constitution

Delors, Jacques, 68–71
devolution
 administrative devolution, 16, 35, 103–4, 107–8, 112, 114–15, 129–30, 156, 157

197

legislative devolution, 35–6, 42, 104, 105, 107–8, 110–13, 115, 122, 157–8, 166
Northern Ireland, 116, 118, 119–22, 126, 155–6
Scotland, 16, 23, 28–9, 35–6, 42, 107–15, 121, 127, 129–30, 154–8
Wales, 42, 103–4, 112, 115–16, 121, 129–30, 157–8
see also Northern Ireland; Scotland; Union; Wales
Disraeli, Benjamin, 1, 10–11
Douglas-Home, Alec, 28, 36

Economic and Monetary Union (EMU), 50, 69–74, 79, 87–8, 165
British policy on, 69–71, 76–7, 97, 99–100, 160
Conservative divisions on, 69–71, 77, 91–3, 94, 96–7, 99–101, 160–2
elections
1955 general election, 35, 105
1964 general election, 28, 35
1970 general election, 34, 40
1974 general election, 36, 41, 105, 109
1979 general election, 105, 135
1983 general election, 150–1
1987 general election, 107, 151
1988 European Parliament elections, 90
1992 general election, 73, 109, 123, 150–3
1994 European Parliament elections, 90
1997 general election, 90–2, 105, 114–15, 116, 124, 130, 150–3, 157, 162
Empire, 3–4, 18
and Conservative politics, 12–15, 19–20, 22–5, 39, 45, 49, 57, 60
decolonization, 21, 22–4, 41, 63
see also imperialism
England
Conservative politics and, 19, 38, 61, 108, 113, 127, 129–30, 157–8, 164

English identity, 1–3, 5–6, 19, 51–2, 54, 60–1
English nationalism, 3, 51, 61, 129, 155, 166
see also Thatcherism; Union
European Community (EC)
British entry, 22–3, 29–33, 34, 39–41, 154
development in 1980s, 67–71, 142
first British application, 24–7
see also European Union
European integration, 31–2, 66–7, 84–9, 165
European Union (EU), 66–7, 72–102, 119–20, 127–8, 142–3, 145, 153, 156, 160–1, 165–6
see also European Community
Euro-scepticism, 73, 77, 79–82, 88, 91–2, 94–100, 160–1, 167
Exchange Rate Mechanism (ERM), 50, 70, 72–4, 80, 87–8, 91, 95, 99

Factortame case, 81–2
Falkland Islands, 56–8, 137, 155
federalism, 18, 36, 129
federal Europe, 68, 73–4, 79
Forsyth, Michael, 106, 110, 113

Gamble, Andrew, 60, 62, 64–5, 93, 99
Gaulle, Charles de, 25–6, 51
Gilmour, Ian, 51, 60
Gladstone, William, 13, 15, 17

Hague, William, 116, 159–61
Hayek, F. A., 52–3
Heath, Edward, 24
and European integration, 29–33, 40, 78, 154
and immigration, 33–5, 154
and Northern Ireland, 23, 36–8, 154
and the politics of nationhood, 22–3, 27, 28–9, 45–7, 154–5
and Scottish devolution, 23, 35–6, 105, 154–5
Heseltine, Michael, 94, 100, 160

Index

Hong Kong, 134, 136–7, 139, 149
Howard, Michael, 72, 92, 160
Howe, Sir Geoffrey, 70, 83, 94, 100, 118
Hurd, Douglas, 71, 100, 118

immigration, 53
  asylum, 65, 139–42, 143, 144, 145–6, 156
  British legislation on, 13, 27–8, 33–5, 138–42, 151
  European Union and, 142–3, 145, 153
  as a political issue, 27–8, 33–5, 42–4, 134–5, 138–9, 144, 149, 152–3, 156, 159
  repatriation, 23, 33–5, 38, 43, 46, 134, 152
  see also race
imperialism, 9–10, 11–15, 19–20, 22–4, 57, 60, 64
  see also Empire
India, 6, 23, 141
  Indian community in UK, 133, 151
Ireland, 1, 3, 6, 154
  Home Rule, 10–11, 14–19
  and Northern Ireland, 37, 41–2, 117–20, 127
  see also Northern Ireland
Irish Republican Army (IRA), 37, 118–20, 127

Joseph, Sir Keith, 50, 147

Labour Party
  and constitutional reform, 158–9
  and devolution, 19, 104, 107, 113, 116, 122, 127, 157, 159
  and European integration, 26, 90–1, 94, 153, 157, 159, 161–2
  and immigration, 27–8, 33–4, 140, 151, 157
  and the politics of nationhood, 20, 158–9, 166–7
Lamont, Norman, 74, 94, 97, 126
Lang, Ian, 108–9
Lawson, Nigel, 70, 79, 94, 95

Letwin, Shirley Robin, 52, 58–9, 60
Liberal Democrats, 109, 113, 150
Liberal Party, 11, 13, 15, 17–19
local government, 36, 42, 89, 108, 110, 112–13, 127–8
  and race relations, 134, 144, 147

Maastricht Treaty, 71–3, 86–7, 88, 127–8, 142–3
  parliamentary ratification of, 73, 87, 94–6, 99, 123
Macmillan, Harold, 22, 24–8, 78
Major, John
  and European integration, 64, 71–7, 86, 90, 94, 96–7, 99–100, 160–2
  and nationhood, 64–5, 80, 162
  and 'race', 64, 145
  and the Union, 65, 108–11, 121–2, 125, 157
Major Governments, 48–9, 62–5
  and European integration, 65, 71–7, 83–4, 86–7, 128, 142–3, 157
  and immigration, 139–44, 152–3
  and Northern Ireland, 65, 118–22
  and the politics of nationhood, 64–5, 74, 128–9, 156
  and race relations, 65, 144–9, 152–3
  and Scotland, 65, 107–15, 121–2
monarchy, 2–4, 9, 11–12, 165, 166
Monday Club, The, 24, 149
Moravcsik, Andrew, 85–6
multiculturalism, 43–4, 49, 132–3, 146, 147, 149, 153, 159, 163, 166

national identity, 1–4, 38–9, 78, 137, 166
  civic accounts of, 1–3, 7–8, 51–6, 63, 124–5, 163–4
  cultural accounts of, 2–3, 7–8, 52, 54–6, 63, 125, 133–4, 153, 163–4
  myths and symbols, 1–4, 8, 38–9, 164
New Right, 3, 29, 162
  and nationhood, 8, 23, 51–6

and 'race', 43–4, 55, 132–3, 152
and Thatcherism, 49–50, 51–2, 56, 58, 133
see also conservatism
Northern Ireland
Anglo-Irish Agreement, 42, 47, 51, 117–18, 121, 123, 126
direct rule, 23, 36–7, 41–2, 104, 116–17, 126–7, 155
Downing Street Declaration, 118–20, 121, 123
Framework Documents, 119–20, 121–2, 127
integrationist perspective, 41–2, 123, 125–7
status in UK, 37, 41–2, 117–19, 121–2, 130, 156
Stormont Parliament, 19, 37, 41–2, 104, 122
see also devolution; Ireland; Union
Norton, Philip, 62, 161

Oakeshott, Michael, 52–4

patriotism, 5, 10, 145, 162–3
patriotic discourse, 1–4, 6, 9, 49, 51, 56–9, 158–9
see also British identity; conservative state patriotism
Powell, Enoch, 29, 50–1
and European integration, 30, 32, 39–41
and immigration, 33–5, 42–5, 132, 134, 152
and the politics of nationhood, 23, 45–7, 155
and the Union, 41–2, 125–6
Powellism
as a nationalist strategy, 38–9, 46–7, 49, 78, 154–5
and 'race', 43–4, 131, 133, 149, 159
and Thatcherism, 46–7, 49, 57, 63, 78, 134
Prior, James, 117, 126
pro-Europeans, 78, 80, 99–101, 161

Qualified Majority Voting (QMV), 68, 75, 86, 90–1, 95, 99, 143, 165

race, 13–14, 43–4, 56, 132–3
politics of 'race', 27–8, 33, 48, 59–60, 131–4, 146–50, 152–3, 159–60
racism, 14, 56, 133, 145, 147, 149
see also immigration
race relations
British legislation, 33–5, 145
government policy, 133–4, 138, 144–9, 152–3, 155
Redwood, John, 73, 94, 100, 116, 160
Referendum Party, 91–2
Ridley, Nicholas, 71, 79, 94
Rushdie affair, 146, 148–9, 159

Salisbury, Lord, 10, 13, 16–18
Scotland
devolution, 16, 23, 35–6, 42, 107–15, 121, 127, 129–30, 154–8
Scottish identity, 3, 106–8
and the Union, 1–4, 13–14, 103–4, 129, 155
see also devolution; Union
Scottish Conservative Party, 16, 19, 35–6, 105–7, 115, 158
Scruton, Roger, 54, 163
Single European Act (SEA), 51, 68–9, 86–7, 97
Single European Market, 64, 68–70, 74, 76, 83–4, 86, 89, 93, 95–6, 98–9, 165
social policy
Maastricht Social Agreement, 72, 74–5
Social Charter, 69–70
sovereignty
and autonomy, 69, 82–3, 84–9, 165
and European integration, 24–6, 29–33, 38–41, 50, 69, 78–84, 89, 91, 95–6, 98–9, 142–3, 165–6
Hong Kong, 139
Northern Ireland, 117–18, 128, 130, 156
parliamentary sovereignty, 2–3, 30, 35, 38–40, 49, 60, 78, 80–3, 108, 113, 122

Index

popular sovereignty, 7, 81–2, 108, 122
statecraft
  analysis of, 9–10, 49–50, 59–61, 63–5, 66–7, 84
  of Conservative Party, 9–11, 28–9, 66–7, 84, 99
  and the politics of nationhood, 23, 24, 32, 46, 49–50, 61, 63–5, 101, 154–6, 166
  and territorial politics, 15–18, 103, 107, 129–30
Suez, 22, 24

tariff reform, 1, 14–15, 18–20, 93, 154
Tebbit, Norman, 95, 149, 159–60
Thatcher, Margaret
  and European integration, 64–5, 67–71, 73, 78–80, 82, 86–8, 90, 96–7, 101
  and imigration, 134–5, 139–40, 149, 151
  and nationhood, 48, 50–1, 57–9, 61, 65, 67, 78–80, 101, 107
  and Northern Ireland, 117–18, 122, 124
  and Scotland, 36, 105–7, 109
Thatcher Governments, 48–50, 59, 62–5
  and European integration, 67–71, 83–4, 142
  and immigration, 135, 138–9, 144, 152
  and Northern Ireland, 117–18, 121–2
  and race relations, 144–9
  and Scotland, 105–8, 114, 129
Thatcherism
  analysis of, 48–65
  Englishnesss of, 51, 54, 56, 59, 60, 64, 108, 129–30, 155
  hegemony, 56, 58, 60–1, 128, 155–6
  ideology, 51, 56, 58, 60
  neo-liberalism, 51–2, 56, 68–9, 95, 106–7, 132, 162
  and the politics of nationhood, 48–65, 125, 128–30, 133–4, 152–3, 155–7
  statecraft, 49–50, 58, 59–61, 63–5, 155
  see also conservatism; England
Tory themes, 1–3, 6, 20

Ulster Unionists, 18, 37–8, 41–2, 117–19, 122–6, 158
Union, 1–3, 10, 15–19, 107–12, 118, 121–2, 155, 156
  see also devolution; England; Northern Ireland; Scotland; Wales
United States of America (USA), 25–6, 41

Wales, 16, 42, 103–4, 112, 115–16, 121, 129–30, 157–8
  see also devolution; Union
Walker, Peter, 115–16
Whig themes, 1–3, 6, 14, 20, 54, 60
Willetts, David, 83–4, 162–3
Wilson, Harold, 28, 31, 33, 42